T0297331

**CAMBRIDGE MONOGRAPHS ON
APPLIED AND COMPUTATIONAL
MATHEMATICS**

Series Editors
M. J. ABLOWITZ, S. H. DAVIS, JOHN HINCH, A. ISERLES, A. MAJDA,
J. OCKENDON, P. J. OLVER

16   Topology for Computing

The *Cambridge Monographs on Applied and Computational Mathematics* reflects the crucial role of mathematical and computational techniques in contemporary science. The series publishes expositions on all aspects of applicable and numerical mathematics, with an emphasis on new developments in this fast-moving area of research.

State-of-the-art methods and algorithms as well as modern mathematical descriptions of physical and mechanical ideas are presented in a manner suited to graduate research students and professionals alike. Sound pedagogical presentation is a prerequisite. It is intended that books in the series will serve to inform a new generation of researchers.

Also in this series:

Topology for Computing

AFRA J. ZOMORODIAN

Dartmouth College

CAMBRIDGE
UNIVERSITY PRESS

32 Avenue of the Americas, New York NY 10013-2473, USA

Cambridge University Press is part of the University of Cambridge.

It furthers the University's mission by disseminating knowledge in the pursuit of
education, learning and research at the highest international levels of excellence.

www.cambridge.org
Information on this title: www.cambridge.org/9780521136099

First published 2005
Reprinted 2009
First paperback edition 2009

A catalogue record for this publication is available from the British Library

Library of Congress Cataloguing in Publication data

Zomorodian, Afra J., 1974–
Topology for computing / Afra J. Zomorodian.
p. cm. – (Cambridge monographs on applied and computational mathematics ; 16)
Includes bibliographical references and index.
ISBN 0-521-83666-2 (hardback)
1. Topology. I. Title. II. Series.
QA611.Z65 2004
514–dc22

2004047311

ISBN 978-0-521-13609-9 Paperback

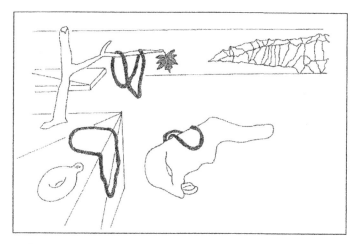

— *Persistence of Homology* — Afra Zomorodian (After Salvador Dali)

On the left, a double-torus and a 1-cycle lie on a triangulated 2-manifold. There is a box-shaped cell-complex above. An unknot hangs from the large branch of the sapless withering tree. Through some exertion, the tree identifies itself as a maple by bearing a single green leaf. A deformed two-sphere, a torus, and a nonbounding loop form a pile in the center. Near the horizon, a 2-manifold is embedded by an associated height field. It divides itself into regions using the 1-cells of its Morse-Smale complex.

Contents

Contents

Color plates follow page

Preface

My goal in this book is to enable a non-specialist to grasp and participate in current research in computational topology. Therefore, this book is not a compilation of recent advances in the area. Rather, the book presents basic mathematical concepts from a computer scientist's point of view, focusing on computational challenges and introducing algorithms and data structures when appropriate. The book also incorporates several recent results from my doctoral dissertation and subsequent related results in computational topology.

The primary motivation for this book is the significance and utility of topological concepts in solving problems in computer science. These problems arise naturally in computational geometry, graphics, robotics, structural biology, and chemistry. Often, the questions themselves have been known and considered by topologists. Unfortunately, there are many barriers to interaction:

- Computer scientists do not know the language of topologists. Topology, unlike geometry, is not a required subject in high school mathematics and is almost never dealt with in undergraduate computer science. The axiomatic nature of topology further compounds the problem as it generates cryptic and esoteric terminology that makes the field unintelligible and inaccessible to non-topologists.
- Topology can be very unintuitive and enigmatic and therefore can appear very complicated and mystifying, often frightening away interested computer scientists.
- Topology is a large field with many branches. Computer scientists often require only simple concepts from each branch. While there are certainly a number of offerings in topology by mathematics departments, the focus of these courses is often theoretical, concerned with deep questions and existential results.

Because of the relative dearth of interaction between topologists and computer scientists, there are many opportunities for research. Many topological questions have large complexity: the best known bound, if any, may be exponential. For example, I once attended a talk on an algorithm that ran in quadruply exponential time! Let me make this clear. It was

$$O\left(2^{2^{2^{2^{2^n}}}}\right).$$

And one may overhear topologists boasting that their software can now handle 14 tetrahedra, not just 13. But better bounds may exist for specialized questions, such as problems in low dimensions, where our interests chiefly lie. We need better algorithms, parallel algorithms, approximation schemes, data structures, and software to solve these problems within our lifetime (or the lifetime of the universe.)

This book is based primarily on my dissertation, completed under the supervision of Herbert Edelsbrunner in 2001. Consequently, some chapters, such as those in Part Three, have a thesis feel to them. I have also incorporated notes from several graduate-level courses I have organized in the area: *Introduction to Computational Topology* at Stanford University, California, during Fall 2002 and Winter 2004; and *Topology for Computing* at the Max-Planck-Institut für Informatik, Saarbrücken, Germany, during Fall 2003.

The goal of this book is to make algorithmically minded individuals fluent in the language of topology. Currently, most researchers in computational topology have a mathematics background. My hope is to recruit more computer scientists into this emerging field.

Stanford, California   A. J. Z.
June 2004

Acknowledgments

I am indebted to Persi Diaconis for the genesis of this book. He attended my very first talk in the Stanford Mathematics Department, asked for a copy of my thesis, and recommended it for publication. To have my work be recognized by such a brilliant and extraordinary figure is an enormous honor for me. I would like to thank Lauren Cowles for undertaking this project and coaching me throughout the editing process and Elise Oranges for copyediting the text.

During my time at Stanford, I have collaborated primarily with Leonidas Guibas and Gunnar Carlsson. Leo has been more than just a post-doctoral supervisor, but a colleague, a mentor, and a friend. He is a successful academic who balances research, teaching, and the mentoring of students. He guides a large animated research group that works on a manifold of significant problems. And his impressive academic progeny testify to his care for their success.

Eleven years after being a freshman in his "honors calculus," I am fortunate to have Gunnar as a colleague. Gunnar astounds me consistently with his knowledge, humility, generosity, and kindness. I continue to rely on his estimation, advice, and support.

I would also like to thank the members of Leo and Gunnar's research groups as well as the Stanford Graphics Laboratory, for inspired talks and invigorating discussions. This book was partially written during a four-month stay at the Max-Planck-Institut. I would like to thank Lutz Kettner and Kurt Mehlhorn for their sponsorship, as well as for coaxing me into teaching a mini-course.

Finally, I would like to thank my research collaborators, whose work appears in this book: Gunnar Carlsson, Anne Collins, Herbert Edelsbrunner, Leonidas Guibas, John Harer, and David Letscher. My research was supported, in part, by ARO under grant DAAG55-98-1-0177, by NSF under grants CCR-00-86013 and DMS-0138456, and by NSF/DARPA under grant CARGO 0138456.

1

Introduction

The focus of this book is capturing and understanding the topological properties of spaces. To do so, we use methods derived from exploring the relationship between geometry and topology. In this chapter, I will motivate this approach by explaining what spaces are, how they arise in many fields of inquiry, and why we are interested in their properties. I will then introduce new theoretical methods for rigorously analyzing topologies of spaces. These methods are grounded in homology and Morse theory, and generalize to high-dimensional spaces. In addition, the methods are robust and fast, and therefore practical from a computational point of view. Having introduced the methods, I end this chapter by discussing the organization of the rest of the book.

1.1 Spaces

Let us begin with a discussion of spaces. A *space* is a set of points as shown in Figure 1.1(a). We cannot define what a *set* is, other than accepting it as a primitive notion. Intuitively, we think of a set as a collection or conglomeration of objects. In the case of a space, these objects are *points*, yet another primitive notion in mathematics. The concept of a space is too weak to be interesting, as it lacks structure. We make this notion slightly richer with the addition of a *topology*. We shall see in Chapter 2 what a topology formally means. Here, we think of a topology as the knowledge of the connectivity of a space: Each point in the space knows which points are near it, that is, in its *neighborhood*. In other words, we know how the space is connected. For example, in Figure 1.1(b), neighbor points are connected graphically by a path in the graph. We call such a space a *topological space*. At first blush, the concept of a topological space may seem contrived, as we are very comfortable with the richer *metric spaces*, as in Figure 1.1(c). We are introduced to the prototypical metric space, the *Euclidean space* $\mathbb{R}^d$, in secondary school, and we often envision our

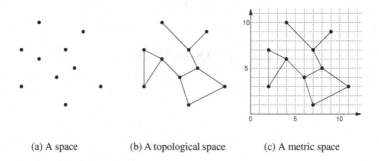

(a) A space   (b) A topological space   (c) A metric space

Fig. 1.1. Spaces.

world as $\mathbb{R}^3$. A metric space has an associated *metric*, which enables us to measure distances between points in that space and, in turn, implicitly define their neighborhoods. Consequently, a metric provides a space with a topology, and a metric space is a topological one. Topological spaces feel alien to us because we are accustomed to having a metric. The spaces arise naturally, however, in many fields.

Example 1.1 (graphics) We often model a real-world object as a set of elements, where the elements are triangles, arbitrary polygons, or B-splines.

Example 1.2 (geography) Planetary landscapes are modeled as elevations over grids, or triangulations, in *geographic information systems*.

Example 1.3 (robotics) A robot must often plan a path in its world that contains many obstacles. We are interested in efficiently capturing and representing the *configuration space* in which a robot may travel.

Example 1.4 (biology) A protein is a single chain of amino acids, which folds into a globular structure. The *Thermodynamics Hypothesis* states that a protein always folds into a state of minimum energy. To predict protein structure, we would like to model the folding of a protein computationally. As such, the *protein folding* problem becomes an optimization problem: We are looking for a path to the global minimum in a very high-dimensional energy landscape.

All the spaces in the above examples are topological spaces. In fact, they are metric spaces that derive their topology from their metrics. However, the questions raised are often topological in nature, and we may solve them easier by focusing on the topology of the space, and not its geometry. I will refer to topological spaces simply as spaces from this point onward.

1.2 Shapes of Spaces

We have seen that spaces arise in the process of solving many problems. Consequently, we are interested in capturing and understanding the *shapes* of spaces. This understanding is really in the form of classifications: We would like to know how spaces agree and differ in shape in order to categorize them. To do so, we need to identify intrinsic properties of spaces. We can try transforming a space in some fixed way and observe the properties that do not change. We call these properties the *invariants* of the space. Felix Klein gave this famous definition for geometry in his *Erlanger Programm* address in 1872. For example, *Euclidean geometry* refers to the study of invariants under rigid motion in $\mathbb{R}^d$, e.g., moving a cube in space does not change its geometry. Topology, on the other hand, studies invariants under continuous, and continuously invertible, transformations. For example, we can mold and stretch a play-doh ball into a filled cube by such transformations, but not into a donut shape. Generally, we view and study geometric and topological properties separately.

1.2.1 Geometry

There are a variety of issues we may be concerned with regarding the geometry of a space. We usually have a finite representation of a space for computation. We could be interested in measuring the quality of our representation, trying to improve the representation via modifications, and analyzing the effect of our changes. Alternatively, we could attempt to reduce the size of the representation in order to make computations viable, without sacrificing the geometric accuracy of the space.

Example 1.5 (decimation) The Stanford Dragon in Figure 1.2(a) consists of 871,414 triangles. Large meshes may not be appropriate for many applications involving real-time rendering. Having *decimated* the surface to 5% of its original size (b), I show that the new surface approximates the original surface quite well (c). The maximum distance between the new vertices and the original surface is 0.08% of the length of the diagonal of the dragon's bounding box.

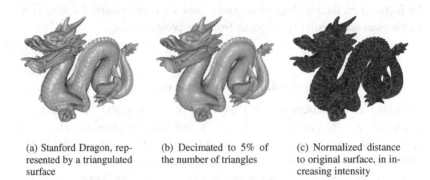

(a) Stanford Dragon, represented by a triangulated surface

(b) Decimated to 5% of the number of triangles

(c) Normalized distance to original surface, in increasing intensity

Fig. 1.2. Geometric simplification.

Fig. 1.3. The string on the left is cut into two pieces. The loop string on the right is cut but still is in one piece.

1.2.2 Topology

While Klein's unifying definition makes topology a form of geometry, we often differentiate between the two concepts. Recall that when we talk about topology, we are interested in how spaces are connected. Topology concerns itself with how things are connected, not how they look. Let's start with a few examples.

Example 1.6 (loops of string) Imagine we are given two pieces of strings. We tie the ends of one of them, so it forms a loop. Are they connected the same way, or differently? One way to find out is to cut both, as shown in Figure 1.3. When we cut each string, we are obviously changing its connectivity. Since the result is different, they must have been connected differently to begin with.

Example 1.7 (sphere and torus) Suppose you have a hollow ball (a sphere) and the surface of a donut (a torus.) When you cut the sphere anywhere, you get two pieces: the cap and the sphere with a hole, as shown in Figure 1.4(a). But there are ways you can cut the torus so that you only get one

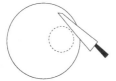

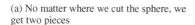

(a) No matter where we cut the sphere, we get two pieces

(b) If we're careful, we can cut the torus and still leave it in one piece.

Fig. 1.4. Two pieces or one piece?

piece. Somehow, the torus is acting like our string loop and the sphere like the untied string.

Example 1.8 (holding hands) Imagine you're walking down a crowded street, holding somebody's hand. When you reach a telephone pole and have to walk on opposite sides of the pole, you let go of the other person's hand. Why?

Let's look back to the first example. Before we cut the string, the two points near the cut are near each other. We say that they are *neighbors* or in each other's *neighborhoods*. After the cut, the two points are no longer neighbors, and their neighborhood has changed. This is the critical difference between the untied string and the loop: The former has two ends. All the points in the loop have two neighbors, one to their left and one to their right. But the untied string has two points, each of whom has a single neighbor. This is why the two strings have different connectivity. Note that this connectivity does not change if we deform or stretch the strings (as if they are made of rubber.) As long as we don't cut them, the connectivity remains the same. Topology studies this connectivity, a property that is *intrinsic* to the space itself.

In addition to studying the *intrinsic* properties of a space, topology is concerned not only with how an object is connected (intrinsic topology), but how it is *placed* within another space (extrinsic topology.) For example, suppose we put a knot on a string and then tie its ends together. Clearly, the string has the same connectivity as the loop we saw in Example 1.6. But no matter how we move the string around, we cannot get rid of the knot (in topology terms, we cannot unknot the knot into the *unknot*.) Or can we? Can we prove that we cannot?

So, topological properties include having tunnels, as shown in Figure 1.5(a), being knotted (b), and having components that are linked (c) and cannot be taken apart. We seek computational methods to detect these properties. Topo-

1 Introduction

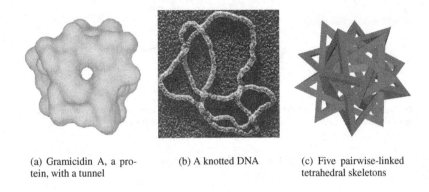

(a) Gramicidin A, a pro-   (b) A knotted DNA   (c) Five pairwise-linked
tein, with a tunnel   tetrahedral skeletons

Fig. 1.5. Topological properties. (b) Reprinted with permission from S Wasserman et al., SCIENCE, 229:171–174 (1985). © 1985 AAAS.

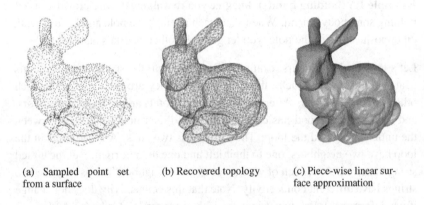

(a) Sampled point set   (b) Recovered topology   (c) Piece-wise linear sur-
from a surface   face approximation

Fig. 1.6. Surface reconstruction.

logical questions arise frequently in many areas of computation. Tools developed in topology, however, have not been used to address these problems traditionally.

Example 1.9 (surface reconstruction) Usually, a computer model is created by sampling the surface of an object and creating a point set, as in Figure 1.6(a). *Surface reconstruction*, a major area of research in computer graphics and computational geometry, refers to the recovery of the lost topology (b) and, in turn, geometry of a space. Once the connectivity is reestablished, the surface is often represented by a piece-wise linear approximation (c).

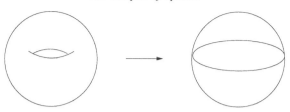

Fig. 1.7. Topological simplification.

As for geometry, we would also like to be able to simplify a space topologically, as in Figure 1.7. I have intentionally made the figures primitive compared to the previous geometric figures to reflect the essential structure that topology captures. To simplify topology, we need a measure of the importance of topological attributes. I provide one such measure in this book.

1.2.3 Relationship

The geometry and topology of a space are fundamentally related, as they are both properties of the same space. Geometric modifications, such as decimation in Example 1.5, could alter the topology. Is the simplified dragon in Figure 1.2(c) connected the same way as the original? In this case, the answer is yes, because the decimation algorithm excludes geometric modifications that have topological impact. We have changed the geometry of the surface without changing its topology.

When creating photo-realistic images, however, appearance is the dominant issue, and changes in topology may not matter. We could, therefore, allow for topological changes when simplifying the geometry. In other words, geometric modifications are possible with, and without, induced changes in topology. The reverse, however, is not true. We cannot eliminate the "hole" in the surface of the donut (torus) to get a sphere in Figure 1.7 without changing the geometry of the surface. We further examine the relationship between topology and geometry by looking at contours of terrains.

Example 1.10 (contours) In Figure 1.8, I show a flooded terrain with the water receding. The boundaries of the components that appear are the *iso-lines* or *contours* of the terrain. Contour lines are used often in map drawings. Noise in sampled data changes the geometry of a terrain, introducing small mountains and lakes. In turn, this influences how contour lines appear and merge as the water recedes.

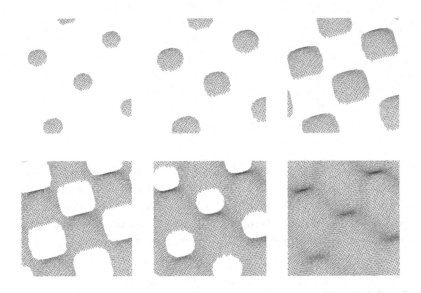

Fig. 1.8. Noah's flood receding.

We may view the spaces shown in Figure 1.8 as a single growing space under-going topological and geometric changes. The history of such a space, called a *filtration*, is the primary object for this book. Note that the topology of the iso-lines within this history is determined by the geometry of the terrain. Gen-eralizing to a $(d+1)$-dimensional surface, we see that there is a relationship between the topology of d-dimensional *level sets* of a space and its geometry, one dimension higher. This relationship is the subject of *Morse theory*, which we will encounter in this book.

1.3 New Results

We will also examine some new results in the area of computational topol-ogy. There are three main groups of theoretical results: persistence, Morse complexes, and the linking number.

Persistence. *Persistence* is a new measure for topological attributes. We call it persistence, as it ranks attributes by their life time in a filtration: their persis-tence in being a feature in the face of growth. Using this definition, we look at the following:

Fig. 1.9. A Morse complex over a terrain.

- **Persistence:** efficient algorithms for computing persistence over arbitrary coefficients.
- **Topological Simplification:** algorithms for simplifying topology, based on persistence. The algorithms remove attributes in the order of increasing persistence. At any moment, we call the removed attributes topological noise, and the remaining ones topological features.
- **Cycles and Manifolds:** algorithms for computing representations. The persistence algorithm tracks the subspaces that express nontrivial topological attributes, in order to compute persistence. We show how to modify this algorithm to identify these subspaces (cycles), as well as the subspaces that eliminate them (manifolds.)

Morse complexes. A *Morse complex* gives a full analysis of the behavior of flow over a space by partitioning the space into cells of uniform flow. In the case of a two-dimensional surface, such as the terrain in Figure 1.8, the Morse complex connects maxima (peaks) to minima (pits) through saddle points (passes) via edges, partitioning the terrain into quadrangles, as shown in Figure 1.9. Morse complexes are defined, however, only for smooth spaces. In this book, we will see how to extend this definition to piece-wise linear surfaces, which are frequently used for computation. In addition, we will learn how to construct hierarchies of Morse complexes.

- **Morse complex:** We give an algorithm for computing the Morse complex by first constructing a complex whose combinatorial form matches that of the Morse complex and then deriving the Morse complex via local transformations. This construction reflects a paradigm we call the *Simulation of Differentiability*.
- **Hierarchy:** We apply persistence to a filtration of the Morse complex to get a hierarchy of increasingly coarser Morse complexes. This corresponds to

modifying the geometry of the space in order to eliminate noise and simplify
the topology of the contours of the surface.

Linking number. The *linking number* is an integer invariant that measures the
separability of a pair of knots. We extend the definition of the linking number
to simplicial complexes. We then develop data structures and algorithms for
computing the linking numbers of the complexes in a filtration.

1.4 Organization

The rest of this book is divided into three parts: mathematics, algorithms, and
applications. Part One, *Mathematics*, contains background on algebra, geometry, and topology, as well as the new theoretical contributions. In Chapter 2,
we describe the spaces we are interested in exploring, and how we examine
them by encoding their geometries in filtrations of complexes. Chapter 3 provides enough group theory background for the definition of homology groups
in Chapter 4. We also discuss other measures of topology and justify our choice
of homology. Switching to smooth manifolds, we review concepts from Morse
Theory in Chapter 5. In Chapter 6, we give the mathematics behind the new
results in this book.

Part Two, *Algorithms*, contains data structures and algorithms for the mathematics presented in Part I. In each chapter, we motivate and present algorithms
and prove they are correct. In Chapter 7, we introduce algorithms for computing persistence: over $\mathbb{Z}_2$ coefficients, arbitrary fields, and arbitrary principal
ideal domains. We then address topological simplification using persistence
in Chapter 8. In Chapter 9, we describe an algorithm for computing two-
dimensional Morse complexes. We end this part by showing how one may
compute linking numbers in Chapter 10.

Part Three, *Applications*, contains issues relating to the application of the
theory and algorithms presented in Parts I and II. To apply theoretical ideas
to real-world problems, we need implementations and software, which we
present in Chapter 11. We give empirical proof of the speed of the algorithms through experiments with our implementations in Chapter 12. We devote Chapter 13 to applications of the work in this book and future work.

Part One

Mathematics

2

Spaces and Filtrations

In this chapter, we describe the input to all of the algorithms described in this book, and the process by which such input is generated. We begin by formalizing the kind of spaces that we are interested in exploring. Then, we introduce the primary approach used for computing topology: growing a space incrementally and analyzing the history of its growth. Naturally, the knowledge we derive from this approach is only as meaningful as the growth process. So, we let the geometry of our space dictate the growth model. In this fashion, we encode geometry into an otherwise topological history. The geometry of our space controls the placement of topological events within this history and, consequently, the life-span of topological attributes. The main assumption of this method is that longevity is equivalent to significance. This approach of exploring the relationship between geometry and topology is not new. It is the hallmark of *Morse theory* (Milnor, 1963), which we will study in more detail in Chapter 5.

The rest of the chapter describes the process outlined in Figure 2.1. We begin with a formal description of topological spaces. We then describe two types of such spaces, manifolds and simplicial complexes, in the next two sections.

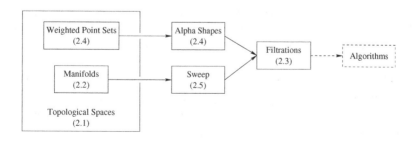

Fig. 2.1. Geometrically ordered filtrations: Topics are labeled with their sections.

These spaces constitute our realm of interest. The latter is more general than the former, and we represent the former with it. We also formalize the notion of a growth history (filtration) within Section 2.3. Finally, we describe two growth processes, alpha shapes and manifold sweeps, which are utilized to spawn filtrations. These *geometrically ordered filtrations* provide the input to the algorithms.

Topology and algebra are both axiomatic studies, necessitating a large number of definitions. My approach will be to start from the very primitive notions, in order to refresh the reader's memory. The titled definitions, however, allow for quick skimming for the knowledgeable reader. My treatment follows Bishop and Goldberg (1980) for point-set topology and Munkres (1984) for algebraic topology. I also used Henle (1997) and McCarthy (1988) for reference and inspiration. I recommend de Berg et al. (1997) for background on computational geometry. I will cite some seminal papers in defining concepts.

2.1 Topological Spaces

A topological space is a set of points who know who their neighbors are. Let's begin with the primitive notion of a set.

2.1.1 Sets and Functions

We cannot define a set formally, other than stating that a *set* is a well-defined collection of objects. We also assume the following:

(i) Set S is made up of *elements* $a \in S$.

(ii) There is only one empty set $\emptyset$.

(iii) We may describe a set by characterizing it ($\{x \mid P(x)\}$) or by enumerating elements ($\{1, 2, 3\}$). Here P is a predicate.

(iv) A set S is *well defined* if, for each object a, either $a \in S$ or $a \notin S$.

Note that "well defined" really refers to the definition of a set, rather than to the set itself. $|S|$ or card S is the size of the set. We may multiply sets in order to get larger sets.

Definition 2.1 (Cartesian) The *Cartesian product of sets* $S_1, S_2, \ldots, S_n$ is the set of all ordered n-tuples $(a_1, a_2, \ldots, a_n)$, where $a_i \in S_i$. The Cartesian product is denoted by either $S_1 \times S_2 \times \ldots \times S_n$ or by $\prod_{i=1}^{n} S_i$. The *i-th Cartesian coordinate function* $u_i \colon \prod_{i=1}^{n} S_i \to S_i$ is defined by

$$u_i(a_1, a_2, \ldots, a_n) = a_i.$$

Having described sets, we now define subsets.

Definition 2.2 (subsets) A set B is a *subset* of a set A, denoted $B \subseteq A$ or $A \supseteq B$, if every element of B is in A. $B \subset A$ or $A \supset B$ is generally used for $B \subseteq A$ and $B \neq A$. If A is any set, then A is the *improper subset* of A. Any other subset is *proper*. If A is a set, we denote by 2^A, the *power set of A*, the collection of all subsets of A, $2^A = \{B \mid B \subseteq A\}$.

We also have a couple of fundamental set operations.

Definition 2.3 (intersection, union) The *intersection $A \cap B$* of sets A and B is the set consisting of those elements that belong to both A and B, that is, $A \cap B = \{x \mid x \in A \text{ and } x \in B\}$. The *union $A \cup B$* of sets A and B is the set consisting of those elements that belong to A or B, that is, $A \cup B = \{x \mid x \in A \text{ or } x \in B\}$.

We indicate a collection of sets by labeling them with subscripts from an index set J, e.g., A_j with $j \in J$. For example, we use $\bigcap_{j \in J} A_j = \bigcap \{A_j \mid j \in J\} = \{x \mid x \in A_j \text{ for all } j \in J\}$ for general intersection. The next definition summarizes functions: maps that relate sets to sets.

Definition 2.4 (relations and functions) A *relation* φ between sets A and B is a collection of ordered pairs (a,b) such that $a \in A$ and $b \in B$. If $(a,b) \in \varphi$, we often denote the relationship by $a \sim b$. A *function* or *mapping φ from a set A into a set B* is a rule that assigns to each element a of A exactly one element b of B. We say that φ *maps a into b* and that φ *maps A into B*. We denote this by $\varphi(a) = b$. The element b is the *image of a under* φ. We show the map as $\varphi \colon A \to B$. The set A is the *domain of* φ, the set B is the *codomain of* φ, and the set $\operatorname{im} \varphi = \varphi(A) = \{\varphi(a) \mid a \in A\}$ is the *image of A under* φ. If φ and ψ are functions with $\varphi \colon A \to B$ and $\psi \colon B \to C$, then there is a natural function mapping A into C, the *composite function*, consisting of φ followed by ψ. We write $\psi(\varphi(a)) = c$ and denote the composite function by $\psi \circ \varphi$. A function from a set A into a set B is *one to one (1-1)* (*injective*) if each element B has at most one element mapped into it, and it is *onto B* (*surjective*) if each element of B has at least one element of A mapped into it. If it is both, it is a *bijection*. A bijection of a set onto itself is called a *permutation*.

A permutation of a finite set is usually specified by its action on the elements of the set. For example, we may denote a permutation of the set $\{1,2,3,4,5,6\}$ by $(6,5,2,4,3,1)$, where the notation states that the permutation maps 1 to 6, 2 to 5, 3 to 2, and so on. We may then obtain a new permutation by a transposition: switching the order of two neighboring elements. In our example, $(5,6,2,4,3,1)$ is a permutation that is one transposition away from $(6,5,2,4,3,1)$. We may place all permutations of a finite set in two sets.

Theorem 2.1 (parity) *A permutation of a finite set can be expressed as either an even or an odd number of transpositions, but not both. In the former case, the permutation is* even; *in the latter, it is* odd.

2.1.2 Topology

We endow a set with structure by using a topology to get a topological space.

Definition 2.5 (topology) A *topology* on a set X is a subset $T \subseteq 2^X$ such that:

(a) If $S_1, S_2 \in T$, then $S_1 \cap S_2 \in T$.
(b) If $\{S_J \mid j \in J\} \subseteq T$, then $\cup_{j \in J} S_j \in T$.
(c) $\emptyset, X \in T$.

The definition states implicitly that only finite intersections, and infinite unions, of the open sets are open. A topology is simply a system of sets that describe the connectivity of the set. These sets have names:

Definition 2.6 (open, closed sets) Let X be a set and T be a topology. $S \in T$ is an *open set*. The *closed sets* are $X - S$, where $S \in T$.

A set may be only closed, only open, both open and closed, or neither. For example, $\emptyset$ is both open and closed by definition. We combine a set with a topology to get the spaces we are interested in.

Definition 2.7 (topological space) The pair (X,T) of a set X and a topology T is a *topological space*.

We often use $\mathbb{X}$ as notation for a topological space X, with T being understood. We next turn our attention to the individual sets.

Definition 2.8 (interior, closure, boundary) The *interior* $\mathring{A}$ of set $A \subseteq \mathbb{X}$ is the union of all open sets contained in A. The *closure* $\overline{A}$ of set $A \subseteq \mathbb{X}$ is the intersection of all closed sets containing A. The *boundary* of a set A is $\partial A = \overline{A} - \mathring{A}$.

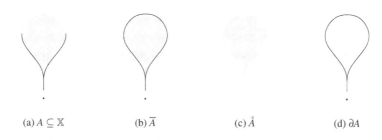

(a) $A \subseteq \mathbb{X}$ (b) $\overline{A}$ (c) $\mathring{A}$ (d) ∂A

Fig. 2.2. A set $A \subseteq \mathbb{X}$ and related sets.

In Figure 2.2, we see a set that is composed of a single point and an upside-down teardrop shape. We also see its closure, interior, and boundary. There are other equivalent ways of defining these concepts. For example, we may think of the boundary of a set as the set of points all of whose neighborhoods intersect both the set and its complement. Similarly, the closure of a set is the minimum closed set that contains the set. Using open sets, we can now define neighborhoods.

Definition 2.9 (neighborhoods) A *neighborhood* of $x \in X$ is any $A \subseteq X$ such that $x \in \mathring{A}$. A *basis of neighborhoods at* $x \in X$ is a collection of neighborhoods of x such that every neighborhood of x contains one of the basis neighborhoods.

We may define basis neighborhoods, and hence a topology, by means of a metric.

Definition 2.10 (metric) A *metric* or *distance function* $d : X \times X \to \mathbb{R}$ is a function satisfying the following axioms:

    (a) For all $x, y \in X$, $d(x,y) \geq 0$ (positivity).
    (b) If $d(x,y) = 0$, then $x = y$ (nondegeneracy).
    (c) For all $x, y \in X$, $d(x,y) = d(y,x)$ (symmetry).
    (d) For all $x, y, z \in X$, $d(x,y) + d(y,z) \geq d(x,z)$ (the triangle inequality).

Definition 2.11 (open ball) The *open ball* $B(x,r)$ with center x and radius $r > 0$ with respect to metric d is defined to be $B(x,r) = \{y \mid d(x,y) < r\}$.

We can show that open balls can serve as basis neighborhoods for a topology of a set X with a metric.

Definition 2.12 (metric space) A set X with a metric function d is called a *metric space*. We give it the *metric topology* of d, where the set of open balls defined using d serve as basis neighborhoods.

A metric space is a topological space. Most of the spaces we are interested in are subsets of metric spaces, in fact, a particular type of metric spaces: the Euclidean spaces. Recall the Cartesian coordinate functions u_i from Definition 2.1.

Definition 2.13 (Euclidean space) The Cartesian product of n copies of $\mathbb{R}$, the set of real numbers, along with the *Euclidean metric*

$$d(x,y) = \sqrt{\sum_{i=1}^{n}(u_i(x) - u_i(y))^2},$$

is the *n-dimensional Euclidean space* $\mathbb{R}^n$.

We may induce a topology on subsets of metric spaces as follows. If $A \subseteq X$ with topology T, then we get the *relative* or *induced* topology T_A by defining

$$T_A \quad = \quad \{S \cap A \mid S \in T\}. \tag{2.1}$$

It is easy to verify that T_A is, indeed, a topology on A, upgrading A a to space $\mathbb{A}$.

Definition 2.14 (subspace) A subset $A \subseteq X$ with topology T_A is a (topological) *subspace* of $\mathbb{X}$.

2.1.3 Homeomorphisms

We noted in Chapter 1 that topology is inherently a classification system. Given the set of all topological spaces, we are interested in partitioning this set into sets of spaces that are connected the same way. We formalize this intuition next.

Definition 2.15 (partition) A *partition of a set* is a decomposition of the set into subsets (*cells*) such that every element of the set is in one and only one of the subsets.

Definition 2.16 (equivalence) Let S be a nonempty set and let $\sim$ be a relation between elements of S that satisfies the following properties for all $a, b, c \in S$:

  (a) (Reflexive) $a \sim a$.
  (b) (Symmetric) If $a \sim b$, then $b \sim a$.

(c) (Transitive) If $a \sim b$ and $b \sim c$, then $a \sim c$.

Then, the relation $\sim$ is an *equivalence relation* on S.

The following theorem allows us to derive a partition from an equivalence relation. We omit the proof, as it is elementary.

Theorem 2.2 *Let S be a nonempty set and let $\sim$ be an equivalence relation on S. Then, $\sim$ yields a natural partition of S, where $\bar{a} = \{x \in S \mid x \sim a\}$. $\bar{a}$ represents the subset to which a belongs to. Each cell $\bar{a}$ is an* equivalence class.

We now define an equivalence relation on topological spaces.

Definition 2.17 (homeomorphism) A *homeomorphism* $f : \mathbb{X} \to \mathbb{Y}$ is a 1-1 onto function, such that both f, f^{-1} are continuous. We say that $\mathbb{X}$ is *homeomorphic* to $\mathbb{Y}$, $\mathbb{X} \approx \mathbb{Y}$, and that $\mathbb{X}$ and $\mathbb{Y}$ have the same *topological type*.

It is clear from Theorem 2.2 that homeomorphisms partition the class of topological spaces into equivalence classes of homeomorphic spaces. A fundamental problem in topology is characterizing these classes. We will see a coarser classification system in Section 2.4, and we further examine this question in Chapter 4, when we encounter yet another classification system, homology.

2.2 Manifolds

Manifolds are a type of topological spaces we are interested in. They correspond well to the spaces we are most familiar with, the Euclidean spaces. Intuitively, a manifold is a topological space that locally looks like $\mathbb{R}^n$. In other words, each point admits a coordinate system, consisting of coordinate functions on the points of the neighborhood, determining the topology of the neighborhood. We use a homeomorphism to define a chart, as shown in Figure 2.3. We also need two additional technical definitions before we may define manifolds.

Definition 2.18 (chart) A *chart* at $p \in \mathbb{X}$ is a function $\varphi : U \to \mathbb{R}^d$, where $U \subseteq \mathbb{X}$ is an open set containing p and φ is a homeomorphism onto an open subset of $\mathbb{R}^d$. The *dimension* of the chart φ is d. The *coordinate functions* of the chart are $x^i = u^i \circ \varphi : U \to \mathbb{R}$, where $u^i : \mathbb{R}^n \to \mathbb{R}$ are the standard coordinates on $\mathbb{R}^d$.

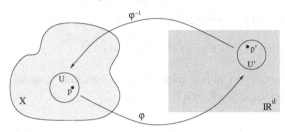

Fig. 2.3. A chart at $p \in \mathbb{X}$. φ maps $U \subset \mathbb{X}$ containing p to $U' \subseteq \mathbb{R}^d$. As φ is a homeomorphism, φ^{-1} also exists and is continuous.

Definition 2.19 (Hausdorff) A topological space $\mathbb{X}$ is *Hausdorff* if, for every $x, y \in X, x \neq y$, there are neighborhoods U, V of x, y, respectively, such that $U \cap V = \emptyset$.

A metric space is always Hausdorff. Non-Hausdorff spaces are rare, but can arise easily, when building spaces by attaching.

Definition 2.20 (separable) A topological space $\mathbb{X}$ is *separable* if it has a countable basis of neighborhoods.

Finally, we can formally define a manifold.

Definition 2.21 (manifold) A separable Hausdorff space $\mathbb{X}$ is called a *(topological) d-manifold* if there is a d-dimensional chart at every point $x \in \mathbb{X}$, that is, if $x \in \mathbb{X}$ has a neighborhood homeomorphic to $\mathbb{R}^n$. It is called a *d-manifold with boundary* if $x \in \mathbb{X}$ has a neighborhood homeomorphic to $\mathbb{R}^d$ or the Euclidean half-space $\mathbb{H}^d = \{x \in \mathbb{R}^d \mid x_1 \geq 0\}$. The *boundary* of $\mathbb{X}$ is the set of points with neighborhood homeomorphic to $\mathbb{H}^d$. The manifold has *dimension* d.

Theorem 2.3 *The boundary of a d-manifold with boundary is a $(d-1)$-manifold without boundary.*

Figure 2.4 displays a 2-manifold and a 2-manifold with boundary. The manifolds shown are compact.

Definition 2.22 (compact) A *covering* of $A \subseteq X$ is a family $\{C_j \mid j \in J\}$ in 2^X, such that $A \subseteq \bigcup_{j \in J} C_j$. An *open covering* is a covering consisting of open sets. A *subcovering* of a covering $\{C_j \mid j \in J\}$ is a covering $\{C_k \mid k \in K\}$, where $K \subseteq J$. $A \subseteq \mathbb{X}$ is *compact* if every open covering of A has a finite subcovering.

Fig. 2.4. The sphere (left) is a 2-manifold. The torus with two holes (right) is a 2-manifold with boundary. Its boundary is composed of the two circles.

Fig. 2.5. The cusp has finite area, but is not compact

Intuitively, you might think any finite area manifold is compact. However, a manifold can have finite area and not be compact, such as the cusp in Figure 2.5.

We are interested in smooth manifolds.

Definition 2.23 (C^∞) Let $U, V \subseteq \mathbb{R}^d$ be open. A function $f : U \to \mathbb{R}$ is *smooth* or C^∞ (*continuous of order ∞*) if f has partial derivatives of all orders and types. A function $\varphi : U \to \mathbb{R}^e$ is a C^∞ *map* if all its components $e^i \circ \varphi : U \to \mathbb{R}$ are C^∞. Two charts $\varphi : U \to \mathbb{R}^d, \psi : V \to \mathbb{R}^e$ are C^∞-*related* if $d = e$ and either $U \cap V = \emptyset$ or $\varphi \circ \psi^{-1}$ and $\psi \circ \varphi^{-1}$ are C^∞ maps. A C^∞ *atlas* is one for which every pair of charts is C^∞-related. A chart is *admissible* to a C^∞ atlas if it is C^∞-related to every chart in the atlas.

C^∞-related charts allow us to pass from one coordinate system to another smoothly in the overlapping region, so we may extend our notions of curves, functions, and differentials easily to manifolds.

Definition 2.24 (C^∞ **manifold**) A C^∞ *manifold* is a topological manifold together with all the admissible charts of some C^∞ atlas.

The manifolds in Figure 2.4 are also orientable.

Definition 2.25 (**orientability**) A pair of charts x^i and y^i is *consistently oriented* if the Jacobian determinant $\det(\partial x^i / \partial y^j)$ is positive whenever defined. A manifold M is *orientable* if there exists an atlas such that every pair of coordinate systems in the atlas is consistently oriented. Such an atlas is *consistently oriented* and determines an *orientation on M*. If a manifold is not orientable, it is *nonorientable*.

In this book, we use the term "manifold" to denote a C^∞-manifold. We are mainly interested in two-dimensional manifolds, or surfaces, that arise as subspaces of $\mathbb{R}^3$, with the induced topology. Equivalently, we are interested in surfaces that are embedded in $\mathbb{R}^3$.

Definition 2.26 (embedding) An embedding $f : \mathbb{X} \to \mathbb{Y}$ is a map whose restriction to its image $f(\mathbb{X})$ is a homeomorphism.

Most of our interaction with manifolds in our lives has been with embedded manifolds in Euclidean spaces. Consequently, we always think of manifolds in terms of an embedding. It is important to remember that a manifold exists independently of any embedding: A sphere does not have to sit within $\mathbb{R}^3$ to be a sphere. This is, by far, the biggest shift in the view of the world required by topology. Before we go on, let's see an example of a nonembedding.

Example 2.1 Figure 2.1(a) shows an map $F : \mathbb{R} \to \mathbb{R}^2$, where

$$F(t) = (2\cos(t - \pi/2), \sin(2(t - \pi/2))).$$

F wraps $\mathbb{R}$ over the figure-eight over and over. Note that while the map is 1-1 locally, it is not 1-1 globally. Using the monotone function

$$g(t) = \pi + 2\tan^{-1}(t)$$

in Figure 2.1(b), we first fit all of $\mathbb{R}$ into the interval $(0, 2\pi)$ and then map it using F once again. We get the same image (figure-eight) but cover it only once, making $\hat{F}$ 1-1. However, the graph of $\hat{F}$ approaches the origin in the limit, at both ∞ and $-\infty$. Any neighborhood of the origin within $\mathbb{R}^2$ will have four pieces of the graph within it and will not be homeomorphic to $\mathbb{R}$. Therefore, the map is not homeomorphic to its image and not an embedding.

The maps shown in Figure 2.1 are both immersions. Immersions are usually defined for smooth manifolds. If our original manifold $\mathbb{X}$ is compact, nothing "nasty" can happen, and an *immersion* $F : \mathbb{X} \to \mathbb{Y}$ is simply a *local* embedding. In other words, for any point $p \in \mathbb{X}$, there exists a neighborhood U containing p such that $F|_U$ is an embedding. However, F need not be an embedding within the neighborhood of $F(p)$ in $\mathbb{Y}$. That is, immersed compact spaces may self-intersect.

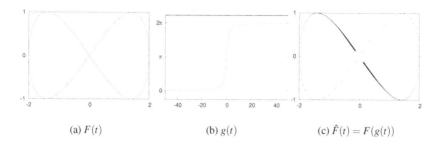

(a) $F(t)$ (b) $g(t)$ (c) $\hat{F}(t) = F(g(t))$

Fig. 2.6. Mapping of $\mathbb{R}$ into $\mathbb{R}^2$ with topological consequences.

2.3 Simplicial Complexes

In general, we are unable to represent surfaces precisely in a computer system, because it has finite storage. Consequently, we sample and represent surfaces with triangulations, as shown in Example 1.9. A triangulation is a simplicial complex, a combinatorial space that can represent a space. With simplicial complexes, we separate the topology of a space from its geometry, much like the separation of syntax and semantics in logic.

2.3.1 Geometric Definition

We begin with a definition of simplicial complexes that seems to mix geometry and topology. Combinations allow us to represent regions of space with very few points.

Definition 2.27 (combinations) Let $S = \{p_0, p_1, \ldots, p_k\} \subseteq \mathbb{R}^d$. A *linear combination* is $x = \sum_{i=0}^{k} \lambda_i p_i$, for some $\lambda_i \in \mathbb{R}$. An *affine combination* is a linear combination with $\sum_{i=0}^{k} \lambda_i = 1$. A *convex combination* is a an affine combination with $\lambda_i \geq 0$, for all i. The set of all convex combinations is the *convex hull*.

Definition 2.28 (independence) A set S is *linearly (affinely) independent* if no point in S is a linear (affine) combination of the other points in S.

Definition 2.29 (k-simplex) A *k-simplex* is the convex hull of $k+1$ affinely independent points $S = \{v_0, v_1, \ldots, v_k\}$. The points in S are the *vertices* of the simplex.

A k-simplex is a k-dimensional subspace of $\mathbb{R}^d$, $\dim \sigma = k$. We show low-dimensional simplices with their names in Figure 2.7.

2 *Spaces and Filtrations*

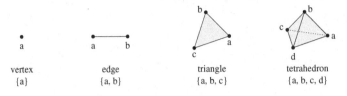

Fig. 2.7. k-simplices, for each $0 \le k \le 3$.

Definition 2.30 (face, coface) Let σ be a k-simplex defined by $S = \{v_0, v_1, \ldots, v_k\}$. A simplex τ defined by $T \subseteq S$ is a *face* of σ and has σ as a *coface*. The relationship is denoted with $\sigma \ge \tau$ and $\tau \le \sigma$. Note that $\sigma \le \sigma$ and $\sigma \ge \sigma$.

A k-simplex has $\binom{k+1}{l+1}$ faces of dimension l and $\sum_{l=-1}^{k} \binom{k+1}{l+1} = 2^{k+1}$ faces in total. A simplex, therefore, is a large, but very uniform and simple combinatorial object. We attach simplices together to represent spaces.

Definition 2.31 (simplicial complex) A *simplicial complex* K is a finite set of simplices such that

(a) $\sigma \in K, \tau \le \sigma \Rightarrow \tau \in K$;
(b) $\sigma, \sigma' \in K \Rightarrow \sigma \cap \sigma' \le \sigma, \sigma'$.

The *dimension* of K is $\dim K = \max\{\dim \sigma \mid \sigma \in K\}$. The *vertices* of K are the zero-simplices in K. A simplex is *principal* if it has no proper coface in K.

Here, *proper* has the same definition as for sets. Simply put, a simplicial complex is a collection of simplices that fit together nicely, as shown in Figure 2.8(a), as opposed to simplices in (b).

Example 2.2 (size of a simplex) As already mentioned, combinatorial topology derives its power from counting. Now that we have a finite description of a space, we can count easily. So, let's use Figure 2.7 to count the number of faces of a simplex. For example, an edge has two vertices and an edge as its faces (recall that a simplex is a face of itself.) A tetrahedron has four vertices, six edges, four triangles, and a tetrahedron as faces. These counts are summarized in Table 2.1. What should the numbers be for a 4-simplex? The numbers in the table may look really familiar to you. If we add a 1 to the left of each row, we get *Pascal's triangle*, as shown in Figure 2.9. Recall that Pascal's triangle encodes the binomial coefficients: the number of different combinations of l objects out of k objects or $\binom{k}{l}$. Here, we have $k+1$ points representing a

(a) The middle triangle shares an edge with the triangle on the left and a vertex with the triangle on the right.

(b) In the middle, the triangle is missing an edge. The simplices on the left and right intersect, but not along shared simplices.

Fig. 2.8. A simplicial complex (a) and disallowed collections of simplices (b).

Table 2.1. *Number of l-simplices in each k-simplex.*

k/l	0	1	2	3
0	1	0	0	0
1	2	1	0	0
2	3	3	1	0
3	4	6	4	1
4	?	?	?	?

k-simplex, any $l + 1$ of which defines an l-simplex. To make the relationship complete, we define the empty set $\emptyset$ as the (-1)-*simplex*. This simplex is part of every simplex and allows us to add a column of 1's to the left side of Table 2.1 to get Pascal's triangle. It also allows us to eliminate the underlined part of Definition 2.31, as the empty set of part of both simplices for nonintersecting simplices. To get the total size of a simplex, we sum each row of

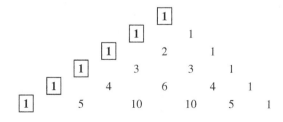

Fig. 2.9. If we add a 1 to the left side of each row in Table 2.1, we get Pascal's triangle.

Pascal's triangle. A k-simplex has $\binom{k+1}{l+1}$ faces of dimension l and

$$\sum_{l=-1}^{k} \binom{k+1}{l+1} = 2^{k+1}$$

faces in total. A simplex, therefore, is a very large object. Mathematicians often do not find it appropriate for "computation," when computation is being done by hand. Simplices are very uniform and simple in structure, however, and therefore provide an ideal computational gadget for computers.

2.3.2 Abstract Definition

The definition of a simplex uses geometry in a fundamental way. It might seem, therefore, that simplicial complexes have a geometric nature. It is possible to define simplicial complexes without using any geometry. We will present this definition next, as it displays the clear separation of topology and geometry that makes simplicial complexes attractive to us.

Definition 2.32 (abstract simplicial complex) An *abstract simplicial complex* is a set K, together with a collection S of subsets of K called *(abstract) simplices* such that:

(a) For all $v \in K, \{v\} \in S$. We call the sets $\{v\}$ the *vertices* of K.
(b) If $\tau \subseteq \sigma \in S$, then $\tau \in S$.

When it is clear from the context what S is, we refer to K as a complex. We say σ is a *k-simplex* of *dimension* k if $|\sigma| = k+1$. If $\tau \subseteq \sigma$, τ is a *face* of σ and σ is a *coface* of τ.

Note that the definition allows for $\emptyset$ as a (-1)-simplex. We now relate this abstract set-theoretic definition to the geometric one by extracting the combinatorial structure of a simplicial complex.

Definition 2.33 (vertex scheme) Let K be a simplicial complex with vertices V and let $\mathcal{K}$ be the collection of all subsets $\{v_0, v_1, \ldots, v_k\}$ of V such that the vertices $v_0, v_1, \ldots, v_k$ span a simplex of K. The collection $\mathcal{K}$ is called the *vertex scheme* of K.

The collection $\mathcal{K}$ is an abstract simplicial complex. It allows us to compare simplicial complexes easily, using isomorphisms.

Definition 2.34 (isomorphism) Let K_1, K_2 be abstract simplicial complexes with vertex sets V_1, V_2, respectively. An *isomorphism* between K_1, K_2 is a bijection $\varphi : V_1 \to V_2$, such that the sets in K_1 and K_2 are the same under the renaming of the vertices by φ and its inverse.

Theorem 2.4 *Every abstract complex S is isomorphic to the vertex scheme of some simplicial complex K. Two simplicial complexes are isomorphic iff their vertex schemes are isomorphic as abstract simplicial complexes.*

The proof is in Munkres (1984).

Definition 2.35 (geometric realization) If the abstract simplicial complex S is isomorphic with the vertex scheme of the simplicial complex K, we call K a *geometric realization* of S. It is uniquely determined up to an isomorphism, linear on the simplices.

Having constructed a simplicial complex, we will divide it into topological and geometric components. The former will be an abstract simplicial complex, a purely combinatorial object that is easily stored and manipulated in a computer system. The latter is a map of the vertices of the complex into the space in which the complex is realized. Again, this map is finite, and it can be approximated in a computer using a floating point representation. This representation of a simplicial complex translates word for word into most common file formats for storing surfaces.

Example 2.3 (Wavefront Object File) One standard format is the *Object File (OBJ)* from *Wavefront*. This format first describes the map that places the vertices in $\mathbb{R}^3$. A vertex with location $(x, y, z) \in \mathbb{R}^3$ gets the line "v x y z" in the file. After specifying the map, the format describes a simplicial complex by only listing its triangles, which are the principal simplices (see Definition 2.31). The vertices are numbered according to their order in the file and numbered from 1. A triangle with vertices v_1, v_2, v_3 is specified with line "f v_1 v_2 v_3". The description in an OBJ file is often called a "triangle soup," as the topology is specified implicitly and must be extracted.

2.3.3 Subcomplexes

Recall that a simplex is the power set of its simplices. Similarly, a natural view of a simplicial complex is that it is a special subset of the power set of all its vertices. The subset is *special* because of the requirements in Definition 2.32. Consider the small complex in Figure 2.11(a). The diagram (b) shows how the simplices connect within the complex: It has a node for each simplex and an

```
v -0.269616 0.228466 0.077226
v -0.358878 0.240631 0.044214
v -0.657287 0.527813 0.497524
v 0.186944 0.256855 0.318011
v -0.074047 0.212217 0.111664
...
f 19670 20463 20464
f 8936 8846 14300
f 4985 12950 15447
f 4985 15447 15448
...
```

Fig. 2.10. Portions of an OBJ file specifying the surface of the Stanford Bunny.

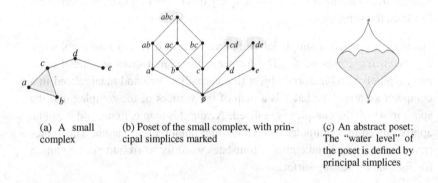

(a) A small complex

(b) Poset of the small complex, with principal simplices marked

(c) An abstract poset: The "water level" of the poset is defined by principal simplices

Fig. 2.11. Poset view of a simplicial complex.

edge indicating a face-coface relationship. The marked principal simplices are the "peaks" of the diagram. This diagram is, in fact, a *poset*.

Definition 2.36 (poset) Let S be a finite set. A *partial order* is a binary relation $\leq$ on S that is reflexive, antisymmetric, and transitive. That is for all $x, y, z \in S$,

(a) $x \leq x$,
(b) $x \leq y$ and $y \leq x$ implies $x = y$, and
(c) $x \leq y$ and $y \leq z$ implies $x \leq z$.

A set with a partial order is a *partially ordered set*, or *poset* for short.

It is clear from the definition that the face relation on simplices is a partial order. Therefore, the set of simplices with the face relation forms a poset. We often abstractly imagine a poset as in Figure 2.11(c). The set is fat around

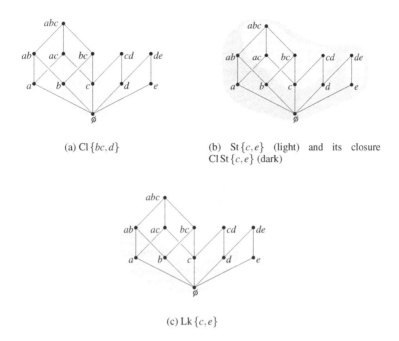

(a) Cl $\{bc, d\}$

(b) St $\{c, e\}$ (light) and its closure Cl St $\{c, e\}$ (dark)

(c) Lk $\{c, e\}$

Fig. 2.12. Closure, star, and link of simplices.

its waist because the number of possible simplices $\binom{n}{k}$ is maximized for $k \approx n/2$. The principal simplices form a level beneath which all simplices must be included. Therefore, we may recover a simplicial complex by simply storing its principal simplices, as in the case with triangulations in Example 2.3. This view also gives us intuition for extensions of concepts in point-set theory to simplicial complexes. A simplicial complex may be viewed as a closed set (it *is* a closed point set, if it is geometrically realized).

Definition 2.37 (subcomplex, closure, link, star) A *subcomplex* is a simplicial complex $L \subseteq K$. The smallest subcomplex containing a subset $L \subseteq K$ is ts *closure*, Cl $L = \{\tau \in K \mid \tau \leq \sigma \in L\}$. The *star of L* contains all of the cofaces of L, St $L = \{\sigma \in K \mid \sigma \geq \tau \in L\}$. The *link of L* is the boundary of its star, Lk $L = $ Cl St $L - $ St (Cl $L - \{\emptyset\}$).

Figure 2.12 demonstrates these concepts within the poset for our complex in Figure 2.11. A subcomplex is the analog of a subset for a simplicial complex. Given a set of simplices, we take all the simplices "below" the set within the poset to get its closure (a), and all the simplices "above" the set to get its star

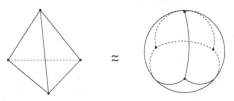

Fig. 2.13. The surface of a tetrahedron is a triangulation of a sphere, as its underlying space is homeomorphic to the sphere.

(b). The face relation is the partial order that defines "above" and "below." Most of the time, the star of a set is an open set (viewed as a point set) and not a simplicial complex. The star corresponds to the notion of a neighborhood for a simplex and, like a neighborhood, it is open. The closure operation completes the boundary of a set as before, making the star a simplicial complex (b). The link operation gives us the boundary. In our example, $\mathrm{Cl}\{c,e\} - \emptyset = \{c,e\}$, so we remove the simplices from the light regions from those in the dark region in (b) to get the link (c). Therefore, the link of c and e is the edge ab and the vertex d. Check on Figure 2.11(a) to see if this matches your intuition of what a boundary should be.

2.3.4 Triangulations

We will use simplicial complexes to represent manifolds.

Definition 2.38 (underlying space) The *underlying space* $|K|$ of a simplicial complex K is $|K| = \cup_{\sigma \in K}\sigma$.

Note that $|K|$ is a topological space.

Definition 2.39 (triangulation) A *triangulation* of a topological space $\mathbb{X}$ is a simplicial complex K such that $|K| \approx \mathbb{X}$.

For example, the boundary of a 3-simplex (tetrahedron) is homeomorphic to a sphere and is a triangulation of the sphere, as shown in Figure 2.13.

The term "triangulation" is used by different fields with different meanings. For example, in computer graphics, the term most often refers to "triangle soup" descriptions of surfaces. The finite element community often refers to triangle soups as a *mesh*, and may allow other elements, such as quadrangles, as basic building blocks. In areas, three-dimensional meshes composed of tetrahedra are called *tetrahedralizations*. Within topology, a triangulation refers to complexes of *any* dimension, however.

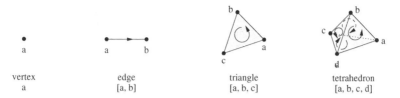

Fig. 2.14. *k*-simplices, $0 \leq k \leq 3$. The orientation on the tetrahedron is shown on its faces.

2.3.5 Orientability

Our earlier definition of orientability (Definition 2.25) depended on differentiability. We now extend this definition to simplicial complexes, which are not smooth. This extension further affirms that orientability is a topological property not dependent on smoothness.

Definition 2.40 (orientation) Let K be a simplicial complex. An *orientation* of a *k*-simplex $\sigma \in K$, $\sigma = \{v_0, v_1, \ldots, v_k\}$, $v_i \in K$, is an equivalence class of orderings of the vertices of σ, where

$$\left(v_0, v_1, \ldots, v_k\right) \sim \left(v_{\tau(0)}, v_{\tau(1)}, \ldots, v_{\tau(k)}\right) \tag{2.2}$$

are equivalent orderings if the parity of the permutation τ is even. We denote an *oriented simplex*, a simplex with an equivalence class of orderings, by $[\sigma]$.

Note that the concept of orientation derives from that fact that permutations may be partitioned into two equivalence classes (if you have forgotten these concepts, you should review Definitions 2.4 and 2.15.) Orientations may be shown graphically using arrows, as shown in Figure 2.14. We may use oriented simplices to define the concept of orientability to triangulated *d*-manifolds.

Definition 2.41 (orientability) Two *k*-simplices sharing a $(k-1)$-face σ are *consistently oriented* if they induce different orientations on σ. A triangulable *d*-manifold is *orientable* if all *d*-simplices can be oriented consistently. Otherwise, the *d*-manifold is *nonorientable*

Example 2.4 (rendering) The surface of a three-dimensional object is a 2-manifold and may be modeled with a triangulation in a computer. In computer graphics, these triangulations are rendered using light models that assign color to each triangle according to how it is situated with respect to the lights in the scene and the viewer. To do this, the model needs the normal for each triangle.

But each triangle has two normals pointing in opposite directions. To get a correct rendering, we need the normals to be consistently oriented.

2.3.6 Filtrations and Signatures

All the spaces explored in this book will be simplicial complexes. We will explore them by building them incrementally, in such a way that all the subsets generated are also complexes.

Definition 2.42 (subcomplex) A *subcomplex* of a simplicial complex K is a simplicial complex $L \subseteq K$.

Definition 2.43 (filtration) A *filtration* of a complex K is a nested sequence of subcomplexes, $\emptyset = K^0 \subseteq K^1 \subseteq K^2 \subseteq \ldots \subseteq K^m = K$. We call a complex K with a filtration a *filtered complex*.

Note that complex $K^{i+1} = K^i \,\dot\cup\, \delta^i$, where δ^i is a set of simplices. The sets δ^i provide a partial order on the simplices of K. Most of the algorithms will require a full ordering. One method to derive a full ordering is to sort each δ^i according to increasing dimension, breaking all remaining ties arbitrarily.

Definition 2.44 (filtration ordering) A *filtration ordering* of a simplicial complex K is a full ordering of its simplices, such that each prefix of the ordering is a subcomplex.

We will index the simplices in K by their rank in a filtration ordering. We may also build a filtration of $n + 1$ complexes from a filtration ordering of n simplices, $\sigma^i, 1 \le i \le n$, by adding one simplex at a time. That is, $K^0 = \emptyset$ and for $i > 0$, $K^i = \{\sigma^j \mid j \le i\}$.

The primary output of algorithms in this book will be a signature function, associating a topologically significant value to each complex.

Definition 2.45 (signature) Let K^i be a filtration of $m + 1$ complexes, and let $[m]$ denote the set $\{0, 1, 2, \ldots, m\}$ of the complex indices. A *signature function* is a map $\lambda : [m] \to \mathbb{R}$.

2.4 Alpha Shapes

We have now seen the types of spaces that will be examined in this book, as well as their representation. What remains is the derivation of meaningful filtrations, encoding the geometry of the space in the ordering. In this section, we

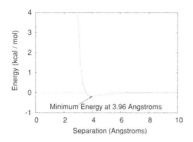

(a) The van der Waals force for two carbon atoms, as modeled by the Leonard-Jones potential function

(b) Gramicidin A, a protein, modeled as the union of spheres with van der Waals radii

Fig. 2.15. The van der Waals model for molecules.

will present a method for generating such filtrations due to Edelsbrunner, Kirkpatrick, and Seidel (1983). The method has a natural affinity to space-filling models of molecules. One such model is the *van der Waals model* (Creighton, 1984). The *van der Waals force* is a weak, but widespread force influencing the structure of molecules. The force arises from the interaction between pairs of atoms. It is extremely repulsive in the short range and weakly attractive in the intermediate range, as shown in Figure 2.15(a) for two carbon atoms. Biologists have captured the repulsive nature of this force by modeling atoms as spheres, as shown in Figure 2.15(b). The radii of atoms are defined to be half the *van der Waals contact distance*, the distance at which the minimum energy is achieved. In reality, atoms should be viewed as balls with fuzzy boundaries. Moreover, interactions of solvents with a molecule are often modeled by growing and shrinking of the balls. Generalizing this model, we could grow and shrink balls to capture all the possible shapes of a molecule. The alpha shapes model formalizes this idea. For a full mathematical exposition of the ideas discussed in this section, see Edelsbrunner (1995).

2.4.1 Dual Complex

We begin with the input to alpha shapes, a set of spherical balls.

Definition 2.46 (spherical balls) A *spherical ball* $\hat{u} = (u, U^2) \in \mathbb{R}^3 \times \mathbb{R}$ is defined by its center u and square radius U^2.

If $U^2 < 0$, the radius is imaginary and so is the ball.

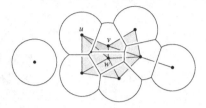

Fig. 2.16. Union of nine disks, convex decomposition using Voronoï regions, and dual complex.

Definition 2.47 (weighted square distance) The *weighted square distance* of a point x from a ball $\hat{u}$ is $\pi_{\hat{u}}(x) = \|x - u\|^2 - U^2$.

The weighted square distance of a point x has geometric meaning. It is the square length of a line segment, tangent to the sphere, that has x as one endpoint and the tangent point as its other endpoint. A point $x \in \mathbb{R}^3$ belongs to the ball iff $\pi_{\hat{u}}(x) \leq 0$, and it belongs to the bounding sphere iff $\pi_{\hat{u}}(x) = 0$. Given a finite set of spherical balls S, we divide the space into regions.

Definition 2.48 (Voronoï region) The *Voronoï region* of $\hat{u} \in S$ is the set of points for which $\hat{u}$ minimizes the weighted distance,

$$V_{\hat{u}} \quad = \quad \{x \in \mathbb{R}^3 \mid \pi_{\hat{u}}(x) \leq \pi_{\hat{v}}(x), \forall \hat{v} \in S\}. \tag{2.3}$$

The diagram of Voronoï regions, as defined above, has been called the *power diagram* and *weighted Voronoï diagram* in the literature, to distinguish it from the Voronoï diagram defined under the Euclidean metric for point sets by Voronoï (1908). It is easy to show that the set of points equally far from two weighted balls $\hat{u}, \hat{v}$ is a hyperplane defined by $\pi_{\hat{u}} = \pi_{\hat{v}}$. The Voronoï regions decompose the union of balls into convex cells of the form $\hat{u} \cap V_{\hat{u}}$, as illustrated in Figure 2.16 for two-dimensional balls or disks. Any two regions are either disjoint or they overlap along a shared portion of their boundary. We assume *general position*, where at most four Voronoï regions can have a nonempty common intersection. This assumption is justified because of a computational technique called *simulation of simplicity* that provides consistent symbolic perturbation of input that is not in general position (Edelsbrunner and Mücke, 1990). This technique is used in the *alpha shapes* software (Edelsbrunner and Mücke, 1994) as well as in my implementations.

Let $T \subseteq S$ have the property that its Voronoï regions have a nonempty common intersection. For example, in Figure 2.16, the regions with centers u, v, w have a common intersection vertex, marked by a small filled circle. Consider

X   A

Fig. 2.17. The deformation retraction of a fat letter "A" onto a thin one, and finally to a cycle.

the convex hull of the centers, in this case, the darker triangle *uvw*. General position implies that the convex hull is a *k*-dimensional simplex, where $k = |T| - 1$. We collect such simplices to construct the dual complex.

Definition 2.49 (dual complex) The *dual complex K* of *S* is the collection of simplices

$$K = \left\{ \operatorname{conv} \{ u \mid \hat{u} \in T \} \mid T \subseteq S, \bigcap_{\hat{u} \in T} (\hat{u} \cap V_{\hat{u}}) \neq \emptyset \right\}. \quad (2.4)$$

The dual complex is a simplicial complex.

2.4.2 Homotopy

We digress briefly here to claim that the dual complex *K* captures the basic topology of the union of balls *S*. In fact, *K* is a deformation retraction of $\bigcup S$ (Edelsbrunner, 1995).

Definition 2.50 (deformation retraction) A *deformation retraction* of a space $\mathbb{X}$ onto a subspace $\mathbb{A}$ is a family of maps $f_t : \mathbb{X} \to \mathbb{A}, t \in [0, 1]$ such that f_0 is the identity map, $f_1(\mathbb{X}) = \mathbb{A}$, and $f_t | \mathbb{A}$ is the identity map, for all t. The family should be continuous, in the sense that the associated map $\mathbb{X} \times [0, 1] \to \mathbb{X}$, $(x,t) \mapsto f_t(x)$ is continuous.

In other words, starting from the original space $\mathbb{X}$ at time 0, we continuously deform the space until it becomes the subspace $\mathbb{A}$ at time 1. We do this without ever moving the subspace $\mathbb{A}$ in the process. In Figure 2.17, the space $\mathbb{X}$ is a fat letter "A", and its subspace $\mathbb{A}$ is a thin letter "A." We retract the fat letter onto the thin letter continuously to get a deformation retraction. Note that the two spaces seem to be connected the same way but are of different dimensions. We may continue this retraction until we get the cycle on the right. Once we get the cycle, we are stuck. We cannot go further and retract the space into a single point. A deformation retraction is a special case of a homotopy where the requirement of the final space being a subspace is relaxed.

Definition 2.51 (homotopy) A *homotopy* is a family of maps $f_t : \mathbb{X} \to \mathbb{Y}, t \in [0,1]$, such that the associated map $F : \mathbb{X} \times [0,1] \to \mathbb{Y}$ given by $F(x,t) = f_t(x)$ is continuous. Then, $f_0, f_1 : \mathbb{X} \to \mathbb{Y}$ are *homotopic* via the homotopy f_t. We denote this as $f_0 \simeq f_1$.

Suppose we have a retraction as in Definition 2.50. If we let $i : \mathbb{A} \to \mathbb{X}$ to be the inclusion map, we have $f_1 \circ i \simeq 1$ and $i \circ f_1 \simeq 1$. This allows us to classify $\mathbb{X}$ and its subspace $\mathbb{A}$ as having the same connectivity using the maps f_1, i. This is just a special case of homotopy equivalence.

Definition 2.52 (homotopy equivalence) A map $f : \mathbb{X} \to \mathbb{Y}$ is called a *homotopy equivalence* if there is a map $g : \mathbb{Y} \to \mathbb{X}$ such that $f \circ g \simeq 1$ and $g \circ f \simeq 1$. Then, $\mathbb{X}$ and $\mathbb{Y}$ are *homotopy equivalent* and have the same *homotopy type*. This fact is denoted as $\mathbb{X} \simeq \mathbb{Y}$.

Earlier in this chapter, in Section 2.1.3, we saw an equivalence class based on homeomorphisms. Homotopy is also an equivalence relation, but it does not have the differentiating power of homeomorphisms: Two spaces with different topological types could have the same homotopy type. As a weaker invariant, homotopy is still quite useful, as homeomorphic spaces are homotopic.

Theorem 2.5 $\mathbb{X} \approx \mathbb{Y} \Rightarrow \mathbb{X} \simeq \mathbb{Y}$.

2.4.3 Alpha Complex

We have seen that the dual complex of a union of balls captures the union's topology. This is significant, because the dual complex is a simplicial complex, a combinatorial object, while the union of balls is a space, described in a set-theoretic fashion. Given a collection of balls S, the growth model for deriving a filtration is to simply grow the balls. We have a choice here as to how fast the growth should be. We choose the following growth model, as it allows for efficient algorithms for its computation. For every real number $\alpha^2 \in \mathbb{R}$, we increase the square radius of a ball $\hat{u}$ by α^2, giving us $\hat{u}(\alpha) = (u, U^2 + \alpha^2)$. We denote the collection of expanded balls $\hat{u}(\alpha)$ as $S(\alpha)$. If $U^2 = 0$, then α is the radius of $\hat{u}(\alpha)$. If $U^2 + \alpha^2 < 0$, then the ball $\hat{u}(\alpha)$ is imaginary.

Definition 2.53 (alpha complex) For a set of spherical balls S, let $S(\alpha) = \{(u, U^2 + \alpha^2) \mid (u, U^2) \in S\}$. The α-*complex* $K(\alpha)$ of S is the dual complex of $S(\alpha)$ (Edelsbrunner and Mücke, 1994).

$K(-\infty)$ is the empty set, $K(0) = K$, and $K(\infty) = D$ is the dual of the Voronoï diagram, also known as the Delaunay triangulation of S (Delaunay, 1934). It is easy to see that the Voronoï regions do not change and simplices are only added as the balls are expanded. Therefore, $K(\alpha_1) \subseteq K(\alpha_2)$ for $\alpha_1 \le \alpha_2$. This implies that the α-complex provides a filtration of the Delaunay triangulation of S. This filtration gives a partial ordering on the simplices of K. For each simplex $\sigma \in D$, there is a unique *birth time* $\alpha^2(\sigma)$ such that $\sigma \in K(\alpha)$ iff $\alpha^2 \ge \alpha^2(\sigma)$. We order the simplices such that $\alpha^2(\sigma) < \alpha^2(\tau)$ implies σ precedes τ in the ordering. More than one simplex may be born at a time, and such cases may arise even if S is in general position. For example, in Figure 2.16, edge *uw* is born at the same moment as triangle *uvw*. As noted before, we may convert this partial ordering into a total ordering easily. In fact, for α-shape filtrations, we always do so, allowing only a single simplex to enter the complex at any time.

In Figure 2.18, we show a few complexes in an alpha-complex filtration for a small protein, Gramicidin A. We have seen this protein before, first modeled as a molecular surface in Figure 1.5(a), and then as a van der Waals surface in Figure 2.15(b). Note that the alpha-complex model has many additional topological attributes at different times in the filtration. One of the main results of this book is the identification of the significant topological features from these attributes.

2.5 Manifold Sweeps

Alpha-shapes allow us to explore the shape of finite point sets and unions of balls. In addition to such spaces, we are interested in exploring manifolds with height functions. In Example 1.10, we saw how the geometry of a manifold dictates the topology of its iso-lines. We use this example to motivate another geometrically ordered filtration in this section, postponing theoretical justification for it until we have been introduced to Morse Theory in Chapter 5.

Let K be a triangulation of a compact 2-manifold without boundary $\mathbb{M}$. Let $h : \mathbb{M} \to \mathbb{R}$ be a function that is linear on every triangle. The function is defined, consequently, by its values at the vertices of K. We will assume that $h(u) \ne h(v)$ for all vertices $u \ne v \in K$. Again, simulation of simplicity is the computational justification for this assumption (Edelsbrunner and Mücke, 1990). It is common to refer to h as the *height function*, because it matches our intuition of a geographic landscape. One needs to be careful, however, not to allow the intuition to limit one's imagination, as h can be any continuous function.

In a simplicial complex, the natural concept of a neighborhood of a vertex

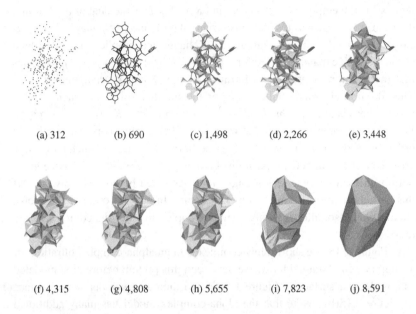

(a) 312   (b) 690   (c) 1,498   (d) 2,266   (e) 3,448

(f) 4,315   (g) 4,808   (h) 5,655   (i) 7,823   (j) 8,591

Fig. 2.18. Gramicidin A, a protein, modeled as a filtration of 8,591 α-complexes of data set *1grm* in Section 12.1. Ten complexes are shown with their indices.

u is the *star*, Stu, that consists of u together with the edges and triangles that share u as a vertex. Since all vertices have different heights, each edge and triangle has a unique lowest and a unique highest vertex. Following Banchoff (1970), we use this to partition the simplices of the star into lower and upper stars. Formally:

Definition 2.54 (upper, lower star) The *lower* star $\underline{\text{St}}u$ and *upper star* $\overline{\text{St}}u$ of vertex u for a height function h are

$$\underline{\text{St}}u \;=\; \{\sigma \in \text{St}u \mid h(v) \leq h(u), \forall \text{ vertices } v \leq \sigma\}, \qquad (2.5)$$

$$\overline{\text{St}}u \;=\; \{\sigma \in \text{St}u \mid h(v) \geq h(u), \forall \text{ vertices } v \leq \sigma\}. \qquad (2.6)$$

These subsets of the star contain the simplices that have u as their highest or their lowest vertex, respectively. As we shall see in Chapter 6, we may examine the lower and upper stars of a vertex to determine if the vertex is a maximum, a minimum, or a saddle point in a triangulated manifold. These points are critical to our understanding of the topology of the iso-lines of a surface, as all topological changes happen when they occur. For example, a maximum vertex u is not the lowest vertex of any simplex, so $\overline{\text{St}}u = \{u\}$ and $\underline{\text{St}}u = \text{St}u$. A

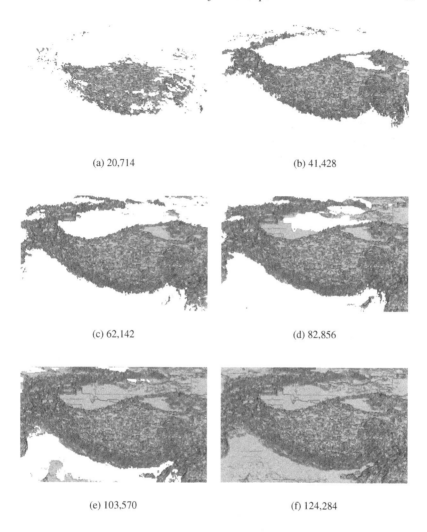

(a) 20,714

(b) 41,428

(c) 62,142

(d) 82,856

(e) 103,570

(f) 124,284

Fig. 2.19. A filtration of the terrain of the Himalayas (data set *Himalayas* in Section 12.5.) Six out of the 124,284 complexes are shown with their indices.

maximum also creates a new component of iso-lines if we sweep the manifold from above, as in Figure 1.8.

We may partition K into a collection of either lower or upper stars, $K = \bigcup_u \underline{\mathrm{St}} u = \bigcup_u \overline{\mathrm{St}} u$. Each partition gives us a filtration. Suppose we sort the n vertices of K in order of increasing height to get the sequence $u^1, u^2, \ldots,$

u^n, $h(u^i) < h(u^j)$, for all $1 \leq i < j \leq n$. We then let K^i be the union of the first i lower stars, $K^i = \bigcup_{1 \leq j \leq i} \underline{\mathrm{St}} u^j$. Each simplex σ has an associated vertex u^i, and we call the height of that vertex the *birth time* $h(\sigma) = h(u^i)$ of σ. This definition mimics the definition of birth times for alpha-shapes. The subcomplex K^i of K consists of the i lowest vertices together with all edges and triangles connecting them. Clearly, the sequence K^i defines a filtration of K. We may define another filtration by sorting in decreasing order and using upper stars. We show an example of such a filtration in Figure 2.19. Either filtration is geometrically ordered and will provide us with filtration orderings and meaningful topological results.

3

Group Theory

Having examined the structure of the input to our computations in the last chapter, we now turn to developing the machinery we need for characterizing the topology of spaces. Recall that we are interested in classification systems. *Group theory* provides us with powerful tools to define equivalence relations using *homomorphisms* and *factor groups*. In the next chapter, we shall utilize these tools to define *homology*, a topological classification system. Unlike homeomorphy and homotopy, homology is discrete by nature. As such, it is the basis for my work.

The rest of this chapter is organized as follows. In Section 3.1, I will introduce groups. I devote Section 3.2 to developing techniques for characterizing a specific type of groups: finitely generated Abelian groups. In Section 3.3, I examine advanced algebraic structures in order to generalize the result from the previous section.

Abstract algebra is beautifully lucid by its axiomatic nature, capturing familiar concepts from arithmetic. The plethora of arcane terms, however, often makes the field inscrutable to nonspecialists. My goal is to make the subject thoroughly accessible by not leaving anything obscure. Consequently, there is a lot of ground to cover in this chapter. My treatment is derived mostly from the excellent introductory book on abstract algebra by Fraleigh (1989), which also contains the proofs to most of the theorems stated in this chapter. I used Dummit and Foote (1999) for the advanced topics.

3.1 Introduction to Groups

Abstract algebra is based on abstracting from algebra its core properties and studying algebra in terms of those properties.

Table 3.1. *A closed binary operation* ∗, *defined on the set* $\{a,b,c\}$.

	a	b	c
a	b	c	b
b	a	c	b
c	c	b	a

3.1.1 Binary Operations

We begin by extending the concept of addition. For a review of sets, see Section 2.1.1.

Definition 3.1 (binary operation) A *binary operation* ∗ *on a set S* is a rule that assigns to each ordered pair (a,b) of elements of S some element in S. It must assign a single element to each pair (otherwise it's *not defined* or *not well-defined*, for assigning zero or more than one elements, respectively), and it must assign an element in S for the operation to be *closed*.

If S is finite, we may display a binary operation ∗ in a table listing the elements of the set on the top and side of the table, and stating $a \ast b$ in row a, column b of the table, as in Table 3.1. Note that the operation defined by that table depends on the order of the pair, as $a \ast b \neq b \ast a$.

Definition 3.2 (commutative) A binary operation ∗ on a set S is *commutative* if $a \ast b = b \ast a$ for all $a, b \in S$.

If S is finite, the table for a commutative binary operation is symmetric with respect to the diagonal from the upper-left to the lower-right.

Definition 3.3 (associative) A binary operation ∗ on a set S is *associative* if $(a \ast b) \ast c = a \ast (b \ast c)$ for all $a, b, c \in S$.

If a binary operation ∗ is associative, we may write unambiguous long expressions without using parentheses.

3.1.2 Groups

The study of groups, as well as the need for new types of numbers, was motivated by solving equations.

Example 3.1 (solving equations) Suppose we were interested in solving the following three equations:

1. $5 + x = 2$
2. $2x = 3$
3. $x^2 = -1$.

The equations imply the need for negative integers $\mathbb{Z}^-$, rational numbers $\mathbb{Q}$, and complex numbers $\mathbb{C}$, respectively. Recalling algebra from eighth grade, I solve equation (1) above, listing the properties needed at each step.

$$
\begin{array}{rcll}
5 + x & = & 2 & \text{Given} \\
-5 + (5 + x) & = & -5 + 2 & \text{Addition property of equality} \\
(-5 + 5) + x & = & -5 + 2 & \text{Associative property of addition} \\
0 + x & = & -5 + 2 & \text{Inverse property of addition} \\
x & = & -5 + 2 & \text{Identity property of addition} \\
x & = & -3 & \text{Addition}
\end{array}
$$

The needed properties motivate the definition of a group.

Definition 3.4 (group) A *group* $\langle G, * \rangle$ is a set G, together with a binary operation $*$ on G, such that the following axioms are satisfied:

(a) $*$ is associative.

(b) $\exists e \in G$ such that $e * x = x * e = x$ for all $x \in G$. The element e is an *identity* element for $*$ on G.

(c) $\forall a \in G, \exists a' \in G$ such that $a' * a = a * a' = e$. The element a' is an *inverse of a with respect to the operation* $*$.

If G is finite, the *order* of G is $|G|$. We often omit the operation and refer to G as the group.

The identity and inverses are unique in a group. We may easily show, furthermore, that $(a * b)' = b' * a'$, for all $a, b \in G$ in group $\langle G, * \rangle$.

Example 3.2 (groups) $\langle \mathbb{Z}, + \rangle$, $\langle \mathbb{R}, \cdot \rangle$, and $\langle \mathbb{R}, + \rangle$ are all groups. Note that only one operation is allowed for groups, so we choose either multiplication or addition for integers, for example.

We are mainly interested in groups with commutative binary operations.

Definition 3.5 (Abelian) A group G is *Abelian* if its binary operation $*$ is commutative.

3 Group Theory

Table 3.2. *Structures for groups of size 2, 3, 4.*

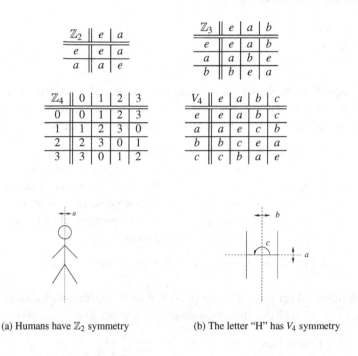

$\mathbb{Z}_2$	e	a
e	e	a
a	a	e

$\mathbb{Z}_3$	e	a	b
e	e	a	b
a	a	b	e
b	b	e	a

$\mathbb{Z}_4$	0	1	2	3
0	0	1	2	3
1	1	2	3	0
2	2	3	0	1
3	3	0	1	2

V_4	e	a	b	c
e	e	a	b	c
a	a	e	c	b
b	b	c	e	a
c	c	b	a	e

(a) Humans have $\mathbb{Z}_2$ symmetry   (b) The letter "H" has V_4 symmetry

Fig. 3.1. Two figures and their symmetry groups.

We usually borrow terminology from arithmetic for Abelian groups, using $+$ or juxtaposition for the operation, 0 or 1 to denote identity, and $-a$ or a^{-1} for inverses. It is easy to list the possible structures for small groups using the following fact, derived from the definition of groups: Each element of a finite group must appear once and only once in each row and column of its table. Using this fact, Table 3.2 shows all possible structures for groups of size two, three, and four. There are, in fact, three possible groups of size four, but only two unique structures: We get the other one by renaming the elements.

Example 3.3 (symmetry groups) An application of group theory is the study of symmetries of geometric figures. An *isometry* is a distance-preserving transformation in a metric space. A *symmetry* is any isometry that leaves the object as a whole unchanged. The symmetries of a figure form a group. A human, abstracted in Figure 3.1(a) as a stick figure, has only two symmetries: the identity and reflection along the vertical line shown. It is immediate that a human's

(a) View of column

(b) Motif   (c) Full design

Fig. 3.2. Tiled design from Masjid-e-Shah in Isfahan, Iran (a) repeats the prophet's name (b) to obtain a figure (c) with $\mathbb{Z}_4$ symmetry.

group of symmetry is $\mathbb{Z}_2$, as this is the only group with two elements. The letter "H" in (b) has three different types of symmetries shown: reflections along the horizontal and vertical axes, and rotation by 180 degrees. If we write down the table corresponding to compositions of these symmetries, we get the group V_4, one of the two groups with four elements, as shown in Table 3.2.

Designers have used symmetries throughout history to decorate buildings. Figure 3.2(a) shows a view of a column of Masjid-e-Shah, a mosque in Isfahan, Iran, that was completed in 1637. The design in the center of the photo pictorializes the name of the prophet of Islam, Mohammad (b), as the motif in a design (c). This figure is unchanged by rotations by multiples of 90 degrees.

Letting e, a, b, c be rotations by 0, 90, 180, and 270 degrees, respectively, and writing down the table of compositions, we get $\mathbb{Z}_4$, the other group with four elements in Table 3.2. That is, the design has $\mathbb{Z}_4$ symmetry.

3.1.3 Subgroups and Cosets

As for sets, we may try to understand groups by examining the building blocks they are composed of. We begin by extending the concept of a subset to groups.

Definition 3.6 (induced operation) Let $\langle G, * \rangle$ be a group and $S \subseteq G$. If S is closed under $*$, then $*$ is the *induced operation on S from G*.

Definition 3.7 (subgroup) A subset $H \subseteq G$ of group $\langle G, * \rangle$ is a *subgroup of G* if H is a group and is closed under $*$. The subgroup consisting of the identity element of G, $\{e\}$ is the *trivial subgroup* of G. All other subgroups are *nontrivial*.

We can identify subgroups easily, using the following theorem.

Theorem 3.1 (subgroups) $H \subseteq G$ *of a group* $\langle G, * \rangle$ *is a subgroup of G iff:*

(a) *H is closed under $*$;*
(b) *the identity e of G is in H;*
(c) *for all $a \in H$, $a^{-1} \in H$.*

Example 3.4 (subgroups) The only nontrivial proper subgroup of $\mathbb{Z}_4$ in Table 3.2 is $\{0, 2\}$. $\{0, 3\}$ is not a subgroup of $\mathbb{Z}_4$ as $3 * 3 = 2 \notin \{0, 3\}$, so the set is not closed under the binary operation stated in the table.

Given a subgroup, we may partition a group into sets, all having the same size as the subgroup. We shall see that if the group satisfies a certain property, we may then regard each set as a single element of a group in a natural way.

Theorem 3.2 (cosets) *Let H be a subgroup of G. Let the relation $\sim_L$ be defined on G by: $a \sim_L b$ iff $a^{-1}b \in H$. Let $\sim_R$ be defined by: $a \sim_R b$ iff $ab^{-1} \in H$. Then $\sim_L$ and $\sim_R$ are both equivalence relations on G.*

Note that $a^{-1}b \in H \Rightarrow a^{-1}b = h \in H \Rightarrow b = ah$. We use these relations to define cosets.

Definition 3.8 (cosets) Let H be a subgroup of group G. For $a \in G$, the subset $aH = \{ah \mid h \in H\}$ of G is the *left coset* of H containing a and $Ha = \{ha \mid h \in H\}$ is the *right coset* of H containing a.

For an Abelian subgroup H of G, $ah = ha, \forall a \in G, h \in H$, so the left and right cosets match. We may easily show that every left coset and every right coset has the same size by constructing a 1-1 map of H onto a left coset gH of H for a fixed element g of G.

Example 3.5 (cosets) As we saw in Example 3.4, $\{0,2\}$ is a subgroup of $\mathbb{Z}_4$. The coset of 1 is $1 + \{0,2\} = \{1,3\}$. The sets $\{0,2\}$ and $\{1,3\}$ exhaust all of $\mathbb{Z}_4$. As $\mathbb{Z}_4$ is Abelian, the sets are both the left and right cosets.

3.2 Characterizing Groups

Having defined groups, a natural question that arises is to characterize groups: How many "different" groups are there? This is yet another classification problem, and it is the fundamental question studied in group theory. Our goal in the rest of this chapter is to fully understand the structure of certain finite groups that are generated in our study of homology.

3.2.1 Structure-Relating Maps

Since we are interested in characterizing the structure of groups, we define maps between groups to relate their structures.

Definition 3.9 (homomorphism) A map φ of a group G into a group G' is a *homomorphism* if $\varphi(ab) = \varphi(a)\varphi(b)$ for all $a, b \in G$. For any groups G and G', there's always at least one homomorphism $\varphi \colon G \to G'$, namely, the *trivial homomorphism* defined by $\varphi(g) = e'$ for all $g \in G$, where e' is the identity in G'.

Homomorphisms preserve the identity, inverses, and subgroups in the following sense.

Theorem 3.3 (homomorphism) *Let φ be a homomorphism of a group G into a group G'.*

(a) If e is the identity in G, then $\varphi(e)$ is the identity e' in G'.
(b) If $a \in G$, then $\varphi(a^{-1}) = \varphi(a)^{-1}$.
(c) If H is a subgroup of G, then $\varphi(H)$ is a subgroup of G'.
(d) If K' is a subgroup of G', then $\varphi^{-1}(K')$ is a subgroup of G.

Homomorphisms also define a special subgroup in their domain.

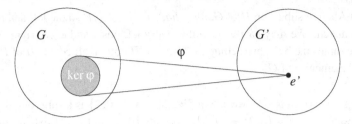

Fig. 3.3. A homomorphism $\varphi: G \to G'$ and its kernel.

Definition 3.10 (kernel) Let $\varphi: G \to G'$ be a homomorphism. The subgroup $\varphi^{-1}(\{e'\}) \subseteq G$, consisting of all elements of G mapped by φ into the identity e' of G', is the *kernel of* φ, denoted by $\ker \varphi$, as shown in Figure 3.3.

Note that $\ker \varphi$ is a subgroup by an application of Theorem 3.3 to the fact that $\{e'\}$ is the trivial subgroup of G'. So, we may use it to partition G into cosets.

Theorem 3.4 (kernel cosets) *Let* $\varphi: G \to G'$ *be a homomorphism, and let* $H = \ker \varphi$. *Let* $a \in G$. *Then the set*

$$\varphi^{-1}\{\varphi(a)\} = \{x \in G \mid \varphi(x) = \varphi(a)\}$$

is the left coset aH *of* H *and is also the right coset* Ha *of* H.

The two partitions of G into left cosets and right cosets of $\ker \varphi$ are the same, according to the theorem. There is a name for subgroups with this property.

Definition 3.11 (normal) A subgroup H of a group G is *normal* if its left and right cosets coincide, that is, if $gH = Hg$ for all $g \in G$.

All subgroups of an Abelian group are normal, as is the kernel of any homomorphism. A simple corollary follows from Theorem 3.4.

Corollary 3.1 *A homomorphism* $\varphi: G \to G'$ *is 1-1 iff* $\ker \varphi = \{e\}$.

Analogs of injections, surjections, and bijections exist for maps between groups. They have their own special names, however.

Definition 3.12 (mono-, epi-, iso-morphism) A 1-1 homomorphism is an *monomorphism*. A homomorphism that is onto is an *epimorphism*. A homomorphism that is 1-1 and onto is an *isomorphism*. We use $\cong$ for isomorphisms.

Isomorphisms between groups are like homeomorphisms between topological spaces. We may use isomorphisms to define an equivalence relationship between groups, formalizing our notion for similar structures for groups.

Theorem 3.5 *Let $\mathcal{G}$ be any collection of groups. Then $\cong$ is an equivalence relation on $\mathcal{G}$.*

All groups of order 4, for example, are isomorphic to one of the two 4 by 4 tables in Table 3.2, so the classification problem is fully solved for that order. We need smarter techniques, however, to settle this question for higher orders.

3.2.2 Cyclic Groups

A method of understanding complex objects is to understand simple objects first. Cyclic groups are simple groups that can be easily classified. We may use cyclic groups as building blocks to form larger groups. On the other hand, we may break larger groups into collections of cyclic groups. Cyclic groups are fundamental to the understanding of Abelian groups.

Theorem 3.6 *Let G be a group and let $a \in G$. Then, $H = \{a^n \mid n \in \mathbb{Z}\}$ is a subgroup of G and is the smallest subgroup of G that contains a, that is, every subgroup containing a contains H.*

Definition 3.13 (cyclic group) The group H of Theorem 3.6 is the *cyclic subgroup of G generated by a* and will be denoted by $\langle a \rangle$. If $\langle a \rangle$ is finite, then the *order of a* is $|\langle a \rangle|$. An element a of a group G *generates* G and is a *generator for G* if $\langle a \rangle = G$. A group G is *cyclic* if it has a generator.

For example, $\mathbb{Z} = \langle 1 \rangle$ under addition and is therefore cyclic. We can also define finite cyclic groups using a new binary operation.

Definition 3.14 (modulo) Let n be a fixed positive integer, and let h and k be any integers. When $h + k$ is divided by n, the remainder is the *sum of h and k modulo n.*

Definition 3.15 ($\mathbb{Z}_n$) The set $\{0, 1, 2, \ldots, n-1\}$ is a cyclic group $\mathbb{Z}_n$ of elements under addition modulo n.

As claimed earlier, we may fully classify cyclic groups using the following theorem.

Theorem 3.7 (classification of cyclic groups) *Any infinite cyclic group is isomorphic to $\mathbb{Z}$ under addition. Any finite cyclic group of order n is isomorphic to $\mathbb{Z}_n$ under addition modulo n.*

Consequently, we may use $\mathbb{Z}$ and $\mathbb{Z}_n$ as the prototypical cyclic groups.

3.2.3 Finitely Generated Abelian Groups

We may form larger groups using simple groups by multiplying them together, forming the Cartesian product of their associated sets.

Theorem 3.8 (direct products) *Let $G_1, G_2, \ldots, G_n$ be groups. For $(a_1, a_2, \ldots, a_n)$ and $(b_1, b_2, \ldots, b_n)$ in $\prod_{i=1}^{n} G_i$, define $(a_1, a_2, \ldots, a_n)(b_1, b_2, \ldots, b_n)$ to be $(a_1 b_1, a_2 b_2, \ldots, a_n b_n)$. Then, $\prod_{i=1}^{n} G_i$ is a group, the* direct product *of the groups G_i, under this binary operation.*

We may also form groups by intersecting subgroups of a group.

Theorem 3.9 (intersection) *The intersection of subgroups H_i of a group G for $i \in I$ is again a subgroup of G.*

Let G be a group and let $a_i \in G$ for $i \in I$. There is at least one subgroup of G containing all the elements a_i, namely, G itself. Theorem 3.9 allows us to take the intersection of all the subgroups of G containing all a_i to obtain a subgroup H of G. Clearly, H is the smallest subgroup containing all a_i.

Definition 3.16 (finitely generated) Let G be a group and let $a_i \in G$ for $i \in I$. The smallest subgroup of G containing $\{a_i \mid i \in I\}$ is the *subgroup generated by* $\{a_i \mid i \in I\}$. If this subgroup is all of G, then $\{a_i \mid i \in I\}$ *generates* G and the a_i are the *generators of* G. If there is a finite set $\{a_i \mid i \in I\}$ that generates G, then G is *finitely generated.*

We are primarily interested in finitely generated Abelian groups. Fortunately, these groups are fully classified by the following theorem.

Theorem 3.10 (fundamental theorem of finitely generated Abelian groups) *Every finitely generated Abelian group G is isomorphic to a direct product of cyclic groups of the form*

$$\mathbb{Z}_{(p_1^{r_1})} \times \mathbb{Z}_{(p_2^{r_2})} \times \cdots \times \mathbb{Z}_{(p_n^{r_n})} \times \mathbb{Z} \times \mathbb{Z} \times \cdots \times \mathbb{Z},$$

where the p_i are primes, not necessarily distinct. The direct product is unique *except for the possible arrangement of factors; that is, the number of factors of $\mathbb{Z}$ is unique and the prime powers $(p_i)^{r_i}$ are unique.*

Note how the product is composed of a number of infinite and finite cyclic group factors. Intuitively, the infinite part captures those generators that are "free" to generate as many elements as they wish. The finite or "torsion" part captures generators with finite order.

Definition 3.17 (Betti numbers, torsion) The number of factors of $\mathbb{Z}$ in Theorem 3.10 is the *Betti number* $\beta(G)$ of G. The subscripts of the finite cyclic factors are called the *torsion coefficients of G*.

3.2.4 Factor Groups

We saw in Theorem 3.4 how the left and right cosets defined by the kernel of a homomorphism were the same. The cosets are also the same for any normal subgroup H by definition. We would like to treat the cosets defined by H as individual elements of another smaller group. To do so, we first derive a binary operation from the group operation of G.

Theorem 3.11 *Let H be a subgroup of a group G. Then, left coset multiplication is well defined by the equation $(aH)(bH) = (ab)H$, iff the left and right cosets coincide.*

The multiplication is well defined because it does not depend on the elements a, b chosen from the cosets. Using left coset multiplication as a binary operation, we get new groups.

Corollary 3.2 *Let H be a subgroup of G whose left and right cosets coincide. Then, the cosets of H form a group G/H under the binary operation $(aH)(bH) = (ab)H$.*

Definition 3.18 (factor group) The group G/H in Corollary 3.2 is the *factor group* (or *quotient group*) *of G modulo H*. The elements in the same coset of H are said to be *congruent modulo H*.

We have already seen a factor group defined by the kernel of a homomorphism φ. The factor group, namely $G/(\ker \varphi)$, is naturally isomorphic to $\varphi(G)$.

Theorem 3.12 (fundamental homomorphism) *Let $\varphi : G \to G'$ be a group homomorphism with kernel H. Then $\varphi(G)$ is a group and the map $\mu : G/H \to$*

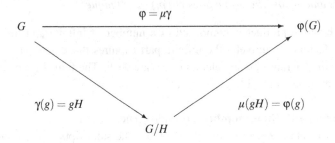

$$\varphi = \mu\gamma$$

$$G \xrightarrow{\hspace{5cm}} \varphi(G)$$

$$\gamma(g) = gH \qquad\qquad \mu(gH) = \varphi(g)$$

$$G/H$$

Fig. 3.4. The fundamental homomorphism theorem. $H = \ker\varphi$, and μ is the natural isomorphism, corresponding to homomorphism γ.

$\mathbb{Z}_6$	0	3	1	4	2	5
0	0	3	1	4	2	5
3	3	0	4	1	5	2
1	1	4	2	5	3	0
4	4	1	5	2	0	3
2	2	5	3	0	4	1
5	5	2	0	3	1	4

Fig. 3.5. $\mathbb{Z}_6/\{0,3\}$ is isomorphic to $\mathbb{Z}_3$.

$\varphi(G)$ *given by* $\mu(gH) = \varphi(g)$ *is an isomorphism. If* $\gamma: G \to G/H$ *is the homomorphism given by* $\gamma(g) = gH$, *then for each* $g \in G$ *we have* $\varphi(g) = \mu\gamma(g)$. μ *is the* natural *or* canonical isomorphism, *and* γ *is the corresponding homomorphism.*

The relationship between φ, μ and γ is shown in a *commutative diagram* in Figure 3.4. Homology characterizes topology using factor groups whose structure is finitely Abelian. So, it is imperative to gain a full understanding of this method before moving on.

Example 3.6 (factoring $\mathbb{Z}_6$) The cyclic group $\mathbb{Z}_6$, on the left, has $\{0,3\}$ as a subgroup. As $\mathbb{Z}_6$ is Abelian, $\{0,3\}$ is normal, so we may factor $\mathbb{Z}_6$ using this subgroup, getting the cosets $\{0,3\}$, $\{1,4\}$, and $\{2,5\}$. Figure 3.5 shows the table for $\mathbb{Z}_6$, ordered and shaded according to the cosets. The shading pattern gives rise to a smaller group, shown on the right, where each coset is collapsed to a single element. Comparing this new group to the structures in Table 3.2,

$\mathbb{Z}_6$	0	2	4	1	3	5
0	0	2	4	1	3	5
2	2	4	0	3	5	1
4	4	0	2	5	1	3
1	1	3	5	2	4	0
3	3	5	1	4	0	2
5	5	1	3	0	2	4

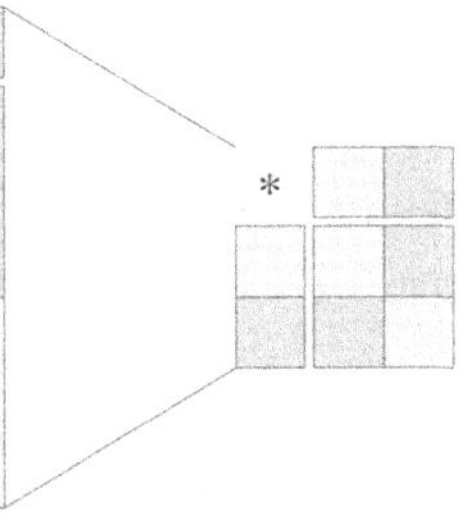

Fig. 3.6. $\mathbb{Z}_6/\{0,2,4\}$ is isomorphic to $\mathbb{Z}_2$.

we observe that it is isomorphic to $\mathbb{Z}_3$, the only group of order 3. Therefore, $\mathbb{Z}_6/\{0,3\} \cong \mathbb{Z}_3$. Moreover, $\{0,3\}$ with binary operation $+_6$ is isomorphic to $\mathbb{Z}_2$, as one may see from the top left corner of the table for $\mathbb{Z}_6$. So, we have $\mathbb{Z}_6/\mathbb{Z}_2 \cong \mathbb{Z}_3$. Similarly, $\mathbb{Z}_6/\mathbb{Z}_3 \cong \mathbb{Z}_2$, as shown in Figure 3.6.

For a beginner, factor groups seem to be one of the hardest concepts in group theory. Given a factor group G/H, the key idea to remember is that each *element* of the factor group has the form aH: It is a set, a coset of H. Now, we could represent each element of a factor group with a representative from the coset. For example, the element 4 could represent the coset $\{1,4\}$ for factor group $\mathbb{Z}_6/\{0,3\}$. However, don't forget that this element is congruent to 1 modulo $\{0,3\}$.

3.3 Advanced Structures

In this section, we delve into advanced algebra by looking at increasingly rich algebraic structures we will encounter in our study of homology. Our goal in this section is to generalize Theorem 3.10, first to modules and then to graded modules.

3.3.1 Free Abelian Groups

Recall that a finitely generated Abelian group is isomorphic to a product of infinite and finite cyclic groups. In this section, we will characterize infinite factors using the notion of free Abelian groups. As we will only deal with Abelian groups, we will use $+$ to denote the group operation and 0 for the identity element. For $n \in \mathbb{Z}^+, a \in G$, we use $na = a + a + \cdots + a$ and $-na = (-a) + (-a) + \cdots + (-a)$ to denote the sum of n copies of a and its inverse, respectively. Finally, $0a = 0$, where the first 0 is in $\mathbb{Z}$, and the second is in G. It is important to realize that G is still a group with a single group operation, addition, even though we use multiplication in our notation. We shall shift our view later in defining modules and vector spaces. Let us start with two equivalent conditions.

Theorem 3.13 *Let X be a subset of a nonzero Abelian group G. The following conditions on X are equivalent.*

  (a) *Each nonzero element a in G can be uniquely expressed in the form $a = n_1 x_1 + n_2 x_2 + \cdots + n_r x_r$ for $n_i \neq 0$ in $\mathbb{Z}$ and distinct $x_i \in X$.*
  (b) *X generates G, and $n_1 x_1 + n_2 x_2 + \cdots + n_r x_r = 0$ for $n_i \in \mathbb{Z}$ and $x_i \in X$ iff $n_1 = n_2 = \cdots = n_r = 0$.*

The conditions should remind the reader of linearly independent vectors. As we will soon find out, this similarity is not accidental.

Definition 3.19 (free Abelian group) An Abelian group having a nonempty generating set X satisfying the conditions in Theorem 3.13 is a *free Abelian group* and X is a *basis* for the group.

We have already seen a free Abelian group: The finite direct product of the group $\mathbb{Z}$ with itself is a free Abelian group with a natural basis. In fact, we may use this group as a prototype.

Theorem 3.14 *If G is a nonzero free Abelian group with a basis of r elements, then G is isomorphic to $\mathbb{Z} \times \mathbb{Z} \times \cdots \times \mathbb{Z}$ for r factors.*

Furthermore, while we may form different bases for a free Abelian group, all of them will have the same size.

Theorem 3.15 (rank) *Let G be a nonzero free Abelian group with a finite basis. Then, every basis of G is finite and all bases have the same number of elements, the rank of G, $\operatorname{rank} G = \log_2 |G/2G|$.*

Subgroups of free Abelian groups are simply smaller free Abelian groups.

Theorem 3.16 *A subgroup K of a free Abelian group G with finite rank n is a free Abelian group of rank $s \leq n$. Furthermore, there exists a basis $\{x_1, x_2, \ldots, x_n\}$ for G and $d_1, d_2, \ldots, d_s \in \mathbb{Z}^+$, such that $\{d_1 x_1, d_2 x_2, \ldots, d_s x_s\}$ is a basis for K.*

All subgroups K of a free Abelian group G are normal as it is Abelian. It is clear from Theorem 3.16 that G/K is finitely generated: K eliminates generators x_i of G when $d_i = 1$ and turns others into generators with finite order $d_i > 1$. This statement extends to finitely generated groups, as their subgroups are finitely generated and a similar factorization occurs. The corollary follows.

Corollary 3.3 *Let G be a finitely generated Abelian group with free part of rank n. Let K be a subgroup of G with free part of rank $s \leq n$. Then, G/K is finitely generated and its free part has rank $n - s$.*

Example 3.7 (factoring finitely generated groups) Theorem 3.10 factors a finitely generated Abelian group as the product of a free Abelian group and a number of finite cyclic groups. Using Theorem 3.14, we may restate the result of Theorem 3.10: Every finitely generated Abelian group G may be factored into a free Abelian group H and the product of finite cyclic groups T, $G = H \times T$. Then, $G/\overline{T} \cong H \cong \mathbb{Z}^\beta$, where β is the Betti number of G. $\overline{T} \cong T$ is often called the *torsion subgroup* of G, and it contains all generators with finite orders.

3.3.2 Rings, Fields, Integral Domains, and Principal Ideal Domains

The concepts of bases and ranks are familiar to most readers from basic linear algebra and vector spaces. There is, indeed, a direct connection, which we will unveil next. We begin by allowing two binary operations for a set.

Definition 3.20 (ring (with unity)) A *ring* $\langle R, +, \cdot \rangle$ is a set R together with two binary operations $+$ and $\cdot$, which we call addition and multiplication, defined on R such that the following axioms are satisfied:

(a) $\langle R, + \rangle$ is an Abelian group.
(b) Multiplication is associative.
(c) For $a, b, c \in R$, the *left distributive law*, $a(b + c) = (ab) + (ac)$, and the *right distributive law*, $(a + b)c = (ac) + (bc)$, hold.

A ring R with a multiplicative identity 1 such that $1x = x1 = x$ for all $x \in R$ is a *ring with unity*.

Definitions and concepts from groups naturally extend to rings, sometimes with different names. Rather than defining them individually, I list the equivalent concepts in Table 3.3. For example, a ring with a commutative multiplication operation is called a *commutative ring*. Using this table, we now define fields, the richest (most restrictive) structure we will encounter.

Table 3.3. *Equivalent concepts for groups and rings.*

groups	rings
Abelian	commutative
subgroup	subring
normal	ideal
cyclic	principal

Definition 3.21 (field) A *field* F is a commutative ring with unity such that, for all $a \in F$, there is an element a^{-1} such that $aa^{-1} = a^{-1}a = 1$.

In other words, multiplicative inverses exist in fields. A sibling structure of a field is an integral domain, where the elements do not necessarily have multiplicative inverses.

Definition 3.22 (integral domain) An *integral domain* D is a commutative ring with unity such that, for all nonzero $a, b \in D$, $ab \neq 0$.

An integral domain captures the properties of the set of integers in abstract algebra, hence the name. Other concepts from the set of integers carry over as well.

Definition 3.23 (unit, irreducible) An element u of an integral domain D is a *unit of D* if u has a multiplicative inverse in D. A nonzero element $p \in D$ that is not a unit of D is an *irreducible of D* if in any factorization $p = ab$ in D either a or b is a unit.

So, the concept of primes in $\mathbb{Z}$ is generalized to the concept of irreducibles for any integral domain. Fields and integral domains are very much related.

Theorem 3.17 *Every field is an integral domain. Every finite integral domain is a field.*

Example 3.8 $\mathbb{Z}, \mathbb{Q}, \mathbb{R}, \mathbb{C}$ are all rings under the operations of addition and multiplication. $\langle \mathbb{Z}_n, +, \cdot_n \rangle$ is a ring where $\cdot_n$ is *multiplication modulo n*. $\mathbb{Z}$ is not a field, because it does not have multiplicative inverses for its elements, but $\mathbb{Z}$ is an integral domain. $\mathbb{Q}$ and $\mathbb{R}$ are fields, and therefore integral domains. $\mathbb{Z}_p$ is an integral domain if p is prime. As $\mathbb{Z}_p$ is finite, Theorem 3.17 implies that $\mathbb{Z}$ is also a field. If p is not a prime, $\mathbb{Z}_p$ is not an integral domain, as it has nonzero elements that divide zero. For example, $2 \cdot_6 3 = 0$ in $\mathbb{Z}_6$.

Another example of a ring we are familiar with is the set of all polynomials with a single variable.

Definition 3.24 (polynomial) Let ring R to be commutative with unity. A *polynomial $f(t)$ with coefficients in R* is a formal sum $\sum_{i=0}^{\infty} a_i t^i$, where $a_i \in R$ and t is the *indeterminate*. The set of all polynomials $f(t)$ over R forms a commutative ring $R[t]$ with unity.

For rings, there exists an analog to cyclic Abelian groups, all of whose subgroups are normal and cyclic.

Definition 3.25 (PID) An integral domain D is a *principal ideal domain (PID)* if every ideal in D is a principal ideal.

Example 3.9 $\mathbb{R}$, $\mathbb{Q}$, $\mathbb{Z}$, $\mathbb{Z}_p$ for p prime are all PIDs. Usually, $R[t]$ is not a PID for an arbitrary ring R. However, when R is a field, $R[t]$ becomes a PID.

3.3.3 Modules, Vector Spaces, and Gradings

Recall the definition of a free Abelian group, where we used multiplication to denote multiple additions. We may also view multiplication as an additional external operation. This makes a free Abelian group a $\mathbb{Z}$-module, as we multiply elements from the group by elements from the ring of integers. Indeed, any Abelian group is a $\mathbb{Z}$-module following this view.

Definition 3.26 (module) Let R be a ring. A *(left) R-module* consists of an Abelian group M together with an operation of external multiplication of each element of M by each element of R on the left such that, for all $\alpha, \beta \in M$ and $r, s \in R$, the following conditions are satisfied:

(a) $(r\alpha) \in M$.
(b) $r(\alpha + \beta) = r\alpha + r\beta$.
(c) $(r+s)\alpha = r\alpha + s\alpha$.
(d) $(rs)\alpha = r(s\alpha)$.

We shall somewhat incorrectly speak of the *R-module M*. If R is a ring with unity and $1\alpha = \alpha$ for all $\alpha \in M$, then M is a *unitary R-module*. M is *cyclic* if there exists $\alpha \in M$ such that $M = \{r\alpha \mid r \in R\}$.

We may also extend the definition of finitely generated groups to modules, following Definition 3.16. A module is very much like a vector space, with which we are familiar from high school algebra.

Definition 3.27 (vector space) Let F be a field and V be an Abelian group. A *vector space over F* is a unitary F-module, where V is the associated Abelian group. The elements of F are called *scalars* and the elements of V are called *vectors*. We often refer to V as the vector space.

We briefly quickly recall some familiar properties of vector spaces.

Theorem 3.18 (basis, dimension) *If we can write any vector in a vector space V as a linear combination of the vectors in a finite linearly independent subset $B = \{\alpha_i \mid i \in I\}$ of V, B forms a basis for V and V is* finite-dimensional *with dimension $|B|$.*

As for free Abelian groups, the dimension is invariant over the set of bases for the vector space.

Our final new concept for this section is that of gradings. Given a ring, we may be able to decompose the structure into a direct sum decomposition, such that multiplication has a nice form with respect to this decomposition.

Definition 3.28 (graded ring) A *graded ring* is a ring $\langle R, +, \otimes \rangle$ equipped with a direct sum decomposition of Abelian groups $R \cong \bigoplus_i R_i$, $i \in \mathbb{Z}$, so that multiplication is defined by bilinear pairings $R_n \otimes R_m \to R_{n+m}$. Elements in a single R_i are *homogeneous* and have *degree i*, $\deg e = i$, for all $e \in R_i$.

If a module is defined over a graded ring as just defined, we may also seek a similar decomposition for the module.

Definition 3.29 (graded module) A *graded module M* over a graded ring R is a module equipped with a direct sum decomposition, $M \cong \bigoplus_i M_i$, $i \in \mathbb{Z}$, so that the action of R on M is defined by bilinear pairings $R_n \otimes M_m \to M_{n+m}$.

Our decomposition may be infinite in size. We will be interested, however, in those gradings that are bounded from below.

Definition 3.30 (non-negatively graded) A graded ring (module) is *non-negatively graded* if $R_i = 0$ ($M_i = 0$, respectively) for all $i < 0$.

Example 3.10 (standard grading) Let $R[t]$ be the ring of polynomials with indeterminate t. We may grade $R[t]$ non-negatively with $(t^n) = t^n \cdot R[t], n \geq 0$. This is called the *standard grading* for $R[t]$.

3.3.4 Structure Theorem

Building upon the concept of a group, we have defined a number of richer structures. A natural question that arises is the classification of these structures. The fundamental theorem (Theorem 3.10) gave a full description of finitely generated Abelian groups in terms of a direct sum of cyclic groups. Amazingly, the theorem generalizes to any PID or graded PID.

Theorem 3.19 (Structure Theorem) *If D is a PID, then every finitely generated D-module is isomorphic to a direct sum of cyclic D-modules. That is, it decomposes uniquely into the form*

$$D^{\beta} \oplus \left(\bigoplus_{i=1}^{m} D / d_i D \right), \tag{3.1}$$

for $d_i \in D, \beta \in \mathbb{Z}$, such that $d_i | d_{i+1}$. Similarly, every graded module M over a graded PID D decomposes uniquely into the form

$$\left(\bigoplus_{i=1}^{n} \Sigma^{\alpha_i} D \right) \oplus \left(\bigoplus_{j=1}^{m} \Sigma^{\gamma_j} D / d_j D \right), \tag{3.2}$$

where $d_j \in D$ are homogeneous elements so that $d_j | d_{j+1}$, $\alpha_i, \gamma_j \in \mathbb{Z}$, and Σ^{α} denotes an α-shift upward in grading.

In both cases, the theorem decomposes the structures into free (left) and torsion (right) parts. In the latter case, the torsional elements are also homogeneous.

In the statement of the theorem, there is some new notation. For example, we write the free part of the module with a a power notation. That is, D^{β} is the direct sum of β copies of D, where β is the *Betti number* for the PID. The shift operator Σ^{α} simply moves an element in grading i to grading $i + \alpha$. Note that if $D = \mathbb{Z}$, we get Theorem 3.10. If $D = F$, where F is a field, then the D-module is a finite-dimensional vector space V over F, and we see that V is isomorphic to a direct sum of vector spaces of dimension 1 over F. These are two of the cases that will concern us in our discussion of homology in the next chapter.

4

Homology

The goal of this chapter is to identify and describe a feasible combinatorial method for computing topology. I use the word "feasible" in a computational sense: We need a method that will provide us with fast implementable algorithms. Our method of choice will be *simplicial homology*, which complements our representation of spaces in simplicial form. Homology utilizes finitely generated Abelian groups for describing the topology of spaces. Fortunately, we fully understand the structure of these groups from Chapter 3. We may now define homology easily, and even venture confidently into some advanced topics.

But first, I need to justify the choice of homology, which is weaker than both forms of topological classification we have seen earlier. I do so in the first section of this chapter. I devote the next section to the definition of simplicial homology, a quick history of the proof of its invariance, and the relationship of homology and the Euler characteristic. In the final section, I examine the Universal Coefficient Theorem in order to develop a faster procedure for computing the topology of subcomplexes of $\mathbb{R}^3$.

I borrow heavily from Hatcher (2001) and Munkres (1984) for the content of this chapter. I am also influenced by great introductory books in algebraic topology, including Giblin (1981), Henle (1997), and, my first encounter with the subject, Massey (1991).

4.1 Justification

The primary goal of topology is to classify spaces according to their connectivity. We have seen that there are different meanings of the word "connectivity," corresponding to finer and coarser levels of classifications. In this section, we examine homeomorphy and homotopy and see how they are not suitable for our purposes. In addition, we look at the powerful framework of categories and functors. A classic functor, the fundamental group, motivates the definition of homology.

A common tool for differentiating between spaces is an invariant.

Definition 4.1 (invariant) A *(topological) invariant* is a map that assigns the same object to spaces of the same topological type.

Note that an invariant may assign the same object to spaces of different topological types. In other words, an invariant need not be *complete*. All that is required by the definition is that if the spaces have the same type, they are mapped to the same object. Generally, this characteristic of invariants implies their utility in contrapositives: If two spaces are assigned different objects, they have different topological types. On the other hand, if two spaces are assigned the same object, we usually cannot say anything about them. A good invariant, however, will have enough differentiating power to be useful through contrapositives.

Rather than classifying all topological spaces, we could focus on interesting subsets of spaces with special structure. One such subset is the set of manifolds, as defined in Section 2.2. Here, we use a famous invariant, the Euler characteristic, defined first for graphs by Euler.

Definition 4.2 (Euler characteristic) Let K be a simplicial complex and $s_i = $ card $\{\sigma \in K \mid \dim \sigma = i\}$. The *Euler characteristic* $\chi(K)$ is

$$\chi(K) = \sum_{i=0}^{\dim K} (-1)^i s_i = \sum_{\sigma \in K - \{\emptyset\}} (-1)^{\dim \sigma}. \tag{4.1}$$

While it is defined for a simplicial complex, the Euler characteristic is an integer invariant for $|K|$, the underlying space of K. Given any triangulation of a space $\mathbb{M}$, we always will get the same integer, which we will call the Euler characteristic of that space $\chi(\mathbb{M})$.

4.1.1 Surface Topology

One of the achievements of topology in the nineteenth century was the classification of all closed compact 2-manifolds using the Euler characteristic. We examine this classification by first looking at a few basic 2-manifolds.

Definition 4.3 (basic 2-manifolds) Figure 4.1 gives the basic 2-manifolds using diagrams. We may also define the sphere geometrically by $\mathbb{S}^2 = \{x \in \mathbb{R}^3 \mid$

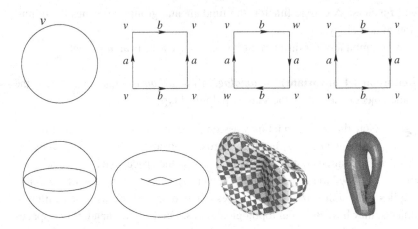

Fig. 4.1. Diagrams (above) and corresponding surfaces. Identifying the boundary of the disk on the left with point v gives us a sphere $\mathbb{S}^2$. Identifying the opposite edges of the squares, as indicated by the arrows, gives us the torus $\mathbb{T}^2$, the real projective plane $\mathbb{RP}^2$, and the Klein bottle $\mathbb{K}^2$, respectively, from left to right. The projective plane and the Klein bottle are not embeddable in $\mathbb{R}^3$. Rather, we show *Steiner's Roman surface*, one of the famous immersions of the former and the standard immersion of the latter.

$|x| = 1\}$. The torus (plural tori) $\mathbb{T}^2$ is the boundary of a donut. The real projective plane $\mathbb{RP}^2$ may be constructed also by identifying opposite (antipodal) points on a sphere. $\mathbb{S}^2$ and $\mathbb{T}^2$ can exist in $\mathbb{R}^3$, as shown in Figures 1.7 and 2.4. Both $\mathbb{RP}^2$ and the Klein bottle $\mathbb{K}^2$, however, cannot be realized in $\mathbb{R}^3$ without self-intersections.

Example 4.1 (χ of basic 2-manifolds) Let's calculate the Euler characteristic for our basic 2-manifolds. Recall that the surface of a tetrahedron triangulates a sphere, as shown in Figure 2.13. So, $\chi(\mathbb{S}^2) = 4 - 6 + 4 = 2$. To compute the Euler characteristic of the other manifolds, we must build triangulations for them. We simply triangulate the square used for the diagrams in Figure 4.1, as shown in Figure 4.2. This triangulation gives us $\chi(\mathbb{T}^2) = 9 - 18 + 27 = 0$. We may complete the table in Figure 4.2(b) in a similar fashion. As $\chi(\mathbb{T}^2) = \chi(\mathbb{K}^2) = 0$, the Euler characteristic by itself is not powerful enough to differentiate between surfaces.

We may connect manifold to form larger manifolds that have complex connectivity.

Definition 4.4 (connected sum) The *connected sum* of two n-manifolds

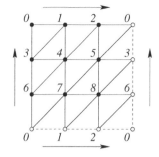

2-Manifold	χ
Sphere $\mathbb{S}^2$	2
Torus $\mathbb{T}^2$	0
Klein bottle $\mathbb{K}^2$	0
Projective plane $\mathbb{RP}^2$	1

(a) A triangulation for the diagram of the torus $\mathbb{T}^2$

(b) The Euler characterics of our basic 2-manifolds

Fig. 4.2. A triangulation of the diagram of the torus $\mathbb{T}^2$

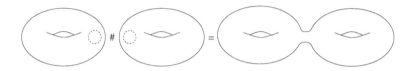

Fig. 4.3. The connected sum of two tori is a genus 2 torus.

$\mathbb{M}_1, \mathbb{M}_2$ is

$$\mathbb{M}_1 \# \mathbb{M}_2 \quad = \quad \mathbb{M}_1 - \mathring{D}_1^n \underset{\partial \mathring{D}_1^n = \partial \mathring{D}_2^n}{\bigcup} \mathbb{M}_2 - \mathring{D}_2^n, \tag{4.2}$$

where D_1^n, D_2^n are n-dimensional closed disks in $\mathbb{M}_1, \mathbb{M}_2$, respectively.

In other words, we cut out two disks and glue the manifolds together along the boundary of those disks using a homeomorphism. In Figure 4.3, for example, we connect two tori to form a sum with two *handles*. Suppose we form the connected sum of two surfaces $\mathbb{M}_1, \mathbb{M}_2$ by removing a single triangle from each and identifying the two boundaries. Clearly, the Euler characteristic should be the sum of the Euler characteristics of the two surfaces minus 2 for the two missing triangles. In fact, this is true for arbitrary shaped disks.

Theorem 4.1 *For compact surfaces* $\mathbb{M}_1, \mathbb{M}_2$,

$$\chi(\mathbb{M}_1 \# \mathbb{M}_2) = \chi(\mathbb{M}_1) + \chi(\mathbb{M}_2) - 2.$$

For a compact surface $\mathbb{M}$, let $g\mathbb{M}$ be the connected sum of g copies of $\mathbb{M}$. If $\mathbb{M}$ is a torus, we get a multi-donut surface, as shown in Figure 4.3.

Definition 4.5 (genus) The connected sum of g tori is called a surface with *genus g*.

The genus refers to how many "holes" the donut surface has. We are now ready to give a complete answer to the homeomorphism problem for closed compact 2-manifolds. Combining this theorem with the table in Figure 4.2(b), we get the following.

Corollary 4.1 $\chi(g\mathbb{T}^2) = 2 - 2g$ *and* $\chi(g\mathbb{R}P^2) = 2 - g$.

We are now ready to fully classify all compact closed 2-manifolds as connected sums, using the Euler characteristic and orientability.

Theorem 4.2 (homeomorphy of 2-manifolds) *Closed compact surfaces* $\mathbb{M}_1$ *and* $\mathbb{M}_2$ *are homeomorphic,* $\mathbb{M}_1 \approx \mathbb{M}_2$, *iff*

   (a) $\chi(\mathbb{M}_1) = \chi(\mathbb{M}_2)$ *and*
   (b) *either both surfaces are orientable or both are nonorientable.*

Observe that the theorem is "if and only if." We can easily compute the Euler characteristic of any 2-manifold by triangulating it. Computing orientability is also easy by orienting one triangle and "spreading" the orientation throughout the manifold if it is orientable. Together, χ and orientability tell us the genus of the surface if we apply Corollary 4.1 Therefore, we have a full computational method for capturing the topology of 2-manifolds.

Our success in classifying all 2-manifolds up to topological type encourages us to seek similar results for higher dimensional manifolds. Unfortunately, Markov showed in 1958 that both the homeomorphism and the homotopy problems are undecidable for n-manifolds, $n \geq 4$: There exist no algorithms for classifying manifolds according to topological or homotopy type (Markov, 1958). We will sketch his result in an extended example later this section. Markov's result leaves the homeomorphism problem unsettled for 3-manifolds. Three-manifold topology is currently an active area in topology. Weeks (1985) provides an accessible view, while Thurston (1997) and Fomenko and Matveev (1997) furnish the theoretical and algorithmic results.

Table 4.1. *Some categories and their morphisms.*

category	morphisms
sets	arbitrary functions
groups	homomorphisms
topological spaces	continuous maps
topological spaces	homotopy classes of maps

4.1.2 Functors

A more powerful technique for studying topological spaces is to form and study algebraic images of them. This idea forms the crux of algebraic topology. Usually, these "images" are groups, but richer structures such as rings and modules also arise. Our hope is that, in the process of forming these images, we retain enough detail to accurately reconstruct the shapes of spaces. As we are interested in understanding how spaces are structurally related, we also want maps between spaces to be converted into maps between the images. The mechanism we use for forming these images is a *functor*. To use functors, we need a concept called categories, which may be viewed as an abstraction of abstractions.

Definition 4.6 (category) A *category* $\mathcal{C}$ consists of:

(a) a collection $\mathrm{Ob}(\mathcal{C})$ of *objects*;

(b) sets $\mathrm{Mor}(X, Y)$ of *morphisms* for each pair $X, Y \in \mathrm{Ob}(\mathcal{C})$; including a distinguished identity morphism $1 = 1_X \in \mathrm{Mor}(X, X)$ for each X.

(c) a composition of morphisms function $\circ \colon \mathrm{Mor}(X, Y) \times \mathrm{Mor}(Y, Z) \to \mathrm{Mor}(X, Z)$ for each triple $X, Y, Z \in \mathrm{Ob}(\mathcal{C})$, satisfying $f \circ 1 = 1 \circ f = f$, and $(f \circ g) \circ h = f \circ (g \circ h)$.

We have already seen a few examples of categories in the previous chapter, as listed in Table 4.1.

Definition 4.7 (functor) A *(covariant) functor* F from a category $\mathcal{C}$ to a category $\mathcal{D}$ assigns to each object $X \in \mathcal{C}$ an object $F(X) \in \mathcal{D}$ and to each morphism $f \in \mathrm{Mor}(X, Y)$ a morphism $F(f) \in \mathrm{Mor}(F(X), F(Y))$ such that $F(1) = 1$ and $F(f \circ g) = F(f) \circ F(g)$.

Figure 4.4 gives an intuitive picture of a functor in action.

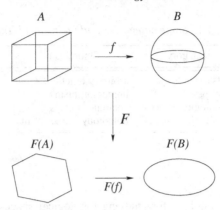

Fig. 4.4. A functor F creates images $F(A), F(B)$ of not only the objects A, B in a category, but also of maps between the objects, such as $F(f)$.

4.1.3 The Fundamental Group

One of the simplest and most important functors in algebraic topology is the fundamental group. We will examine it here briefly to see why it's not a viable option for the computation of topology. In addition, the fundamental group motivates the definition of homology.

We saw in Section 2.4.2 that two maps are homotopic if one may be deformed continuously into another. The fundamental group is concerned with homotopic maps on a surface, where these maps are paths and loops.

Definition 4.8 (fundamental group) A *path* in $\mathbb{X}$ is a continuous map $f : [0,1] \to \mathbb{X}$. The equivalence class of a path f under the equivalence relation of homotopy is $[f]$. Given two paths $f, g : [0,1] \to \mathbb{X}$, the product path $f \cdot g$ is a path that traverses f and then g. The speed of traversal is doubled in order for $f \cdot g$ to be traversed in unit time. This product operation respects homotopy classes. A *loop* is a path f with $f(0) = f(1)$, i.e., a loop starts and ends at the same *basepoint*. The *fundamental group* $\pi_1(\mathbb{X}, x_0)$ of $\mathbb{X}$ and x_0 has the homotopy classes of loops in $\mathbb{X}$ based at x_0 as its elements and $[f][g] = [f \cdot g]$ as its binary operation.

Example 4.2 ($\pi_1(\mathbb{T}^2)$) Figure 4.5 shows three loops on a torus. The loops on the right are homotopic to each other and may be deformed to the basepoint through the highlighted surface. The thick loop, however, goes around the neck of the torus and may not be deformed to the basepoint, as it does not bound any surface around the neck. Because a torus is connected, the basepoint may be moved around, so we can omit it from our notation. The thick loop is one

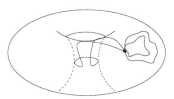

Fig. 4.5. The thick loop goes around the neck of the torus and is not homotopic to the other two loops, which are homotopic through the highlighted surface.

of the generators of $\pi_1(\mathbb{T}^2)$. The other generator goes around the width of the torus. The two generators are not homotopic, and $\pi_1(\mathbb{T}^2) \cong \mathbb{Z} \times \mathbb{Z}$, although this result is not immediate.

Example 4.3 (Markov's proof) The definition of the fundamental group enables us to give a sketch of Markov's proof of the undecidability of the homeomorphism problem in dimensions greater than 4. In 1912, Dehn proposed the following problem: Given two finitely presented groups, decide whether or not they are isomorphic. In 1955, Adyan showed that, for any fixed group, Dehn's problem is undecidable. Markov knew that homeomorphic manifolds have the same fundamental group. So, he described a procedure for building a manifold whose fundamental group was related to a given finitely presented group. In particular, its fundamental group would not be the trivial group unless the manifold itself was contractible. In this fashion, Markov reduced the homeomorphism problem to the isomorphism of groups, proving its undecidability.

Markov uses *group presentations* in his proof, a method for specifying finitely generated groups. We think of each generator of such a group as a *letter* in an *alphabet*. Any symbol of the form $a^n = aaaa \cdots a$ (a string of $n \in \mathbb{Z}$ a's) is a *syllable* and a finite string of syllables is a *word*. The *empty word* 1 does not have any syllables. We modify words naturally using *elementary contractions*, replacing $a^m a^n$ by a^{m+n}. The torsional part of the group also gives us *relations*, equations of the form $r = 1$. For example, the cyclic group $\mathbb{Z}_6$ may be presented by a single generator a and the relation $a^6 = 1$. We use $(a : a^6)$ for denoting this presentation of one generator and one relation.

Suppose we have a presentation of a group $G : (a_1, \ldots, a_n : r_1, \ldots, r_m)$ with n generators and m relations. Markov maps each generator to an equivalence class of homotopic loops in a 4-manifold. To do so, he attaches n handles to $\mathbb{B}^4$, the four-dimensional closed ball, as shown in Figure 4.6. This base manifold $\mathbb{M}$ is like the connected sum of n four-dimensional tori. The fundamental group of this manifold, then, is generated by n generators, each of which is represented by one of the handles. We name each handle, with one of the two

Fig. 4.6. A four-dimensional closed ball $\mathbb{B}^4$ with four handles, corresponding to generators α_1 through α_4 with the indicated directions. The loop corresponds to loop $\alpha_1^{-1}\alpha_3\alpha_4\alpha_2$.

directions, as a generator. The inverse of each generator is when we travel in the opposite direction in each handle.

Having constructed a manifold with the appropriate generators, Markov next considers the relations. Each relation states $r_i = 1$, that is, the word r_i is equivalent to the identity element. Markov maps the relation r_i into an equivalence class of homotopic loops in $\mathbb{M}$, as shown for the loop $\alpha_1^{-1}\alpha_3\alpha_4\alpha_2$ in Figure 4.6. Any loop C_i associated to r_i in $\mathbb{M}$ should be bounding and equivalent to the trivial loop. To establish this, we begin by taking a tubular N_i neighborhood of C_i. We make sure these neighborhoods do not intersect each other. We carve N_i out of $\mathbb{M}$ to get $\mathbb{M}'$, leaving a tunnel that represents the relation r_i.

To turn C_i into the trivial loop, we need to "sew in" an appropriate disk whose boundary is C_i, thereby turning C_i into a boundary. Each loop C_i is homeomorphic to $\mathbb{S}^1$ by definition. When creating the neighborhoods N_i, we place a copy of $\mathbb{B}^3$ at every point of C_i. This action corresponds to getting the product of the two spaces.

Definition 4.9 (products of manifolds) The *product* of two topological spaces consists of the Cartesian product of their sets, along with the *product topology* that consists of the Cartesian product of their open sets.

Figure 4.7 displays three product spaces. This means that we may glue the two spaces on the sides along their common boundaries, shown in the middle. We follow this procedure to glue a disk along the first loop C_1. According to the definition, our tubular neighborhood is $N_1 \approx \mathbb{S}^1 \times \mathbb{B}^3$. Consequently, its boundary is $\partial N_1 \approx \mathbb{S}^1 \times \mathbb{S}^2$, with the closed ball contributing the boundary. We now use a trick we used in creating connected sums of 2-manifolds, as shown in Figure 4.7, in lower dimensions. That is, we find another space whose boundary is homeomorphic to ∂N_1. We have $\partial N_1 \approx \mathbb{S}^1 \times \mathbb{S}^2 \approx \partial(\mathbb{B}^2 \times \mathbb{S}^2)$. So,

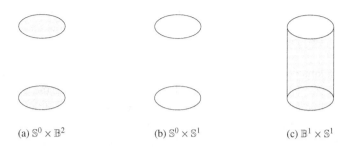

(a) $\mathbb{S}^0 \times \mathbb{B}^2$ (b) $\mathbb{S}^0 \times \mathbb{S}^1$ (c) $\mathbb{B}^1 \times \mathbb{S}^1$

Fig. 4.7. The two circles in (b) constitute the boundary of both disks in (a) and the cylinder in (c). This fact allowed us to construct connected sums of 2-manifolds: we carved out two disks (a) and connected a handle (c) on the boundary (b).

we glue the boundary of $\mathbb{B}^2 \times \mathbb{S}^2$ to the boundary left by N_1 to get $\mathbb{M}_1$. Within $\mathbb{M}_1$, the loop corresponding to relation r_1 is retractable, because we just gave it a disk through which it can contract to a point. So, by performing a *Dehn surgery*, we have killed r_1. But we have also killed several other relations too. For example, in Figure 4.6, we have also killed $\alpha_3\alpha_4\alpha_2\alpha_1^{-1}$. This is equivalent to adding relations to the finitely presented group. We perform this surgery on the other relations, arriving at $\mathbb{M}_m$, a topological space whose fundamental group has the relations of the presented group G as well as some others.

But now, we are done. By Adyan's result, the isomorphism problem for any fixed group is undecidable. In particular, we may pick the trivial group, the fundamental group of the sphere. Given a group presentation, we build a manifold $\mathbb{M}_m$ according to Markov's directions. This manifold has a fundamental group equivalent to the presented group with some additional relations. But the presented group is isomorphic to the trivial group; the additional relations do not change anything. Therefore, if we could decide whether $\mathbb{M}_m$ is homeomorphic to $\mathbb{S}^4$, we could decide whether the group is the trivial group. As the latter problem is undecidable, so is the former problem.

The same proof works if we go back and replace all occurrences of "homeomorphism" by "homotopy," making the latter classification undecidable. It also works for higher dimensional manifolds. Markov eventually extended his undecidability proof to any "interesting property," although this result is known as *Rice's Theorem*, as it was independently proven and published by Rice in the West.

An English translation of the result (Markov, 1958) is available off my Web site. He worked during the golden age of Soviet mathematics at the Steklov Institute. Matiyasevich (1986) and Adyan and Makanin (1986) discuss the

Markov and Novikov schools of mathematics, respectively. Adyan (1955) is only available in Russian, but one may substitute Rabin's independent proof (Rabin, 1958). For a history of undecidability theory, see Davis (1965).

The fundamental group is, in fact, one in a series of *homotopy groups* $\pi_n(\mathbb{X})$ for a space $\mathbb{X}$. The higher dimensional homotopy groups extend the notion of a loop to n-dimensional cycles and capture the homotopy classes of these cycles. The groups are useful only in contrapositive statements: $\pi_n(\mathbb{X}) = \pi_n(\mathbb{Y})$, for all n, does not imply that $\mathbb{X} \approx \mathbb{Y}$. We may still use these groups to differentiate between spaces. We do not, however, on the following grounds:

1. The definition of the fundamental group is inherently noncombinatorial, as it depends on smooth maps and the topology of the space.
2. The higher dimensional homotopy groups are very complicated and hard to compute. In particular, they are not directly computable from a cell decomposition of a space, such as a simplicial decomposition.
3. Even if we were able to compute the homotopy groups, we may get an infinite description of a space: Only a finite number of homotopy groups may be nontrivial for an n-dimensional space. Infinite descriptions are certainly not viable for computational purposes.

We would like a combinatorial computable functor that gives us a finite description of the topology of a space. Homology provides us with one such functor.

4.2 Homology Groups

Homology groups may be regarded as an algebraization of the first layer of geometry in cell structures: how cells of dimension n attach to cells of dimension $n - 1$ (Hatcher, 2001). Mathematically, the homology groups have a less transparent definition than the fundamental group, and require a lot of machinery to be set up before any calculations. We focus on a weaker form of homology, simplicial homology, that both satisfies our need for a combinatorial functor and obviates the need for this machinery. Simplicial homology is defined only for simplicial complexes, the spaces we are interested in. Like the Euler characteristic, however, homology is an invariant of the underlying space of the complex.

Homology groups, unlike the fundamental group, are Abelian. In fact, the first homology group is precisely the Abelianization of the fundamental group. We pay a price for the generality and computability of homology groups: Homology has less differentiating power than homotopy. Once again, however, homology respects homotopy classes and, therefore, classes of homeomorphic spaces.

4.2.1 Chains and Cycles

To define homology groups, we need simplicial analogs of paths and loops. Recalling free Abelian groups from Section 3.3.1, we create the chain group of oriented simplices.

Definition 4.10 (chain group) The *kth chain group* of a simplicial complex K is $\langle C_k(K), + \rangle$, the free Abelian group on the oriented k-simplices, where $[\sigma] = -[\tau]$ if $\sigma = \tau$ and σ and τ have different orientations. An element of $C_k(K)$ is a *k-chain*, $\sum_q n_q[\sigma_q], n_q \in \mathbb{Z}, \sigma_q \in K$.

We often omit the complex in the notation. A simplicial complex has a chain group in every dimension. As stated earlier, homology examines the connectivity between two immediate dimensions. To do so, we define a structure-relating map between chain groups.

Definition 4.11 (boundary homomorphism) Let K be a simplicial complex and $\sigma \in K$, $\sigma = [v_0, v_1, \ldots, v_k]$. The boundary homomorphism $\partial_k : C_k(K) \to C_{k-1}(K)$ is

$$\partial_k \sigma = \sum_i (-1)^i [v_0, v_1, \ldots, \hat{v}_i, \ldots, v_n], \qquad (4.3)$$

where $\hat{v}_i$ indicates that v_i is deleted from the sequence.

It is easy to check that ∂_k is well defined, that is, ∂_k is the same for every ordering in the same orientation.

Example 4.4 (boundaries) Let us take the boundary of the oriented simplices in Figure 2.14.

- $\partial_1[a,b] = b - a$.
- $\partial_2[a,b,c] = [b,c] - [a,c] + [a,b] = [b,c] + [c,a] + [a,b]$.
- $\partial_3[a,b,c,d] = [b,c,d] - [a,c,d] + [a,b,d] - [a,b,c]$.

Note that the boundary operator orients the faces of an oriented simplex. In the case of the triangle, this orientation corresponds to walking around the triangle on the edges, according to the orientation of the triangle.

If we take the boundary of the boundary of the triangle, we get:

$$\partial_1\partial_2[a,b,c] = [c] - [b] - [c] + [a] + [b] - [a] = 0. \tag{4.4}$$

This is intuitively correct: The boundary of a triangle is a cycle, and a cycle does not have a boundary. In fact, this intuition generalizes to all dimensions.

Theorem 4.3 $\partial_{k-1}\partial_k = 0$, *for all k.*

Proof The proof is elementary:

$$
\begin{aligned}
\partial_{k-1}\partial_k[v_0,v_1,\ldots,v_k] &= \partial_{k-1}\sum_i(-1)^i[v_0,v_1,\ldots,\hat{v}_i,\ldots,v_k]\\
&= \sum_{j<i}(-1)^i(-1)^j[v_0,\ldots,\hat{v}_j,\ldots,\hat{v}_i,\ldots,v_k]\\
&\quad + \sum_{j>i}(-1)^i(-1)^{j-1}[v_0,\ldots,\hat{v}_i,\ldots,\hat{v}_j,\ldots,v_k]\\
&= 0,
\end{aligned}
$$

as switching i and j in the second sum negates the first sum. $\square$

Using the boundary homomorphism, we have the following picture for an n-dimensional complex K:

$$0 \longrightarrow C_n \xrightarrow{\partial_n} C_{n-1} \xrightarrow{\partial_{n-1}} \ldots \longrightarrow C_1 \xrightarrow{\partial_1} C_0 \xrightarrow{\partial_0} 0, \tag{4.5}$$

with $\partial_k\partial_{k+1} = 0$ for all k. Note that the sequence is augmented on the right by a 0, with $\partial_0 = 0$. On the left, $C_{n+1} = 0$, as there are no $(n+1)$-simplices in K. Such a sequence is called a *chain complex*. Chain complexes are common in homology, but this is the only one we will see here. The images and kernels of these maps are subgroups of C_k.

Theorem 4.4 $\mathrm{im}\,\partial_{k+1}$ *and* $\ker\partial_k$ *are free Abelian normal subgroups of* C_k. $\mathrm{im}\,\partial_{k+1}$ *is a normal subgroup of* $\ker\partial_k$.

Proof As in Section 3.2, both are subgroups by application of Theorem 3.3: A homomorphism preserves subgroups C_{k+1} and $\{0\} \in C_k$, respectively. As C_k is Abelian, both groups are normal. By Theorem 3.16, both groups are free Abelian. For the second statement, note that $\partial_k\partial_{k+1} = 0$ implies $\mathrm{im}\,\partial_{k+1} \subseteq \ker\partial_k$. We have already seen this subset is a group. Let $\partial_{k+1}\sigma, \partial_{k+1}\tau \in \mathrm{im}\,\partial_{k+1}$. Then, $\partial_{k+1}\sigma + \partial_{k+1}\tau = \partial_{k+1}(\sigma+\tau) \in \mathrm{im}\,\partial_{k+1}$, by the homomorphism property of ∂. Therefore, the set is closed and is a subgroup by definition. $\square$

These subgroups are important enough to be named.

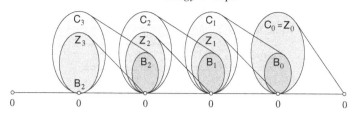

Fig. 4.8. A chain complex for a three-dimensional complex.

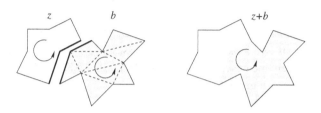

Fig. 4.9. A nonbounding oriented 1-cycle $z \in Z_k, z \notin B_k$ is added to an oriented 1-boundary $b \in B_k$. The resulting cycle $z + b$ is homotopic to z. The orientation on the cycles is induced by the arrows.

Definition 4.12 (cycle, boundary) The *kth cycle group* is $Z_k = \ker \partial_k$. A chain that is an element of Z_k is a *k-cycle*. The *kth boundary group* is $B_k = \operatorname{im} \partial_{k+1}$. A chain that is an element of B_k is a *k-boundary*. We also call boundaries *bounding cycles* and cycles not in B_k *nonbounding cycles*.

These names are self-explanatory: Bounding cycles *bound* higher dimensional cycles, as otherwise they would not be in the image of the boundary homomorphism. We can think of them as "filled" cycles, as opposed to "empty" nonbounding cycles. Figure 4.8 shows a chain complex for a three-dimensional complex, along with the cycle and boundary subgroups.

4.2.2 Simplicial Homology

Chains and cycles are simplicial analogs of the maps called paths and loops in the continuous domain. Following the construction of the fundamental group, we now need a simplicial version of a homotopy to form equivalent classes of cycles. Consider the sum of the nonbounding 1-cycle and a bounding 1-cycle in Figure 4.9. The two cycles z, b have a shared boundary. The edges in the shared boundary appear twice in the sum $z + b$ with opposite signs, so they are eliminated. The resulting cycle $z + b$ is homotopic to z: We may slide the shared portion of the cycles smoothly across the triangles that b bounds. But

Table 4.2. *Homology of basic 2-manifolds.*

2-manifold	H_0	H_1	H_2
sphere	$\mathbb{Z}$	$\{0\}$	$\mathbb{Z}$
torus	$\mathbb{Z}$	$\mathbb{Z} \times \mathbb{Z}$	$\mathbb{Z}$
projective plane	$\mathbb{Z}$	$\mathbb{Z}_2$	$\{0\}$
Klein bottle	$\mathbb{Z}$	$\mathbb{Z} \times \mathbb{Z}_2$	$\{0\}$

such homotopies exist for any boundary $b \in B_1$. Generalizing this argument to all dimensions, we look for equivalent classes of $z + B_k$ for a k-cycle. But these are precisely the cosets of B_k in Z_k by Definition 3.8. As B_k is normal in Z_k, the cosets form a group under coset addition.

Definition 4.13 (homology group) The *kth homology group* is

$$H_k = Z_k/B_k = \ker \partial_k / \operatorname{im} \partial_{k+1}. \tag{4.6}$$

If $z_1 = z_2 + B_k, z_1, z_2 \in Z_k$, we say z_1 and z_2 are *homologous* and denote it with $z_1 \sim z_2$.

By Corollary 3.3, homology groups are finitely generated Abelian, as they are factor groups of two free Abelian groups. Therefore, the fundamental theorem of finitely generated Abelian groups (Theorem 3.10) applies. Homology groups describe spaces through their Betti numbers and the torsion subgroups.

Definition 4.14 (kth Betti number) The *kth* Betti number β_k of a simplicial complex K is $\beta(H_k)$, the rank of the free part of H_k.

By Corollary 3.3, $\beta_k = \operatorname{rank} H_k = \operatorname{rank} Z_k - \operatorname{rank} B_k$. The description given by homology is finite, as an n-dimensional simplicial space has at most $n + 1$ nontrivial homology groups.

4.2.3 Understanding Homology

The description provided by homology groups may not be transparent at first. In this section, we look at a few examples to gain an intuitive understanding of what homology groups capture. Table 4.2 lists the homology groups of our basic 2-manifolds shown in Figure 4.1. Because they are 2-manifolds, the highest nontrivial homology group for any of them is H_2. *Torsion-free* spaces have homology that does not have a torsion subgroup, that is, terms that are

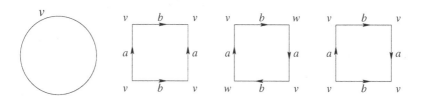

Fig. 4.10. Diagrams for our basic 2-manifolds from Figure 4.1.

finite cyclic groups $\mathbb{Z}_m$. Most of the spaces we are interested are torsion-free. In fact, any space that is a subcomplex of $\mathbb{S}^3$, the three-dimensional sphere, is torsion-free. We deal with $\mathbb{S}^3$ as it is compact and does not create special boundary cases that need to be resolved in algorithms. To avoid these difficulties, we add a point at infinity and *compactify* $\mathbb{R}^3$ to get $\mathbb{S}^3$. This construction mirrors that of the two-dimensional sphere in Figure 4.1. Algorithmically, the *one point compactification of* $\mathbb{R}^3$ is easy, as we have a simplicial representation of space.

So what does homology capture? For torsion-free spaces in three dimensions, the Betti numbers (the number of $\mathbb{Z}$ terms in the description) have intuitive meaning as a consequence of the *Alexander duality*. β_0 measures the number of components of the complex. β_1 is the rank of a basis for the *tunnels*. As H_1 is free, it is a vector-space and β_1 is its rank. β_2 counts the number of *voids* in the complex. Tunnels and voids exist in the complement of the complex in $\mathbb{S}^3$. The distinction might seem tenuous, but this is merely because of our familiarity with the terms. For example, the complex *encloses* a void, and the void is the empty space *enclosed* by the complex.

Using this understanding, we may now examine Table 4.2. All four spaces have a single component, so $H_0 = \mathbb{Z}$ and $\beta_0 = 1$. The sphere and the torus enclose a void, so $H_2 = \mathbb{Z}$ and $\beta_2 = 1$. The nonorientable spaces, on the other hand, are one-sided and cannot enclose any voids, so they have trivial homology in dimension 2. To see what H_1 captures, we look again at the diagrams for the 2-manifolds, as shown in Figure 4.1 for convenience. We may, of course, triangulate these diagrams to obtain abstract simplicial complexes for computing simplicial homology. For now, though, we assume that whatever curve we draw on these manifolds could be "snapped" to some triangulation of the diagrams. To understand 1-cycles and torsion, we need to pay close attention to the boundaries in the diagrams. Recall that a boundary is simply a cycle that *bounds*. In each diagram, we have a boundary, simply, the boundary of the diagram! The manner in which this boundary is labeled determines how the space is connected, and therefore the homology of the space.

It is clear that any simple closed curve drawn on the disk for the sphere is a boundary. Therefore, its homology is trivial in dimension 1. The torus has two classes of nonbounding cycles. When we glue the edges marked "a", edge "b" becomes a nonbounding 1-cycle and forms a class with all 1-cycles that are homologous to it. We get a different class of cycles when we glue the edges marked "b." Each class has a generator, and each generator is free to generate as many *different* classes of homologous 1-cycles as it pleases. Therefore, the homology of a torus in dimension 1 is $\mathbb{Z} \times \mathbb{Z}$ and $\beta_1 = 2$.

There is a 1-boundary in the diagram, however: the boundary of the disk that we are gluing. Going around this 1-boundary, we get the description $aba^{-1}b^{-1}$. That is, the disk makes the cycle with this description a boundary. Equivalently, the disk adds the relation $aba^{-1}b^{-1} = 1$ to the presentation of the group. But this relation is simply stating that the group is Abelian, and we already knew that.

Continuing in this manner, we look at the boundary in the diagram for the projective plane. Going around, we get the description $abab$. If we let $c = ab$, the boundary is c^2 and we get the definition of the cross-cap used in Conway's ZIP. The disk adds the relation $c^2 = 1$ to the group presentation. In other words, we have a cycle c in our manifold that is nonbounding but becomes bounding when we go around it twice. If we try to generate all the different cycles from this cycle, we just get two classes: the class of cycles homologous to c and the class of boundaries. But any group with two elements is isomorphic to $\mathbb{Z}_2$, hence the description of H_1. You should convince yourself of the verity of the description of H_1 for the Klein bottle in a similar fashion.

4.2.4 Invariance

Like the Euler characteristic before it, we defined homology using simplicial complexes. From the definition, it seems that homology is capturing extrinsic properties of our representation of a space. We are interested in intrinsic properties of the space, however. We hope that any two different simplicial complexes K and L with homeomorphic underlying spaces $|K| \approx |L|$ have the same homology, the homology of the space itself. Poincaré stated this hope in terms of "the principal conjecture" in 1904.

Conjecture 4.1 (Hauptvermutung) *Any two triangulations of a topological space have a common refinement.*

In other words, the two triangulations can be subdivided until they are the same. This conjecture, like Fermat's last lemma, is deceptively simple. Papakyriakopoulos (1943) verified the conjecture for polyhedra of dimension ≤ 2 and Moïse (1953) proved it for three-dimensional manifolds. Unfortunately, the conjecture is false in higher dimensions for general spaces. Milnor (1961) obtained a counterexample for dimensions 6 and greater using Lens spaces. Kirby and Siebenmann (1969) produced manifold counterexamples in 1969. The conjecture fails to show the invariance of homology (Ranicki, 1997).

To settle the question of topological invariance of homology, a more general theory was introduced, that of *singular homology*. This theory is defined using maps on general spaces, thereby eliminating the question of representation. Homology is axiomatized as a sequence of functors with specific properties. Much of the technical machinery required is for proving that singular homology satisfies the axioms of a homology theory, and that simplicial homology is equivalent to singular homology. Mathematically speaking, this machinery makes homology less transparent than the fundamental group. Algorithmically, however, simplicial homology is the ideal mechanism to compute topology.

4.2.5 The Euler-Poincaré Formula

To end this section, we derive the invariance of the Euler characteristic (Definition 4.2) from the invariance of homology. The machinery of homology is intrinsically beautiful by itself. To catch a glimpse of this beauty, we scrutinize this relationship with a bit more algebra than we might otherwise need. Recall that a simplicial complex K gives us a chain complex of finite length. We denote it by C_*. We may now define the Euler characteristic of a chain complex.

Definition 4.15 (Euler characteristic of chain complex)

$$\chi(C_*) = \sum_i (-1)^i \operatorname{rank}(C_i).$$

This definition is trivially equivalent to Definition 4.2 as k-simplices are the generators of C_k, or $\operatorname{rank}(C_i) = s_i$ in that definition. So, $\chi(K) = \chi(C_*(K))$. If C_i is finitely Abelian and not free, we mean by *rank* the rank of the free part of the group, or its Betti number. We now denote the sequence of homology functors as H_* (Hatcher, 2001). Then, $H_*(C_*)$ is another chain complex:

$$0 \longrightarrow H_n \longrightarrow H_{n-1} \longrightarrow \ldots \longrightarrow H_1 \longrightarrow H_0 \longrightarrow 0. \tag{4.7}$$

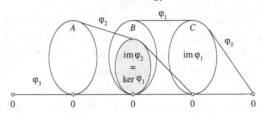

Fig. 4.11. Groups in Lemma 4.1. φ_2 is injective and φ_1 is surjective.

The operators between the homology groups are induced by the boundary operators: We map a homology class to the class of the boundary of one of its members. The Euler characteristic of $H_*(C_*)$, according to the new definition, is simply $\sum_i(-1)^i \operatorname{rank}(H_i) = \sum_i(-1)^i \beta_i$. Surprisingly, the homology functor preserves the Euler characteristic of a chain complex.

Theorem 4.5 (Euler-Poincaré) $\chi(C_*) = \chi(H_*(C_*))$.

The theorem states that $\sum_i(-1)^i s_i = \sum_i(-1)^i \beta_i$ for a simplicial complex K, deriving the invariance of the Euler characteristic from the invariance of homology. To prove the theorem, we need a lemma.

Lemma 4.1 *Let A, B, C be finitely generated Abelian groups related by the sequence of maps φ_i:*

$$0 \xrightarrow{\varphi_3} A \xrightarrow{\varphi_2} B \xrightarrow{\varphi_1} C \xrightarrow{\varphi_0} 0, \qquad (4.8)$$

where $\operatorname{im}\varphi_i = \ker\varphi_{i-1}$. *Then,* $\operatorname{rank} B = \operatorname{rank} A + \operatorname{rank} C$.

Proof The sequence is shown in Figure 4.11. First, we establish two facts.

   (a) φ_1 is surjective: $\operatorname{im}\varphi_1 = \ker\varphi_0 = C$.
   (b) φ_2 is injective: $\ker\varphi_2 = \operatorname{im}\varphi_3 = \{e\}$, so by Corollary 3.1, φ_2 is 1-1.

By the fundamental homomorphism theorem (Theorem 3.10), $(B/\ker\varphi_1) \cong \operatorname{im}\varphi_1$. By fact (a), $(B/\ker\varphi_1) \cong C$. Corollary 3.3 gives $\operatorname{rank}(B/\ker\varphi_1) = \operatorname{rank} B - \operatorname{rank}(\ker\varphi_1)$, so $\operatorname{rank} C = \operatorname{rank} B - \operatorname{rank}(\ker\varphi_1)$. By fact (b), $A \cong \operatorname{im}(\varphi_2)$ and $\operatorname{rank} A = \operatorname{rank}(\operatorname{im}\varphi_2)$. But $\operatorname{im}\varphi_2 = \ker\varphi_1$, so $\operatorname{rank} A = \operatorname{rank}(\ker\varphi_1)$. Substituting, we get the desired result. $\qquad\square$

The sequence in the lemma has a name.

Definition 4.16 (short exact sequence) The sequence in Lemma 4.1 is a *short exact sequence*.

We use the lemma to prove the Euler-Poincaré relation.

Proof [Euler-Poincaré] Consider the following sequences:

$$0 \xrightarrow{0} \mathsf{Z}_n \xrightarrow{i} \mathsf{C}_n \xrightarrow{\partial_n} \mathsf{B}_{n-1} \xrightarrow{0} 0$$
$$0 \xrightarrow{0} \mathsf{B}_n \xrightarrow{i} \mathsf{Z}_n \xrightarrow{\varphi} \mathsf{H}_n \xrightarrow{0} 0,$$

where 0 is the zero map, i is the inclusion map, and φ assigns to a cycle $z \in \mathsf{Z}_n$ its homology class $[z] \in \mathsf{H}_n$. Both sequences are short exact. Applying Lemma 4.1, we get:

$$\operatorname{rank} \mathsf{C}_n = \operatorname{rank} \mathsf{Z}_n + \operatorname{rank} \mathsf{B}_{n-1}, \tag{4.9}$$

$$\operatorname{rank} \mathsf{Z}_n = \operatorname{rank} \mathsf{B}_n + \operatorname{rank} \mathsf{H}_n. \tag{4.10}$$

Substituting the second equation into the first, multiplying by $(-1)^n$, and summing over n gives the theorem. $\qquad \square$

4.3 Arbitrary Coefficients

We spent a considerable amount of energy in Sections 3.3.3 and 3.3.4 extending the fundamental theorem of finitely generated Abelian groups to arbitrary R-modules. We now take advantage of our effort to generate additional homology groups rather quickly. Recall that any finitely generated group is also a $\mathbb{Z}$-module. In this view, we are multiplying elements of a homology group with *coefficients* from the ring of integers. We may replace this ring with any PID D, such as $\mathbb{Z}_2$, and the fundamental theorem of finitely generated D-modules (Theorem 3.19) would give us a factorization of the homology groups in terms of the module. This fact generates a large number of homology groups, for which we need new notation.

Definition 4.17 (homology with coefficients) The kth homology group with ring of *coefficients* D is $\mathsf{H}_k(K;D) = \mathsf{Z}_k(K;D)/\mathsf{B}_k(K;D)$.

If we choose a field F as set of coefficients, the homology groups become vector spaces with no torsion: $\mathsf{H}_k(K;F) \cong F^r$, where r is the rank of the vector space. A natural question is whether homology groups generated with different coefficients are related. The *Universal Coefficient Theorem for Homology* answers in the affirmative, relating all types of homology to $\mathbb{Z}$ homology. Before stating the theorem, we need to look at two new functors that the theorem uses. I will not define these functors formally, as they are large and very interesting topics by themselves. Rather, I aim here to state the properties of these functors that allow us to understand the theorem and use it for computation.

Table 4.3. *Rules for computing tensor and torsion products, given for general Abelian groups G and certain type of groups:* $\mathbb{Z}_m$ *and F (fields).*

	tensor $\otimes$	torsion $*$
G	$\mathbb{Z} \otimes G \cong G$	$\mathbb{Z} * G \cong \{0\}$
G	$\mathbb{Z}_n \otimes G \cong G/nG$	$\mathbb{Z}_n * G \cong \ker(G \xrightarrow{n} G)$
$\mathbb{Z}_m$	$\mathbb{Z} \otimes \mathbb{Z}_m \cong \mathbb{Z}_m$	$\mathbb{Z} * \mathbb{Z}_m \cong \{0\}$
$\mathbb{Z}_m$	$\mathbb{Z}_n \otimes \mathbb{Z}_m \cong \mathbb{Z}/d\mathbb{Z}, d = \gcd(n,m))$	$\mathbb{Z}_n * \mathbb{Z}_m \cong \mathbb{Z}/d\mathbb{Z}, d = \gcd(n,m))$
F	$\mathbb{Z} \otimes F \cong F$	$\mathbb{Z} * F \cong \{0\}$
F	$\mathbb{Z}_n \otimes F \cong \{0\}$	$\mathbb{Z}_n * F \cong \{0\}$

The first functor we need is the *tensor product*, which maps two Abelian groups to an Abelian group. The tensor product of Abelian groups A and B, denoted $A \otimes B$, is like the product $A \times B$, except that all functions on $A \otimes B$ are bilinear. The tensor is commutative, associative, and has distributive properties with respect to group products. The distributive properties are easier to grasp by thinking of direct products as direct sums, as is often the case when the groups are Abelian. The universal theorem uses the tensor product to rename the factors of a product.

The other functor we need is the *torsion product*, which also maps two Abelian groups to an Abelian group. Intuitively, the torsion product of Abelian groups A, B, denoted $A * B$, captures the torsion elements of A with respect to B. The torsion functor is also commutative and has distributive properties. If either A or B is torsion-free (that is, it is free), $A * B = 0$, the trivial group. Table 4.3 gives rules for computing using the torsion and tensor products. The rules look cryptic, but they match our intuition of these functors. For example, note how the tensor product translates between $\mathbb{Z}$ and a group G. Along with the distributive properties, we use the tensor product to translate between direct products representing the structure of homology groups. We are now ready to tackle the universal theorem.

Theorem 4.6 (universal coefficient) *Let G be an Abelian. The following sequence is short exact:*

$$0 \longrightarrow H_k(K) \otimes G \longrightarrow H_k(K;G) \longrightarrow H_{k-1}(K) * G \longrightarrow 0. \qquad (4.11)$$

Let us use the rules from Table 4.3 to see what the theorem states for the following two cases: homology with coefficients in $\mathbb{Z}_p$, where p is prime, and a field F. We know by Theorem 3.10 that

$$H_k(K) \cong \mathbb{Z}_{d_1} \times \mathbb{Z}_{d_2} \times \cdots \times \mathbb{Z}_{d_n} \times \mathbb{Z}^{\beta_k}, \qquad (4.12)$$

where d_i is the appropriate prime power and β_k is the kth Betti number. We would like to know how the ring of coefficients changes this result in $H_k(K;\mathbb{Z}_p)$ and $H_k(K;F)$.

1. Case $H_k(K;\mathbb{Z}_p)$: Applying the tensor with $\mathbb{Z}_p$ and distributing over the factors, we get

$$H_k(K) \otimes \mathbb{Z}_p \cong \mathbb{Z}_{d_1}/p\mathbb{Z}_{d_1} \times \cdots \times \mathbb{Z}_{d_n}/p\mathbb{Z}_{d_n} \times (\mathbb{Z}_p)^{\beta_k}. \qquad (4.13)$$

On the right side of sequence (4.11), the torsion functor eliminates the $\mathbb{Z}$ factors and modifies the torsion coefficients, giving us

$$H_{k-1}(K) * \mathbb{Z}_p \cong \mathbb{Z}_{c_1} \times \mathbb{Z}_{c_2} \times \cdots \times \mathbb{Z}_{c_m}, \qquad (4.14)$$

where c_i are the corresponding gcd's. In this case, the sequence *splits* and we get:

$$H_k(K;\mathbb{Z}_p) \cong (H_k(K) \otimes \mathbb{Z}_p) \times (H_{k-1}(K) * \mathbb{Z}_p) \qquad (4.15)$$
$$\cong \mathbb{Z}_{d_1}/p\mathbb{Z}_{d_1} \times \cdots \times \mathbb{Z}_{d_n}/p\mathbb{Z}_{d_n} \times \qquad (4.16)$$
$$\mathbb{Z}_{c_1} \times \cdots \times \mathbb{Z}_{c_m} \times (\mathbb{Z}_p)^{\beta_k}.$$

Therefore, by using $\mathbb{Z}_p$ as the ring of coefficients, we get the same Betti numbers as before, but different torsion coefficients.

2. Case $H_k(K;F)$: According to the rules, $H_{k-1}(K) * F \cong \{0\}$, reducing sequence (4.11) to

$$0 \longrightarrow H_k(K) \otimes F \xrightarrow{\varphi} H_k(K;F). \longrightarrow 0 \qquad (4.17)$$

Applying the facts in the proof of Lemma 4.1 shows that φ is both injective and surjective. In other words, $H_k(K) \otimes F \cong H_k(K;F)$. The tensor product eliminates the torsion factors from H_k and renames the $\mathbb{Z}$ factors, so $H_k(K;F) \cong H_k(K) \otimes F \cong F^{\beta_k}$. We lose the torsion and get the same Betti numbers whenever we use a field of coefficients for computation.

We restate our results in a corollary.

Corollary 4.2 *Let p be a prime and F be a field. Then,*

$$H_k(K;\mathbb{Z}_p) \cong (H_k(K) \otimes \mathbb{Z}_p) \times (H_{k-1}(K) * \mathbb{Z}_p), \qquad (4.18)$$
$$H_k(K;F) \cong F^{\beta_k}. \qquad (4.19)$$

While the results from the universal coefficient theorem are theoretically beautiful, our motivation in examining them has a computational nature. We have seen that some rings of coefficients, such as $\mathbb{R}$, are unable to capture torsion. If a space does not have torsion, then we may be able to craft faster algorithms for computing topology by using such rings. The field of real numbers, $\mathbb{R}$, is not an option, because we do not have infinite precision on computers. The field of rational numbers, $\mathbb{Q}$, does not provide any advantage, as we will need to represent each rational exactly with two integers. The simplest principal ring, $\mathbb{Z}_2$, however, simplifies computation greatly. Here, the coefficients are either 0 or 1, so there is no need for orienting simplices or maintaining coefficients. A k-chain is simply a list of simplices, those with coefficient 1. Each simplex is its own inverse, reducing the group operation to the *symmetric difference*, where the sum of two k-chains c, d is $c + d = (c \cup d) - (c \cap d)$. Consequently, $\mathbb{Z}_2$ provides us with a best system for computing homology of torsion-free spaces.

In fact, nearly all of the spaces in this book are torsion-free. The processes described in Chapter 2 generate subcomplexes of $\mathbb{R}^3$. $\mathbb{R}^3$ is not compact and creates special cases that need to be handled in algorithms. To avoid these difficulties, we add a point at infinity and *compactify* $\mathbb{R}^3$ to get $\mathbb{S}^3$, the three-dimensional sphere. This construction mirrors that of the two-dimensional sphere in Definition 4.3. Algorithmically, the *one point compactification of* $\mathbb{R}^3$ is easy, as we have a simplicial representation of space. Subcomplexes of a triangulation of $\mathbb{S}^3$ do not have torsion.

5

Morse Theory

In the last two chapters, we studied combinatorial methods for describing the topology of a space. One reason for our interest in understanding topology is *topological simplification*: removing topological "noise," using a measure that defines what "noise" is. But as we saw in Section 1.2.3, the geometry and topology of a space are intricately related, and modifying one may modify the other. We need to understand this relationship in order to develop intelligent methods for topological simplification. *Morse theory* provides us with a complete analysis of this relationship when the geometry of the space is given by a function. The theory identifies points at which level-sets of the function undergo topological changes and relates these points via a complex. The theory is defined, however, on smooth domains, requiring us to take a radical departure from our combinatorial focus. We need these differential concepts to guide our development of methods for nonsmooth domains. Our exposition of Morse theory, consequently, will not be as thorough and axiomatic as the accounts in the last two chapters. Rather, we rely on the reader's familiarity with elementary calculus to focus on the concepts we need for analyzing 2-manifolds in $\mathbb{R}^3$.

We begin this chapter by extending some ideas from calculus to manifolds in Sections 5.1 and 5.2. These ideas enable us to identify the *critical points* of a manifold in Section 5.3. The critical points become the vertices of a complex. We define this complex by first decomposing the manifold into regions associated with the critical points in Section 5.4. We then construct the complex in Section 5.5 and look at a couple of examples.

Spivak and Well's notes on Milnor's lectures provide the basis for Morse theory (Milnor, 1963). As an introduction to Riemannian manifolds, Morgan (1998) is beautifully accessible. O'Neill (1997) and Boothby (1986) provide good overviews of differential geometry and differential manifolds, respectively. I also use Bruce and Giblin (1992) for inspiration.

5.1 Tangent Spaces

In this chapter, we will generally assume that M is a smooth, compact, 2-manifold without boundary, or a *surface*. We will also assume, for simplicity, that the manifold is embedded in $\mathbb{R}^3$, that is, $M \subset \mathbb{R}^3$ without self-intersections. The embedded manifold derives subspace topology and a metric from $\mathbb{R}^3$. These assumptions are not necessary, however. The ideas presented in this chapter generalize to higher dimensional abstract manifolds with Riemannian metrics.

We begin by attaching tangent spaces to each point of a manifold. As always, we derive our notions about manifolds from the Euclidean spaces.

Definition 5.1 ($T_p(\mathbb{R}^3)$) A *tangent vector* v_p to $\mathbb{R}^3$ consists of two points of $\mathbb{R}^3$: its *vector part* v and its *point of application* p. The set $T_p(\mathbb{R}^3)$ consists of all tangent vectors to $\mathbb{R}^3$ at p and is called the *tangent space of* $\mathbb{R}^3$ *at* p.

Note that $\mathbb{R}^3$ has a different tangent space at every point. Each tangent space is a vector space isomorphic to $\mathbb{R}^3$ itself. We may also attach a vector space to each point of a manifold.

Definition 5.2 ($T_p(M)$) Let p be a point on M in $\mathbb{R}^3$. A tangent vector v_p to $\mathbb{R}^3$ at p is *tangent to* M *at* p if v is the velocity of some curve in M. The set of all tangent vectors to M at p is called the *tangent plane of M at p* and is denoted by $T_p(M)$.

Recall from Chapter 2 that a 2-manifold is covered with a number of charts, which map the neighborhood of a point to an open subset of $\mathbb{R}^2$. Each map is a homeomorphism, and we may parameterize the manifold using the inverses of these maps, which are often called *patches*.

Theorem 5.1 *Let* $p \in M \subset \mathbb{R}^3$, *and let* φ *be a path in* M *such that* $\varphi(u_0, v_0) = p$. *A tangent vector* v *to* $\mathbb{R}^3$ *at* p *is tangent to* M *iff* v *can be written as a linear combination of* $\varphi_u(u_0, v_0)$ *and* $\varphi_v(u_0, v_0)$.

In other words, the tangent plane at a point of the manifold is a two-dimensional vector subspace of the tangent space $T_p(\mathbb{R}^3)$, as shown in Figure 5.1. Based on the properties of derivatives, the tangent plane $T_p(M)$ is the best linear approximation of the surface M near p. Given tangent planes, we may select vectors at each point of the manifold to create a vector field.

Definition 5.3 (vector field) A *vector field* or *flow* on V is a function that assigns a vector $v_p \in T_p(M)$ to each point $p \in M$.

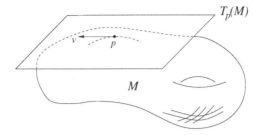

Fig. 5.1. The tangent plane $T_p(\mathbb{M})$ to $\mathbb{M}$ at p with tangent vector $v \in T_p(\mathbb{M})$.

5.2 Derivatives and Morse Functions

Intuitively, a tangent vector gives us a direction to move on a surface. If we have a real-valued smooth function h defined on a manifold, we may ask how h changes as we move in the direction specified by the tangent vector.

Definition 5.4 (derivative) Let $v_p \in T_p(\mathbb{M})$ and let $h\colon \mathbb{M} \to \mathbb{R}$. The *derivative* $v_p[h]$ *of h with respect to* v_p is the common value of $(d/dt)(h \circ \gamma)(0)$, for all curves $\gamma \in \mathbb{M}$ with initial velocity v_p.

Here, we are using the Euclidean metric to measure the length of v_p. This definition is a generalization of the derivative of functions on $\mathbb{R}$, except that now we can travel in many different directions for different rates of changes. The differential of a function captures all rates of change of h in all possible directions on a surface. The possible directions are precisely vectors in $T_p(\mathbb{M})$.

Definition 5.5 (differential) The *differential* dh_p *of* $h\colon \mathbb{M} \to \mathbb{R}$ at $p \in \mathbb{M}$ is a linear function on $T_p(\mathbb{M})$ such that $dh_p(v_p) = v_p[h]$, for all tangent vectors $v_p \in T_p(\mathbb{M})$.

We may view the differential as a machine that converts vector fields into real-valued functions (O'Neill, 1997).

Given a function h and a surface $\mathbb{M}$, we are interested in understanding the geometry h gives our manifold. We travel in all directions, starting from a point p, and note the rate of change. If there is no change in any direction, we have a found a special point, critical to our understanding of the geometry.

Definition 5.6 (critical) A point $p \in \mathbb{M}$ is *critical* for map $h\colon \mathbb{M} \to \mathbb{R}$ if dh_p is the zero map. Otherwise, p is *regular*.

To further classify a critical point, we have to look at how the function's derivative changes in each direction. The *Hessian* is a symmetric bilinear form on the tangent space $T_p(\mathbb{M})$, measuring this change. Like the derivative, it is independent of the parameterization of the surface. We may state it explicitly, however, given local coordinates on the manifold.

Definition 5.7 (Hessian) Let x,y be a patch on $\mathbb{M}$ at p. The *Hessian* of h : $\mathbb{M} \to \mathbb{R}$ is

$$H(p) = \begin{bmatrix} \frac{\partial^2 h}{\partial x^2}(p) & \frac{\partial^2 h}{\partial y \partial x}(p) \\ \frac{\partial^2 h}{\partial x \partial y}(p) & \frac{\partial^2 h}{\partial y^2}(p) \end{bmatrix}. \tag{5.1}$$

The definition gives the Hessian in terms of the basis $(\frac{\partial}{\partial x}(p), \frac{\partial}{\partial y}(p))$ for $T_p(\mathbb{M})$. We may classify the critical points of a manifold, and an associated real-valued function, using the Hessian.

Definition 5.8 (degeneracy) A critical point $p \in \mathbb{M}$ is *nondegenerate* if the Hessian is nonsingular at p, i.e., $\det H(p) \neq 0$. Otherwise, it is degenerate.

We are interested in functions that only give us nondegenerate critical points.

Definition 5.9 (Morse function) A smooth map $h : \mathbb{M} \to \mathbb{R}$ is a *Morse function* if all its critical points are nondegenerate.

Any twice differentiable function h may be unfolded to a Morse function. That is, there is Morse a function that is as close to h as we would like it to be. Sometimes, the definition of Morse functions also requires that the critical values of h, that is—values h takes at its critical points—are distinct. We do not need this requirement here.

5.3 Critical Points

We may, in fact, fully classify the critical points of a Morse function by the geometry of their neighborhood. We do so for a 2-manifold in this section.

Lemma 5.1 (Morse lemma) *It is possible to choose local coordinates x,y at a critical point $p \in \mathbb{M}$ so that a Morse function h takes the form:*

$$h(x,y) = \pm x^2 \pm y^2. \tag{5.2}$$

Figure 5.2 shows the four possible graphs of h, near the critical point $(0,0)$. The existence of these neighborhoods means that the critical points are *isolated*: They have neighborhoods that are free of critical points. Using the Morse characterization, we name the critical points using an index.

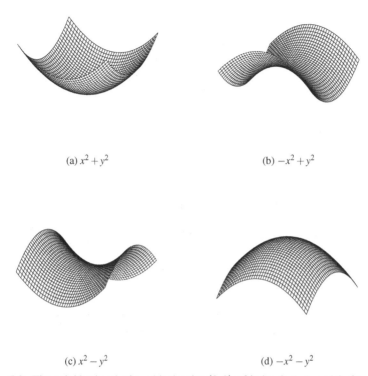

(a) $x^2 + y^2$ (b) $-x^2 + y^2$

(c) $x^2 - y^2$ (d) $-x^2 - y^2$

Fig. 5.2. The neighborhood of a critical point $(0,0)$ of index 0, 1, 1, and 2, from the left, corresponding to the possible forms of h. (a) is a minimum, (b) and (c) are saddles, and (d) is a maximum.

Definition 5.10 (index) The *index $i(p)$ of h at* critical point $p \in \mathbb{M}$ is the number of minuses in Equation (5.2).

Equivalently, the index at p is the number of the negative eigenvalues of $H(p)$.

Definition 5.11 (minimum, saddle, maximum) A critical point of index 0, 1, or 2, is called a *minimum*, *saddle*, or *maximum*, respectively.

The Morse lemma states that the neighborhood of a critical point of a Morse function cannot be more complicated than those in Figure 5.2. For example, the neighborhood shown in Figure 5.3 is not possible. A point with this neighborhood is often called a *monkey saddle*, as its geometry as a saddle allows for a monkey's tail.

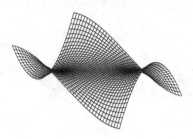

Fig. 5.3. The monkey saddle at $(0,0)$ is a degenerate critical point.

5.4 Stable and Unstable Manifolds

The critical points of a Morse function are locations on a 2-manifold where the
function is stationary. To fully understand a Morse function, we need to extract
more structure. To do so, we first define a vector field called the gradient.

Definition 5.12 (gradient) Let γ be any curve passing through p, tangent to
$v_p \in T_p(\mathbb{M})$. The *gradient* ∇h of a Morse function h is

$$\frac{d\gamma}{dt} \cdot \nabla h = \frac{d(h \circ \gamma)}{dt}. \qquad (5.3)$$

In the general setting, the inner product above is replaced by an arbitrary
Riemannian metric (Boothby, 1986). The gradient is related naturally to the
derivative, as $v_p[h] = v_p \cdot \nabla h(p)$. It is always possible to choose coordinates
(x,y) so that the tangent vectors $\frac{\partial}{\partial x}(p)$, $\frac{\partial}{\partial y}(p)$ are orthonormal with respect to
the chosen metric. For such coordinates, the gradient is given by the familiar
formula $\nabla h = (\frac{\partial h}{\partial x}(p), \frac{\partial h}{\partial y}(p))$.

The gradient of a Morse function h is a vector field on $\mathbb{M}$. We integrate this
vector field, in order to decompose $\mathbb{M}$ into regions of uniform flow.

Definition 5.13 (integral line) An *integral line* $\gamma \colon \mathbb{R} \to \mathbb{M}$ is a maximal path
whose tangent vectors agree with the gradient, that is, $\frac{\partial}{\partial s}p(s) = \nabla h(p(s))$ for
all $s \in \mathbb{R}$. We call $\operatorname{org} p = \lim_{s \to -\infty} p(s)$ the *origin* and $\operatorname{dest} p = \lim_{s \to +\infty} p(s)$
the *destination* of the path p.

Each integral line is open at both ends, and the limits at each end exist, as $\mathbb{M}$
is compact. Note that a critical point is an integral line by itself.

Theorem 5.2 *Integral lines have the following properties:*

 (a) *Two integral lines are either disjoint or the same.*
 (b) *The integral lines cover all of* $\mathbb{M}$.
 (c) *And the limits org p and dest p are critical points of h.*

The properties follow from standard differential calculus.

Definition 5.14 (stable and unstable manifolds) The *stable manifold $S(p)$* and the *unstable manifold $U(p)$* of a critical point p are defined as

$$S(p) = \{p\} \cup \{y \in \mathbb{M} \mid y \in \text{im}\,\gamma, \text{dest}\,\gamma = p\}, \qquad (5.4)$$

$$U(p) = \{p\} \cup \{y \in \mathbb{M} \mid y \in \text{im}\,\gamma, \text{org}\,\gamma = p\}, \qquad (5.5)$$

where $\text{im}\,\gamma$ is the image of the path $\gamma \in \mathbb{M}$.

Both sets of manifolds decompose $\mathbb{M}$ into open cells.

Definition 5.15 (open cell) An *open d-cell* σ is a space homeomorphic to $\mathbb{R}^d$.

We can predict the dimension of the open cell associated to a critical point p.

Theorem 5.3 *The stable manifold $S(p)$ of a critical point p with index $i = i(p)$ is an open cell of dimension $\dim S(p) = i$.*

The unstable manifolds of h are the stable manifolds of $-h$ as $\nabla(-h) = -\nabla h$. Therefore, the two types of manifolds have the same structural properties. That is, the unstable manifolds of h are also open cells, but with dimension $\dim U(p) = 2 - i$, where i is the index of a critical point. The closure of a stable or unstable manifold, however, is not necessarily homeomorphic to a closed ball. We see this in Figure 5.4, where a stable 2-cell is pinched at a minimum.

 By the properties in Theorem 5.2, the stable manifolds are pairwise disjoint and decompose $\mathbb{M}$ into open cells. The cells form a *complex*, as the boundary of every cell $S(a)$ is a union of lower dimensional cells. We may view a cellular complex as a generalization of a simplicial complex, where we allow for arbitrarily shaped cells and relax restrictions on how they are connected to each other.

 The unstable manifolds similarly decompose $\mathbb{M}$ into a complex dual to the complex of stable manifolds: For $a, b \in \mathbb{M}$, $\dim S(a) = 2 - \dim U(a)$ and $S(a)$ is a face of $S(b)$ iff $U(b)$ is a face of $U(a)$.

Example 5.1 (manifolds) Figure 5.4 displays the stable and unstable manifolds of a sphere and a Morse function h. We show an uncompactified sphere: The boundary of the terrain is a minimum at negative infinity. Note that the stable manifold of a minimum and the unstable manifold of a maximum, are the critical points themselves, respectively. On the other hand, both the unstable manifold of a minimum and the stable manifold of a maximum are 2-cells. A saddle has 1-cells as both stable and unstable manifolds. Also, observe that the stable manifolds of the saddles decompose $\mathbb{M}$ into the stable manifolds of the maxima. The unstable manifolds provide such a decomposition for the minima.

5.5 Morse-Smale Complex

We place one more restriction on Morse functions in order to be able to construct Morse-Smale complexes.

Definition 5.16 (Morse-Smale) A Morse function is a *Morse-Smale function* if the stable and unstable manifolds intersect only transversally.

In two dimensions, this means that stable and unstable 1-manifolds cross when they intersect. Their crossing point is necessarily a saddle, since crossing at a regular point would contradict property (a) in Theorem 5.2. Given a Morse-Smale function h, we intersect the stable and unstable manifolds to obtain the Morse-Smale complex.

Definition 5.17 (Morse-Smale complex) Connected components of sets $U(p) \cap S(q)$ for all critical points $p, q \in \mathbb{M}$ are *Morse-Smale cells*. We refer to the cells of dimension 0, 1, and 2 as *vertices*, *arcs*, and *regions*, respectively. The collection of Morse-Smale cells form a complex, the *Morse-Smale complex*.

Note that $U(p) \cap S(p) = \{p\}$, and if $p \neq q$, then $U(p) \cap S(q)$ is the set of regular points $r \in \mathbb{M}$ that lie on integral lines γ with $\text{org}\,\gamma = p$ and $\text{dest}\,\gamma = q$. It is possible that the intersection of stable and unstable manifolds consists of more than one component, as seen in Figure 5.5.

Example 5.2 (Morse-Smale complex) We continue with the manifold and Morse function in Example 5.1. Figure 5.5 shows the Morse-Smale complex we get by intersecting the stable and unstable manifolds displayed in Figure 5.4. Each vertex of the Morse-Smale complex is a critical point, each arc is

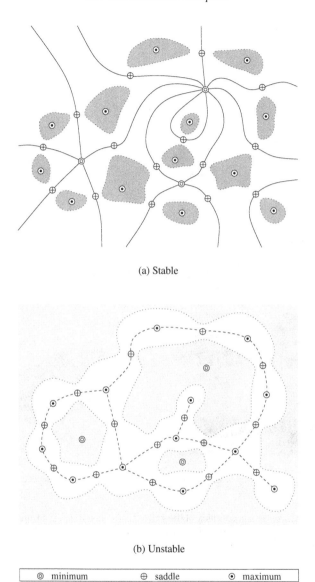

(a) Stable

(b) Unstable

| ◎ minimum | ⊕ saddle | ⊙ maximum |

Fig. 5.4. The stable (a) and unstable (b) 1-manifolds, with dotted iso-lines $h^{-1}(c)$, for constants c. In the diagrams, all the saddle points have height between all minima and maxima. Regions of the 2-cells of maxima and minima are shown, including the critical point, and bounded by the dotted iso-lines. The underlying manifold is $\mathbb{S}^2$, and the outer 2-cell in (b) corresponds to the minimum at negative infinity.

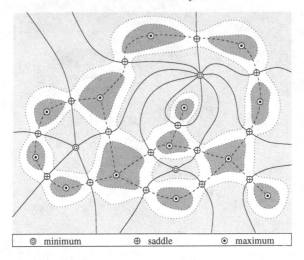

| ◎ minimum | ⊕ saddle | ⊙ maximum |

Fig. 5.5. The Morse-Smale complex of Figure 5.4.

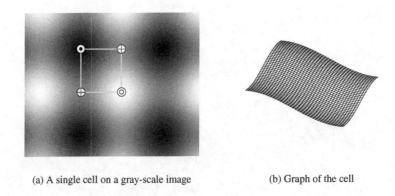

(a) A single cell on a gray-scale image   (b) Graph of the cell

Fig. 5.6. The Morse-Smale complex of the graph of $sin(x) + sin(y)$ is a tiling into copies of the cell shown in (a), along with its reflections and rotations. Each cell has simple geometry (b).

half of a stable or unstable 1-manifold of a saddle, and each region is a component of the intersection of a stable 2-manifold of a maximum and an unstable 2-manifold of a minimum.

Example 5.3 ($sin(x) + sin(y)$) Figure 5.6 shows a single cell of the Morse-Smale complex for the graph of $h(x,y) = sin(x) + sin(y)$. The cell is superimposed on a gray-scale image, mapping $h(x,y)$ to an intensity value for pixel

(x, y). The figure shows that each cell has simple geometry: The gradient flows from the maximum to the minimum, after being attracted by the saddles on each side. We saw the Morse-Smale complex for this function on a triangulated domain in Figure 1.9.

6

New Results

This chapter concludes the first part of this book by introducing the nonalgorithmic aspects of some of the recent results in computational topology. In Chapter 1, we established the primary goal of this book: the computational exploration of topological spaces. Having laid the mathematical foundation required for this study in the previous four chapters, we now take steps toward this goal through

- persistence;
- hierarchical Morse-Smale complexes;
- and the linking number for simplicial complexes.

The three sections of this chapter elaborate on these topics. In Section 6.1, we introduce a new measure of importance for topological attributes called *persistence*. Persistence is simple, immediate, and natural. Perhaps precisely because of its naturalness, this concept is powerful and applicable in numerous areas, as we shall see in Chapter 13. Primarily, persistence enables us to simplify spaces topologically. The meaning of this simplification, however, changes according to context. For example, topological simplification of Morse-Smale complexes corresponds to geometric smoothing of the associated function. To apply persistence to sampled density functions, we extend Morse-Smale complexes to piece-wise linear (PL) manifolds in Section 6.2. This extension will allow us to construct hierarchical PL Morse-Smale complexes, providing us with an intelligent method for noise reduction in sampled data. Finally, in Section 6.3, we extend the linking number, a topological invariant detecting entanglings, to simplicial complexes. Naturally, we care about the computational aspects of these ideas and their applications. We dedicate Parts Two and Three of this book to examining these concerns.

6.1 Persistence

In this section, we introduce a new concept called *persistence* (Edelsbrunner et al., 2002; Zomorodian and Carlsson, 2004). This notion may be placed within the framework of spectral sequences, the by-product of a divide-and-conquer method for computing homology (McCleary, 2000). We will show how persistence arises out of our need for feature discernment in Section 6.1.1. This discussion motivates the formulation of persistence in terms of homology groups in Section 6.1.2. In order to better comprehend the meaning of persistence, we visualize the theoretical definition in Section 6.1.3. We next briefly discuss persistence in relation to spaces we are most interested in: subspaces of $\mathbb{R}^3$. In the last section, we take a more algebraic view of persistent homology using the advanced structures we discussed in Section 3.3. This view is necessary for understanding the persistence algorithm for spaces of arbitrary dimensions and arbitrary coefficient rings, as developed in Chapter 7. The reader may skip this section safely, however, without any loss of understanding of the algorithms for subspaces of $\mathbb{R}^3$.

6.1.1 Motivation

In Chapter 2, we examined an approach for exploring the topology of a space. This approach used a geometrically grown filtration as the representation of the space. In Chapter 4, we studied a combinatorial method for computing topology using homology groups. Applying homology to filtrations, we get some signature functions for a space.

Definition 6.1 (homology of filtration) Let K^l be a filtration of a space $\mathbb{X}$. Let $\mathsf{Z}_k^l = \mathsf{Z}_k(K^l)$ and $\mathsf{B}_k^l = \mathsf{B}_k(K^l)$ be the kth cycle and boundary group of K^l, respectively. The kth homology group of K^l is $\mathsf{H}_k^l = \mathsf{Z}_k^l / \mathsf{B}_k^l$. The kth Betti number β_k^l of K^l is the rank of H_k^l.

The kth Betti numbers describe the topology of a growing simplicial complex by a sequence of integers. Our hope is that these numbers contain topological information about the original space. Unfortunately, as Figure 6.1 illustrates, our representation scheme generates a lot of additional topological attributes, all of which are captured by homology. We cannot distinguish between the *features* of the original space and the *noise* spawned by the representation. The primary topological feature of the space in the figure is a single tunnel. The graph of β_k^l in Figure 6.1, however, gives up to 43 tunnels for complexes in the filtration of this space. The evidence of the feature is buried in a heap of topological noise. To be able to derive any meaningful information about a

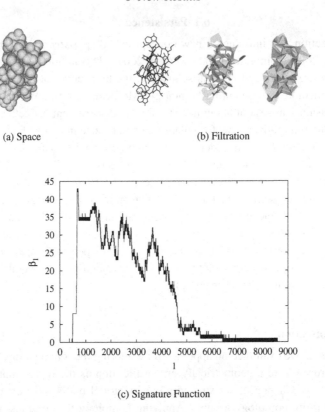

(a) Space   (b) Filtration

(c) Signature Function

Fig. 6.1. From a space (a) (van der Waals model of Gramicidin A) to its filtration (b), to a signature function β_1^l (c). The evidence of the single tunnel in the middle of this protein is engulfed by topological noise.

space from our combinatorial approach, we need a measure of significance for the captured attributes. This measure would enable us to differentiate between noise and features. One such measure is persistence.

6.1.2 Formulation

The main premise of persistence is that a significant topological attribute must have a long life-time in a filtration: The attribute *persists* in being a feature of the growing complex. Alternatively, we may call persistence *space-time analysis* or *historical analysis*, where the filtration is the history of the topological and geometric changes the spaces undergo in time. Consequently, persistence may be defined only in terms of a filtration, and filtrations, as defined in Chapter 2, are the primary input to all the algorithms in this book.

Recall that homology captures equivalent classes of cycles by factoring out the boundary cycles. We wish to capture nonbounding cycles with long lives, so we look for cycles that are nonbounding now and will not turn into boundaries in the near future, say for at least the next p complexes. These cycles persist for p steps in time, so they are significant. Formally, we factor K^l's kth cycle group by the kth boundary group of K^{l+p} p complexes later in the filtration.

Definition 6.2 (persistent homology) Let K^l be a filtration. The *p-persistent kth homology group of K^l* is

$$H_k^{l,p} = Z_k^l / (B_k^{l+p} \cap Z_k^l). \tag{6.1}$$

The *p-persistent kth Betti number $\beta_k^{l,p}$ of K^l* is the rank of $H_k^{l,p}$.

This group is well defined because $B_k^{l+p} \cap Z_k^l$ is the intersection of two subgroups of C_k^{l+p} and thus a group itself by Theorem 3.9. We may kill short-lived attributes, the topological noise of the complex, by increasing p sufficiently. The p-persistent homology groups may also be defined using injective homomorphisms between ordinary homology groups. If two cycles are homologous in K^l, they also exist and are homologous in K^{l+p}. Consider the homomorphism $\eta_k^{l,p} : H_k^l \to H_k^{l+p}$ that maps a homology class into one that contains it. The image of the homomorphism is isomorphic to the p-persistent homology group of K^l, $\mathrm{im}\, \eta_k^{l,p} \simeq H_k^{l,p}$.

Suppose a nonbounding k-cycle z is created at time i with the arrival of simplex σ into the complex. The homology class of this cycle, $[z]$, is an element of H_k^i. Assume that the arrival of simplex τ at time $j \geq i$ turns a cycle z' in $[z]$ into a boundary. That is, $z' \in B_k^j$. This event merges $[z]$ with an older class of cycles, decreasing the rank of the homology group. Equivalently, we may say that $[z]$ exists independently for all $i \leq q < j$, that is, for $j - i - 1$ steps. The half-open interval $[i, j)$ is the life-time of this class in the filtration.

Definition 6.3 (persistence) Let z be a nonbounding k-cycle that is created at time i by simplex σ, and let $z' \sim z$ be a homologous k-cycle that is turned into a boundary at time j by simplex τ. The *persistence* of z, and its homology class $[z]$, is $j - i - 1$. σ is the *creator* and τ is the *destroyer* of $[z]$. We say that τ *destroys* z and the cycle class $[z]$. We also call a creator a *positive* simplex and a destroyer a *negative* simplex. If a cycle class does not have a destroyer, its persistence is ∞.

Often, a filtration has an associated map $\rho : S(K) \to \mathbb{R}$, which maps simplices in the final complex to real numbers. In α-shapes, ρ is precisely α^2, the map we use to construct α-complex filtrations. For filtrations generated by manifold sweeps, ρ is the associated function h. We may also define persistence in terms of the birth times of the two simplices: $\rho(\sigma_j) - \rho(\sigma_i)$.

Definition 6.4 (time-based persistence) Let K be a simplicial complex and let $K^\rho = \{\sigma^i \in K \mid \rho(\sigma^i) \leq \rho\}$ be a filtration defined for an associated function $\rho : S(K) \to \mathbb{R}$. Then for every real $\pi \geq 0$, the π-persistent kth homology group of K^ρ is

$$H_k^{\rho,\pi} \;=\; Z_k^\rho / (B_k^{\rho+\pi} \cap Z_k^\rho). \qquad (6.2)$$

The π-persistent kth Betti number $\beta_k^{\rho,\pi}$ of K^ρ is the rank of $H_k^{\rho,\pi}$. The persistence of a k-cycle, created at time ρ_i and destroyed at time ρ_j, is $\rho_j - \rho_i$.

Time-based persistence is useful in the context of iso-surfaces of density functions. Index-based persistence is appropriate for alpha-complexes, as most interesting activity occurs in a small range of α.

6.1.3 Visualization

Right now, it is not clear at all that we can actually associate distinct pairs of simplices – creators and destroyers – to homology classes of cycles. The persistence equation merely indicates the existence of the persistent Betti numbers. We will see that such pairs do exist, however, when we look at the persistence algorithm in Chapter 7. In this section, I assume the existences of such pairs for a visualization exercise that will further enhance our understanding of persistence.

Suppose a space does not have any torsion. This implies that each bounding k-cycle z in the final complex K is associated with a pair of simplices (σ, τ) that create and destroy it at times i, j, respectively. We may visualize each such pair on the index axis by a half-open interval $[i, j)$, which we call the k-interval of cycle z. A nonbounding cycle in K created at time i has the infinite k-interval $[i, \infty)$. Intuitively, the graph of β_k^l is composed of the amalgamation of these intervals, as shown in Figure 6.2.

We now extend these intervals to two dimensions spanned by the index and persistence axes. The k-interval of (σ, τ) is extended into a k-triangle spanned by $(i,0)$, $(j,0)$, $(i, j-i)$ in the index-persistence plane. The k-triangle is closed along its vertical and horizontal edges and open along the diagonal connecting $(j,0)$ to $(i, j-i)$. It represents the k-cycle z that is created by σ and is destroyed

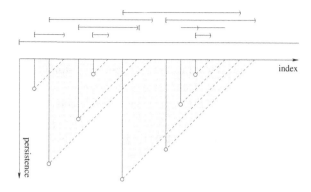

Fig. 6.2. Visualizing persistence as k-intervals and k-triangles. The k-triangle of the infinite k-interval is not shown.

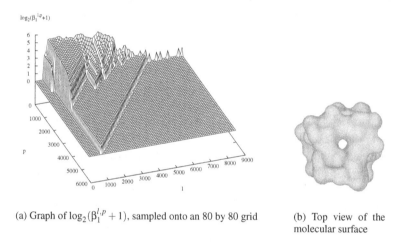

(a) Graph of $\log_2(\beta_1^{l,p} + 1)$, sampled onto an 80 by 80 grid

(b) Top view of the molecular surface

Fig. 6.3. The 1-triangles (a) of data set *1grm* and weighted balls for protein Gramicidin A (b). The single highly persistent 1-cycle represents the tunnel that is the primary topological feature of this protein. The data set is introduced in Section 12.1.

by τ progressively earlier as we increase the persistence. It seems reasonable that $\beta_k^{l,p}$ is the number of k-triangles that contain point (l, p), as each triangle covers the region for which the cycle is nonbounding. We will validate this claim, as well as the one involving k-intervals, in Chapter 7.

Example 6.1 (Gramicidin A) Figure 6.3(a) shows the overlapped 1-triangles for the filtration of protein Gramicidin A (b). We saw the graph of $\beta_1^{l,p}$ earlier in Figure 6.1. That graph corresponds to the cross-section of this three-dimensional plot at $p = 0$. The added dimension enables us to differentiate between topological noise and features according to persistence. The single 1-cycle with large persistence defines the tunnel through Gramicidin A, the only one-dimensional topological feature of this protein. Any simplification process that eliminates 1-cycles of persistence less than 2,688 succeeds in separating this tunnel from the remaining topological attributes detected by homology.

Example 6.2 (index-based vs. time-based) Figure 6.4 displays the overlapped 0-triangles for the filtration of a terrain data set, computed by a manifold sweep (see Section 2.5.)

The figure compares index-based and time-based persistence for this terrain data set. The latter method seems appropriate, as it utilizes the sampled density function (height) for making the noise-feature differentiation.

6.1.4 In $\mathbb{R}^3$

Recall from Section 4.2.3 that we are mostly interested in subcomplexes of triangulations of compactified $\mathbb{R}^3$. Such complexes are composed of vertices, edges, triangles, and tetrahedra, and they may only contain k-cycles, $0 \leq k \leq 2$, and no torsion. The simplices (σ, τ) that create and destroy k-cycles are k- and $(k+1)$-dimensional, respectively. For example, a 0-simplex or vertex always creates a 0-cycle, as it has no faces. Therefore, a vertex is always positive. The 0-cycle created by the vertex is destroyed by a negative 1-simplex or edge. This argument may be extended to develop an algorithm for computing Betti numbers of subcomplexes of $\mathbb{S}^3$ (Delfinado and Edelsbrunner, 1995). We will describe this algorithm in Chapter 7 to motivate the persistence algorithm.

6.1.5 The Persistence Module

In this section, we take a different view of persistent homology in order to understand its structure (Zomorodian and Carlsson, 2004). Intuitively, the computation of persistence requires compatible bases for H_k^i and H_k^{i+p}. It is not clear when a succinct description is available for the compatible bases. We begin this section by combining the homology of all the complexes in the filtration into a single algebraic structure. We then establish a correspondence that reveals a simple description over fields. We end this section by illustrating the relationship of our view to the persistence equation (Equation (6.1)).

Definition 6.5 (persistence complex) A *persistence complex* C is a family of

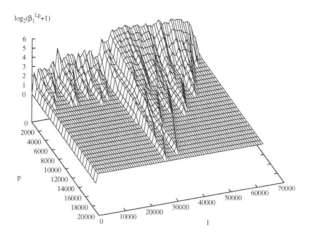

(a) Graph of $\log_2(\beta_1^{l,p} + 1)$

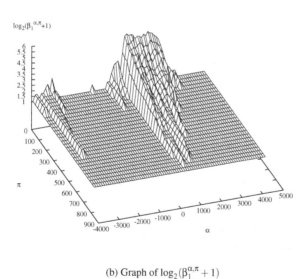

(b) Graph of $\log_2(\beta_1^{\alpha,\pi} + 1)$

Fig. 6.4. The 0-triangles of data set *Iran*, introduced in Section 12.5, for index-based (a) and time-based (b) persistence.

chain complexes $\{C_*^i\}_{i \geq 0}$ over R, together with chain maps $f^i \colon C_*^i \to C_*^{i+1}$, so that we have the following diagram:

$$C_*^0 \xrightarrow{f^0} C_*^1 \xrightarrow{f^1} C_*^2 \xrightarrow{f^2} \cdots .$$

Our filtered complex K with inclusion maps for the simplices becomes a persistence complex. Below, we show a portion of a persistence complex with the chain complexes expanded. The filtration index increases horizontally to the right under the chain maps f^i, and the dimension decreases vertically to the bottom under the boundary operators ∂_k.

$$
\begin{array}{ccccccc}
\partial_3 \downarrow & & \partial_3 \downarrow & & \partial_3 \downarrow & & \\
C_2^0 & \xrightarrow{f^0} & C_2^1 & \xrightarrow{f^1} & C_2^2 & \xrightarrow{f^2} & \cdots \\
\partial_2 \downarrow & & \partial_2 \downarrow & & \partial_2 \downarrow & & \\
C_1^0 & \xrightarrow{f^0} & C_1^1 & \xrightarrow{f^1} & C_1^2 & \xrightarrow{f^2} & \cdots \\
\partial_1 \downarrow & & \partial_1 \downarrow & & \partial_1 \downarrow & & \\
C_0^0 & \xrightarrow{f^0} & C_0^1 & \xrightarrow{f^1} & C_0^2 & \xrightarrow{f^2} & \cdots
\end{array}
$$

Definition 6.6 (persistence module) A *persistence module* $\mathcal{M}$ is a family of R-modules M^i, together with homomorphisms $\varphi^i \colon M^i \to M^{i+1}$.

For example, the homology of a persistence complex is a persistence module, where φ^i simply maps a homology class to the one that contains it.

Definition 6.7 (finite type) A persistence complex $\{C_*^i, f^i\}$ (persistence module $\{M^i, \varphi^i\}$) is of *finite type* if each component complex (module) is a finitely generated R-module and if the maps f^i (φ^i, respectively) are isomorphisms for $i \geq m$ for some integer m.

As our complex K is finite, it generates a persistence complex $\mathcal{C}$ of finite type whose homology is a persistence module $\mathcal{M}$ of finite type.

Correspondence. Suppose we have a persistence module $\mathcal{M} = \{M^i, \varphi^i\}_{i \geq 0}$ over ring R. We now equip $R[t]$ with the standard grading and define a graded module over $R[t]$ by

$$\alpha(\mathcal{M}) = \bigoplus_{i=0}^{\infty} M^i,$$

where the R-module structure is simply the sum of the structures on the individual components and where the action of t is given by

$$t \cdot (m^0, m^1, m^2, \ldots) = (0, \varphi^0(m^0), \varphi^1(m^1), \varphi^2(m^2), \ldots).$$

That is, t simply shifts elements of the module up in the gradation.

Theorem 6.1 (structure of persistence) *The correspondence α defines an equivalence of categories between the category of persistence modules of finite type over R and the category of finitely generated non-negatively graded modules over $R[t]$.*

Proof It is clear that α is functorial. We only need to construct a functor β that carries finitely generated non-negatively graded $k[t]$-modules to persistence modules of finite type. But this is readily done by sending the graded module $M = \bigoplus_{i=0}^{\infty} M^i$ to the persistence module $\{M^i, \varphi^i\}_{i \geq 0}$, where $\varphi^i \colon M^i \to M^{i+1}$ is multiplication by t. It is clear that $\alpha\beta$ and $\beta\alpha$ are canonically isomorphic to the corresponding identity functors on both sides. This proof is the Artin-Rees theory in commutative algebra (Eisenbud, 1995). $\qquad\square$

Decomposition. The correspondence established by Theorem 6.1 shows that there exists no simple classification of persistence modules over a ground ring, such as $\mathbb{Z}$, that is not a field. It is well known in commutative algebra that the classification of modules over $\mathbb{Z}[t]$ is extremely complicated. While it is possible to assign interesting invariants to $\mathbb{Z}[t]$-modules, a simple classification is not available, nor is it likely ever to be available.

On the other hand, the correspondence gives us a simple decomposition when the ground ring is a field F. Here, the graded ring $F[t]$ is a PID and its only graded ideals are homogeneous of form (t^n), so the structure of the $F[t]$-module is described by sum (3.2) in Theorem 3.19:

$$\left(\bigoplus_{i=1}^{n} \Sigma^{\alpha_i} F[t] \right) \oplus \left(\bigoplus_{j=1}^{m} \Sigma^{\gamma_j} F[t]/(t^{n_j}) \right). \tag{6.3}$$

We wish to parametrize the isomorphism classes of $F[t]$-modules by suitable objects.

Definition 6.8 ($\mathcal{P}$-interval) A $\mathcal{P}$-interval is an ordered pair (i, j) with $0 \leq i < j \in \mathbb{Z}^{\infty} = \mathbb{Z} \cup \{+\infty\}$.

We associate a graded $F[t]$-module to a set $\mathcal{S}$ of $\mathcal{P}$-intervals via a bijection

Q. We define $Q(i,j) = \Sigma^i F[t]/(t^{j-i})$ for $\mathcal{P}$-interval (i,j). And, $Q(i,+\infty) = \Sigma^i F[t]$. For a set of $\mathcal{P}$-intervals $\mathcal{S} = \{(i_1,j_1),(i_2,j_2)\ldots,(i_n,j_n)\}$, we define

$$Q(\mathcal{S}) = \bigoplus_{l=1}^{n} Q(i_l,j_l).$$

Our correspondence may now be restated as follows.

Corollary 6.1 *The correspondence $\mathcal{S} \to Q(\mathcal{S})$ defines a bijection between the finite sets of $\mathcal{P}$-intervals and the finitely generated graded modules over the graded ring $F[t]$. Consequently, the isomorphism classes of persistence modules of finite type over F are in bijective correspondence with the finite sets of $\mathcal{P}$-intervals.*

Interpretation. Before proceeding any further, let us recap our work so far. Recall that our input is a filtered complex K and we are interested in its kth homology. In each dimension, the homology of complex K^i becomes a vector space over a field, described fully by its rank β_k^i. We need to choose compatible bases across the filtration in order to compute persistent homology for the entire filtration. So, we form the persistence module corresponding to K, a direct sum of these vector spaces. The structure theorem states that a basis exists for this module that provides compatible bases for all the vector spaces. In particular, each $\mathcal{P}$-interval (i,j) describes a basis element for the homology vector spaces starting at time i until time $j-1$. This element is a k-cycle e that is completed at time i, forming a new homology class. It also remains nonbounding until time j, at which time it joins the boundary group B_k^j. While component homology groups are torsion-less, persistence appears as torsional and free elements of the persistence module.

Our interpretation also allows us to ask when $e + B_k^l$ is a basis element for the persistent groups $H_k^{l,p}$. Recall Equation (6.1). As $e \notin B_k^l$ for all $l < j$, we know that $e \notin B_k^{l+p}$ for $l+p < j$. Along with $l \geq i$ and $p \geq 0$, the three inequalities define a triangular region in the index-persistence plane, as shown in Figure 6.5. The region gives us the values for which the k-cycle e is a basis element for $H_k^{l,p}$. In other words, we have just shown a proof of why our visualization in the last section was correct.

Theorem 6.2 *Let $\mathcal{T}$ be the set of triangles defined by $\mathcal{P}$-intervals for the k-dimensional persistence module. The rank $\beta_k^{l,p}$ of $H_k^{l,p}$ is the number of triangles in $\mathcal{T}$ containing the point (l,p).*

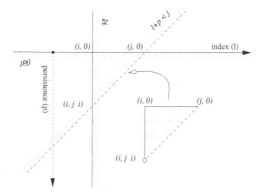

Fig. 6.5. The inequalities $p \geq 0$, $l \geq i$, and $l + p < j$ define a triangular region in the index-persistence plane. This region defines when the cycle is a basis element for the homology vector space.

We give an alternate characterization of this theorem in Chapter 7 while developing the persistence algorithm. By this lemma, computing persistent homology over a field is equivalent to finding the corresponding set of $\mathcal{P}$-intervals.

6.2 Hierarchical Morse-Smale Complexes

We would like to use persistence to simplify the iso-lines of a 2-manifold and an associated function. But persistence requires a suitably defined filtration. In Chapter 2, we looked at filtrations generated by manifold sweeps. In this section, we will see that the generated filtrations are appropriate for computing persistence and eliminating critical points combinatorially. To modify the function, however, we need control over the geometry. The Morse-Smale complex, defined in Chapter 5, provides us with the geometric description that we need.

In practice, our function is sampled. This sampling introduces noise into our data and provides the motivation for utilizing persistence for noise-feature differentiation. No matter how dense the sampling, however, our theoretical notions, based on smooth structures, are no longer valid. Triangulating the 2-manifold, we get a piece-wise linear (PL) function. The gradient of a PL function is not continuous and does not generate the pair-wise disjoint integral lines that are needed to define stable and unstable manifolds. To extend smooth notions to PL manifolds, we use differential structures to guide our computations. We call this method the *simulation of differentiability* or *SoD* paradigm. Using SoD, we first guarantee that the computed complexes have the same structural form as those in the smooth case. We then achieve numerical accuracy by means of transformations that maintain this structural integrity. The separation of combinatorial and numerical aspects of computation is similar to many algorithms in computational geometry (de Berg et al., 1997). It is also the hallmark of the SoD paradigm.

We show in this section how to extend the ideas from the last chapter to PL manifolds. We will first motivate and define the *quasi Morse-Smale complex* in Section 6.2.1. A quasi Morse-Smale complex has the same combinatorial structure as the Morse-Smale complex. In Section 6.2.2, I discuss and resolve the artifacts encountered in the PL domain. We then justify the filtrations defined in Chapter 2 and relate them to the Morse-Smale complex. We end this section by applying persistence to PL Morse-Smale complexes to get a hierarchy of progressively coarser Morse-Smale complexes.

6.2.1 Quasi Morse-Smale Complex

We begin by examining the structure of a Morse-Smale complex for a smooth, compact, connected 2-manifold. For brevity, we will call the Morse-Smale complex the *MS complex*. The following theorem establishes a fact implied by the examples in Chapter 5.

Theorem 6.3 (quadrangle) *Each region of the MS complex is a quadrangle with vertices of index 0, 1, 2, 1, in this order around the region. The boundary is possibly glued to itself along vertices and arcs.*

Proof The vertices on the boundary of any region alternate between saddles and other critical points, which, in turn, alternate between maxima and minima. The shortest possible cyclic sequence of vertices around a boundary is therefore 0, 1, 2, 1, a quadrangle. The argument below shows that longer sequences force a critical point in the interior of the region, a contradiction.

Take a region whose boundary cycle has length $4k$ for $k \geq 2$ and glue two copies of the region together along their boundary to form a sphere. Glue each critical point to its copy, so saddles become regular points. Maxima and minima remain as before. The Euler characteristic of the sphere is 2, and so is the alternating sum of critical points, $\sum_a (-1)^{i(a)}$. However, the number of minima and maxima together is $2k > 2$, which implies that there is at least one saddle inside the region. $\qquad \square$

Intuitively, a quasi Morse-Smale complex (QMS complex, for short) is a complex with the structural form of a MS complex, as described by Theorem 6.3.

The QMS complex is combinatorially a quadrangulation, with vertices at the critical points of h and with edges that strictly ascend or descend as measured by h. But it differs in that its edges may not necessarily be the edges of maximal ascent or descent.

Definition 6.9 (splitable) A subset of the vertices in a complex Q is *independent* if no two are connected by an arc. The complex Q is *splitable* if we can partition the vertices into three sets U, V, W and the arcs into two sets A, B, so that

(a) $U \cup W$ and V are both independent;
(b) arcs in A have endpoints in $U \cup V$; and arcs in B have endpoints in $V \cup W$, and
(c) each vertex $v \in V$ belongs to four arcs, which in a cyclic order around v alternate between A and B.

We may then *split* Q (Q *splits*) into two complexes defined by U, A and W, B.

Not surprisingly, the MS complex is a splitable quadrangulation.

Theorem 6.4 *The Morse-Smale complex splits.*

Proof Following Definition 6.9: (a) U, V, and W are maxima, saddles, and minima; (b) set A contains arcs connecting maxima to saddles and set B contains arcs connecting minima to saddles; and (c) saddles have degree 4 and alternate as required. The MS complex then splits into the complex of stable manifolds and the complex of unstable manifolds. □

A QMS complex splits like the MS complex but does not have the geometric characteristics of that complex. It is like the triangulation of a point set, which has the same combinatorics as the Delaunay triangulation but fails the geometric *in-circle* test (de Berg et al., 1997).

Definition 6.10 (quasi Morse-Smale complex) A *splitable quadrangulation* is a splitable complex whose regions are quadrangles. A *quasi Morse-Smale complex (QMS complex)* of a 2-manifold $\mathbb{M}$ and a function h is a splitable quadrangulation whose vertices are the critical points of h and whose arcs are monotone in h.

In Chapter 9, we will describe an algorithm for constructing a QMS complex, as well as local transformations that transform the complex into the MS complex.

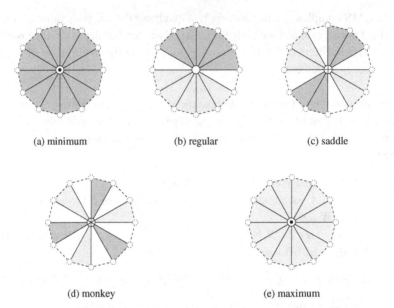

(a) minimum   (b) regular   (c) saddle

(d) monkey   (e) maximum

Fig. 6.6. Classifying vertices by their stars. The light-shaded lower wedges are connected by white triangles to the dark-shaded upper wedges The dotted vertices and
dashed edges on the boundary do not belong to the open star.

6.2.2 Piece-Wise Linear Artifacts

As in the last chapter, we assume that we have a smooth, compact, connected
2-manifold $\mathbb{M}$ without boundary, embedded in $\mathbb{R}^3$. In this section, moreover,
we represent the manifold with a triangulation K. We also assume that function
$h\colon \mathbb{M} \to \mathbb{R}$ is linear on every triangle in K. The function is defined, therefore,
by its values at the vertices of K. It will be convenient to assume $h(u) \neq h(v)$
for all vertices $u \neq v$ in K. We simulate simplicity to justify this assumption
computationally (Edelsbrunner and Mücke, 1990). In order to extend the concept of MS complexes to the piece-wise linear domain, we need to look at the
artifacts created by the lack of smoothness in a triangulation.

Stars. We have already encountered the analog of a neighborhood of a vertex
in Section 2.5: the *star* of a vertex in Definition 2.54, as shown in Figure 6.6.
We also looked at the lower and upper stars of a vertex to define filtrations. We
may use these to classify a vertex as regular or critical.

Definition 6.11 (wedge) A *wedge* is a contiguous section of St u that begins
and ends with an edge.

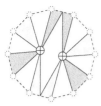 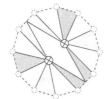 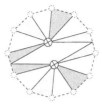

Fig. 6.7. A monkey saddle may be unfolded into two simple saddles in three different ways.

In Figure 6.6, the lower star either contains the entire star or some number $k + 1$ of wedges, and the same is true for the upper star. If $\underline{St}u = St u$, then $k = -1$ and u is a maximum. Symmetrically, if $\overline{St}u = St u$, then $k = -1$ and u is a minimum. Otherwise, u is regular if $k = 0$ and a saddle if $k = 1$. Unlike the smooth case, monkey saddles and even more complicated configurations are possible in triangulations.

Definition 6.12 (multiple saddle) A vertex u is a *k-fold saddle* or a saddle with *multiplicity* k if $\underline{St}u$ has $k + 1$ wedges. A 2-fold saddle is often called a *monkey saddle*. For $k \geq 2$, k-fold saddles are also called *multiple saddles*.

We can unfold a k-fold saddle into two saddles of multiplicity $1 \leq i, j < k$ with $i + j = k$ by the following procedure. We split a wedge of $\underline{St}u$ (through a triangle, if necessary) and similarly split a nonadjacent wedge of $\overline{St}u$. The new number of (lower and upper) wedges is $2(k+1) + 2 = 2(i+1) + 2(j+1)$, as required. By repeating the process, we eventually arrive at k simple saddles. The combinatorial process is ambiguous, but it is usually sufficient to pick an arbitrary unfolding from the set of possibilities. There are three minimal unfoldings for a monkey saddle, as shown in Figure 6.7.

Merging and forking. The definition of integral lines is inherently dependent on the smoothness of the space. In their place, we construct monotonic curves that never cross in K. Such curves can merge together and fork after a while. Moreover, it is possible for two curves to alternate between merging and forking an arbitrary number of times. To resolve this, when two curves merge, we will pretend that they maintain an infinitesimal separation, running side by side without crossing. Figure 6.8 illustrates the two PL artifacts and the corresponding simulated smooth resolution. As always, we will only simulate the smooth resolution combinatorially.

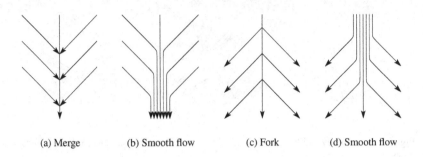

(a) Merge   (b) Smooth flow   (c) Fork   (d) Smooth flow

Fig. 6.8. Merging (a) and forking (c) PL curves and their corresponding smooth flow pictures (b, d).

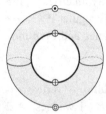

Fig. 6.9. Nontransversality: The unstable 1-manifold of the lower saddle approaches the upper saddle.

Nontransversal intersections. Another artifact of PL domains is nontransversal intersections. We illustrate this artifact via the standard example in Morse theory: the height function over a torus, standing on its side. The lowest and highest points of the inner ring are the only saddles, as shown in Figure 6.9. Both the unstable 1-manifold of the lower saddle and the stable 1-manifold of the upper saddle follow the inner ring and overlap in two open half-circles. The characteristic property of a nontransversal intersection is that the unstable 1-manifold of one saddle approaches another saddle, and vice versa. Generically, such nontransversal intersections do not happen. If they do happen, an arbitrarily small perturbation of the height function suffices to make the two 1-manifolds miss the other saddles and approach a maximum and a minimum without meeting each other. The PL counterpart of a nontransversal intersection is an ascending or descending path that ends at a saddle. Once again, we will simulate the generic case by extending the path beyond the saddle.

6.2.3 Filtration

Having discussed the resolution of PL artifacts, we may now return to our original goal of applying persistence to 2-manifolds. In Section 2.5, we introduced two filtrations, constructed by sorting the vertices of K according to the associated function h and taking the first j lower or upper stars, respectively. Without loss of generality, we will focus on the filtration of lower stars, that is, $K^i = \bigcup_{1 \leq j \leq i} \underline{\mathrm{St}}\, u^j$. Our goal is to show this filtration is meaningful with respect to persistence and the MS complex. To do so, we show a correspondence between the critical points of a triangulated 2-manifold and the persistence pairs discussed in Section 6.1. As in that section, we will assume that such pairs exist and that the underlying space is torsion-free.

Let us consider the topological changes that occur at time i in a filtration. As $|K|$ is a closed connected 2-manifold, only $\beta_0, \beta_1, \beta_2$ are nonzero and β_2 is at most 1 during the manifold sweep. When vertex u^i enters complex K^i, it brings along its lower star $\underline{\mathrm{St}}\, u^i$. As shown in Figure 6.6, the lower star consists of a number of wedges. It is clear by induction that each wedge has one more edge than it has triangles. Applying the Euler-Poincaré Theorem (Theorem 4.2.5) to our 2-manifold, we get:

$$\chi = v - e + t = \beta_0 - \beta_1 + \beta_2, \qquad (6.4)$$

where v, e, f are the number of vertices, edges, and triangles in the filtration, respectively. Once we have unfolded the multiple saddles, vertex u^i may be one of the following types:

minimum: $\underline{\mathrm{St}}\, u^i = u^i$, so a minimum vertex is a new component and $\chi^i = \chi^{i-1} + 1$. We know that $\beta_0^i = \beta_0^{i-1} + 1$ because of the new component and $\beta_1^i = \beta_1^{i-1}$ and $\beta_2^i = \beta_2^{i-1}$, as there are no other simplices to create such cycles. Substituting, we get $\chi^i = \beta_0^{i-1} + 1 + \beta_1^{i-1} + \beta_2^{i-1} = \chi^{i-1} + 1$, as expected. So, a minimum creates a new 0-cycle and acts like a positive vertex in the filtration of a complex. The negative simplex that destroys this 0-cycle is added at a time $j > i$. Therefore, the vertex is *unpaired* at time i.

regular: $\underline{\mathrm{St}}\, u^i$ is a single wedge, bringing in one more edge than triangles, giving us $\chi^i = \chi^{i-1} + 1 - 1 = \chi^{i-1}$. As $\underline{\mathrm{St}}\, u^i$ is nonempty, no new component has been created and $\beta_0^i = \beta_0^{i-1}$. $\overline{\mathrm{St}}\, u^i$ is also nonempty, no 2-cycle is created either, and $\beta_2^i = \beta_2^{i-1}$. Substituting into Equation (6.4), we get $\beta_1^i = \beta_1^{i-1}$. Therefore, no topological changes occur at regular vertices. All the cycles created at time i are also destroyed at time i. That is, the positive and negative simplices in $\underline{\mathrm{St}}\, u^i$ cancel each other, leaving no unpaired simplices.

Table 6.1. *Critical points, the unpaired simplex in their lower star, and the induced topological change. The last is specified in* C *notation, where* $\beta_{k++} \Leftrightarrow \beta_k^i = \beta_k^{i-1} + 1$, *and* β_{k--} *is defined similarly.*

critical	unpaired	action
minimum	vertex	β_{0++}
saddle	edge	β_{0--} or β_{1++}
maximum	triangle	β_{1--} or β_{2++}

saddle: $\underline{St}\,u^i$ has two wedges, bringing in two more edges than triangles. The new vertex and two extra edges give us $\chi^i = \chi^{i-1} + 1 - 2 = \chi^{i-1} - 1$. A saddle does not create a new component, being connected in two directions to the manifold through its lower star. If this saddle connects two components, it destroys a 0-cycle and $\beta_0^i = \beta_0^{i-1} - 1$. Otherwise, it creates a new 1-cycle and $\beta_1^i = \beta_1^{i-1} + 1$. This means that all the simplices in a saddle are paired, except for a single edge whose sign corresponds to the action of the saddle. We have $\chi^i = \chi^{i-1} - 1$ in either case.

maximum: $\underline{St}\,u^i = St\,u^i$ and has the same number of edges and triangles. So, $\chi^i = \chi^{i-1} + 1$ for the single vertex. If the maximum is the global maximum, $\beta_2^i = \beta_2^{i-1} + 1 = 1$. Otherwise, the lower star covers a 1-cycle and $\beta_1^i = \beta_1^{i-1} - 1$. As no new component is created, the positive vertex is paired with a negative edge, leaving a single unpaired triangle that is positive or negative, depending on the action of the maximum. We have $\chi^i = \chi^{i-1} + 1$ in both cases.

Table 6.1 displays the association between critical points and simplices that do not arrive at the same time with their persistence counterparts. We call a critical point positive or negative, according to the sign of its associated unpaired simplex. A 0-cycle is created by a positive minimum and destroyed by a negative saddle. A 1-cycle is created by a positive saddle and destroyed by a negative maximum. This association gives us persistence intervals for critical points, as shown in Figure 6.10.

There is a natural relationship between these filtrations and the MS complex. If we relax the definition of a filtration to include k-cells, then we may construct a filtration of an MS complex for applying persistence. In this filtration, a minimum is still a vertex, a saddle is represented by an arc (a path of edges), and a maximum is represented by a region (a set of triangles). Once again,

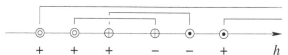

Fig. 6.10. Each critical point is either positive or negative. We use time-based persistence to measure the life-time of critical points.

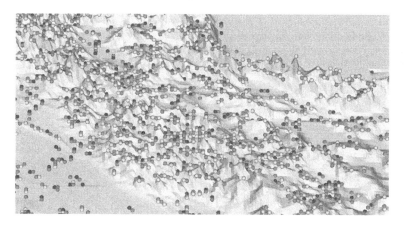

Fig. 6.11. The critical points of a section of data set *Iran* in Section 12.5. Minima (pits), saddles (passes), and maxima (peaks) are in increasingly lighter shades of gray. *Damāvand*, the highest peak in Iran, is visible over the Caspian sea in the northeast corner. The Mesopotamian valley, in the southwest corner, is bordered by the *Zagros* mountain range.

we get the same persistence intervals as above, since the MS complex captures the critical points and their connectivity. The filtration of simplices is a refined version of the filtration of the MS complex. Both filtrations contain geometry in the ordering of their components. Persistence correctly identifies the critical points through the unpaired simplices. In fact, this is precisely how we will identify critical points for terrains in Chapter 9, as shown in Figure 6.11 for the critical points of the data set *Iran*.

Finally, note that we may also use the filtration composed of upper stars for computation. In this filtration, minima and maxima exchange roles, and saddles change signs. The persistence of critical points remains unchanged, however, as the same pairs of critical points define cycles.

6.2.4 Hierarchy

The length of the persistence intervals of critical points gives us a measure of their importance. We use this measure to create a hierarchy of progres-

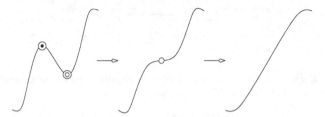

Fig. 6.12. From the left, the maximum and minimum approach and cancel each other to form a degenerate critical point in the middle. This point is perturbed into a regular point on the right.

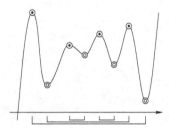

Fig. 6.13. The intervals defined by critical point pairs are either disjoint or nested.

sively coarser MS complexes. Each step in the process cancels a pair of critical points, and the sequence of cancellations is determined by the persistence of the pairs.

Motivation. To simplify the discussion, consider first a generic one-dimensional function $h\colon \mathbb{R} \to \mathbb{R}$. Its critical points are minima and maxima in an alternating sequence from left to right. In order to eliminate a maximum, we locally modify h so that the maximum moves toward an adjacent minimum. When the two points meet, they momentarily form a degenerate critical point and then disappear, as illustrated in Figure 6.12. Clearly, only adjacent critical points can be canceled, but adjacency is not sufficient unless we are willing to modify f globally. Figure 6.13 shows that the persistence intervals of the critical points are either disjoint or nested. We cancel pairs of critical points in the order of increasing persistence. The nesting structure is unraveled in this manner from inside out, the innermost pair being removed each time.

Simplification. We now return to function h over $\mathbb{M}$. The critical points of h can be eliminated in a similar manner by locally modifying the height function. In the generic case, the critical points cancel in pairs of contiguous indices.

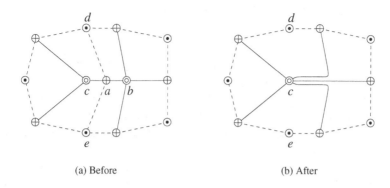

(a) Before   (b) After

Fig. 6.14. The cancellation of a and b deletes the arcs ad and ae and contracts the arcs ca and ab. The contraction effectively extends the remaining arcs of b to c.

More precisely, positive minima cancel with negative saddles and positive saddles cancel with negative maxima. We may simulate the cancellation process combinatorially by removing critical points in pairs from the MS complex. Figure 6.14 illustrates the operation for a minimum b paired with a saddle a. The operation requires that ab be an arc in the complex. Let c be the other minimum and d, e the two maxima connected to a. The operation deletes the two ascending paths from a to d and e, and contracts the two descending paths from a to b and c. In the symmetric case in which b is a maximum, the operation deletes the descending and contracts the ascending paths. The contraction pulls a and b into the critical point c, which inherits the connections of b.

Definition 6.13 (cancellation) The combinatorial operation described above and shown in Figure 6.14 for critical points a and b is the *cancellation* of a and b.

Cancellation is the only operation needed in the construction of the hierarchy. There are two special cases, namely, when $d = e$ and when $b = c$, which cannot occur at the same time. In the latter case, we prohibit the cancellation because it would change the topology of the 2-manifold.

The sequence of cancellations is again in the order of increasing persistence. In general, paired critical points may not be adjacent in the MS complex. The theorem below shows, however, that they will be adjacent just before they are canceled, even if the initial QMS complex Q is a poor approximation of the MS complex.

Theorem 6.5 (adjacency) *For every positive i, the i-th pair of critical points* *ordered by persistence forms an arc in the complex obtained by canceling the first i − 1 pairs.*

Proof Assume without loss of generality that the i-th pair consists of a negative saddle $a = u^{j+1}$ and a positive minimum z. Consider the component of K^j that contains z. One of the descending paths originating at a enters this component, and because it cannot ascend, it eventually ends at some minimum b in the same component. Either $b = z$, in which case we are done, or b has already been paired with a saddle $c \neq a$. In the latter case, c has height less than a; it belongs to the same component of K^j as b and z; and the pair b, c is one of the first $i − 1$ pairs of critical points. It follows that when b gets canceled, the path from a to b gets extended to another minimum d, which again belongs to the same component. Eventually, all minima in the component other than z are canceled, implying that the initial path from a to b gets extended all the way to z. The claim follows.   □

We may cancel pairs of critical points combinatorially without the need of an MS complex, using the simplification algorithms given in Chapter 8. For simplifying terrains, however, we would like to modify the geometry so that critical points actually disappear. The MS complex provides us with the geometric control we need for this modification.

6.3 Linking Number

In the last two sections, we described a measure for topological attributes and showed how it may be applied to simplify a sampled density function. In this section, we discuss another topological property: *linking*. Figure 6.15 shows the five linked tetrahedral skeletons we last saw in Chapter 1. Intuitively, we say an object is linked if components of the object cannot be separated from each other. In this section, we consider the *linking number*, a topological invariant that detects linking. As before, we are interested in computing linking in a filtration. To do so, we need to extend the definition of the linking number to simplicial complexes.

The mathematical background needed for this section is rather brief, so I present it here in the first two sections instead of placing it in a separate chapter. My treatment follows Adams (1994), a highly readable introductory book, as well as Rolfsen (1990), the classic textbook on knots and links. The last section includes new results. I extend the linking number to graphs and define a canonical basis for the set of homological 1-cycles in a simplicial complex.

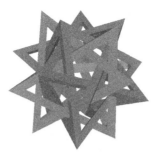

Fig. 6.15. The skeletons of 5 regular tetrahedra defined by the 20 vertices of the regular dodecahedron. The tetrahedra are linked pair-wise.

6.3.1 Knots and Links

We begin by examining a few basic definitions of knot theory.

Definition 6.14 (knot) A *knot* is an embedding of a circle in three-dimensional Euclidean space, $k : \mathbb{S}^1 \to \mathbb{R}^3$.

That is, k does not have self-intersections. As before, we define an equivalence relation on knots in order to classify their topologies.

Definition 6.15 (knot equivalence) Two knots are *equivalent* if there is an ambient isotopy that maps the first to the second.

In other words, we may deform a knot to an equivalent knot by a continuous motion in $\mathbb{R}^3$ that does not cause intersections in the knot at any time.

Definition 6.16 (link) A *link l* is a collection of knots with disjoint images.

For example, the union of two circles whose projections onto a plane are disjoint is a link called the *unlink*.

Definition 6.17 (separable) A link is *separable (splitable)* if it can be continuously deformed via an ambient isotopy so that one or more components can be separated from the other components by a plane that itself does not intersect any of the components.

The unlink is separable; linked knots are not. We often visualize a link l by a *link diagram*, a the projection of a link onto a plane, such that the over- and undercrossings of knots are presented clearly. Figure 6.16(a) is one commonly used diagram of the Whitehead link. The knots in the figure are also oriented arbitrarily. For a formal definition of a link diagram, see (Hass et al., 1999).

(a) A link diagram for the Whitehead link   (b) Crossing label convention

Fig. 6.16. The Whitehead link (a) is labeled according to the convention (b) that the crossing label is $+1$ if the rotation of the overpass by 90 degrees counter-clockwise aligns its direction with the underpass, and -1 otherwise.

6.3.2 The Linking Number

As before, we may use invariants as tools for detecting whether a link is separable. Seifert first defined an integer link invariant, the linking number, in 1935 to detect link separability (Seifert, 1935). There are several equivalent definitions for the linking number. I give the most accessible definition below for intuition. Given a link diagram for a link l, we first choose orientations for each knot in l. We then assign integer labels to each crossing between any pair of knots k, k', following the convention in Figure 6.16(b). Let $\lambda(k, k')$ of the pair of knots to be one-half the sum of these labels. A standard argument using Reidemeister moves shows that λ is an invariant for equivalent pairs of knots up to sign.

Definition 6.18 (linking number) The *linking number* $\lambda(l)$ of a link l is

$$\lambda(l) \quad = \quad \sum_{k \neq k' \in l} |\lambda(k, k')|, \qquad (6.5)$$

where $\lambda(k, k')$ is one-half the sum of labels on oriented knots k, k' according to the convention in Figure 6.16(b).

Note that $\lambda(l)$ is independent of knot orientations. Also, the linking number has the characteristic of invariants that it does not completely recognize linking. The Whitehead link in Figure 6.16(a), for example, has linking number zero but is not separable. If the linking number is nonzero, however, we know that the link is not the unlink.

I will use an alternate definition for developing algorithms for computing the linking number in Chapter 10. This definition is based on surfaces whose boundaries are the knots in the link.

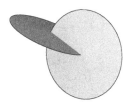 

Fig. 6.17. The Hopf link and Seifert surfaces of its two unknots are shown on the left. Clearly, $\lambda = 1$. The spanning surface for the cycle on the right is a Möbius strip and therefore nonorientable.

Definition 6.19 (spanning, Seifert) A *spanning surface* for a knot k is an embedded surface with boundary k. An orientable spanning surface is a *Seifert surface*.

Figure 6.17 shows examples of spanning surfaces for the Hopf link and Möbius strip. Since a Seifert surface is orientable, we may label its two sides as positive and negative. Given a pair of oriented knots k, k' and a Seifert surface s for k, we label s by using the orientation of k. We then adjust k' via a homotopy h until it meets s in a finite number of points. Following along k' according to its orientation, we add $+1$ whenever k' passes from the negative to the positive side and -1 whenever k' passes from the positive to the negative side. The following theorem asserts that this sum is independent of our the choice of h and s, and it is, in fact, the linking number.

Theorem 6.6 (Seifert surface) $\lambda(k, k')$ *is the sum of the signed intersections between k' and any Seifert surface for k.*

The proof is by the standard Seifert surface construction. If the spanning surface is nonorientable, we can still count how many times we pass through the surface, giving us the following weaker result.

Theorem 6.7 (spanning surface) $\lambda(k, k')$ (mod 2) *is the parity of the number of times k' passes through any spanning surface for k.*

6.3.3 Graphs

In order to compute the linking number of a simplicial complex, we need to first define what we mean by a knot in a complex. Not surprisingly, we decide to use the homology cycles of a simplicial complex, as defined in Chapter 4.

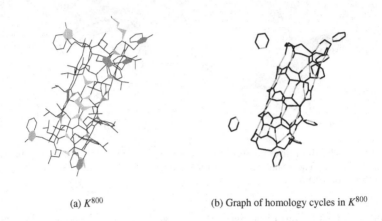

(a) K^{800} (b) Graph of homology cycles in K^{800}

Fig. 6.18. The homology cycles of the 800th complex K^{800} of a filtration for data set *1grm* (a) form a graph (b). The darker negative edges form a spanning forest that defines a canonical basis for the cycles.

These cycles form a graph within the simplicial complex, as shown in Figure 6.18. We need to extend the linking number to graphs, in order to use the theorems in the last section in computing linking numbers for simplicial complexes.

Let $G = (V,E), E \subseteq \binom{V}{2}$ be a simple undirected graph in $\mathbb{R}^3$ with c components $G^1, \ldots, G^c$. A graph may be viewed as a vector space of cycles. For example, the graph in Figure 6.18(b) has rank 35. Let $z^1, \ldots, z^m$ be a fixed basis for the cycles in G, where $m = |E| - |V| + c$ is the rank of G. We then define the linking number between two components of G to be $\lambda(G^i, G^j) = \sum |\lambda(z^p, z^q)|$ for all cycles z^p, z^q in G^i, G^j, respectively. The linking number of G is then defined by summing the total interactions between pairs of components.

Definition 6.20 (linking number of graphs) The *linking number* $\lambda(G)$ *of a graph G is*

$$\lambda(G) \;\; = \;\; \sum_{i \neq j} \lambda(G^i, G^j),$$

where $\lambda(G^i, G^j) = \sum |\lambda(z^p, z^q)|$ for ball basis cycles z^p, z^q in different components G^i, G^j, respectively.

The linking number is computed only between pairs of components following Seifert's original definition. Linked cycles within the same component may be unlinked by a homotopy (Prasolov, 1995).

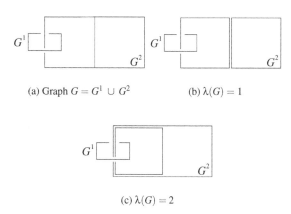

(a) Graph $G = G^1 \cup G^2$ (b) $\lambda(G) = 1$

(c) $\lambda(G) = 2$

Fig. 6.19. We get different $\lambda(G)$ for graph G (a) depending on our choice of basis for G^2: two small cycles (b) or one large and one small cycle (c).

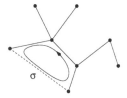

Fig. 6.20. Solid negative edges combine to form a spanning tree. The dashed positive edge σ creates a canonical cycle.

Figure 6.19 shows that the linking number for graphs is dependent on the chosen basis. While it may seem that we want $\lambda(G) = 1$ in the figure, there is no clear answer in general. We need a canonical basis for defining a canonical linking number. The definition of the canonical basis is similar to the one used for the fundamental group of a graph (Hatcher, 2001). Recall that persistence marks simplices as positive or negative, depending on whether they create or destroy cycles. Each negative edge connects two components. Therefore, the set of all negative edges gives us a spanning forest of the complex, as shown in Figures 6.20 and Figure 6.18(b). Every time a positive edge σ is added to the complex, it creates a new cycle. We choose the unique cycle that contains σ and no other positive edge as a new basis cycle.

Definition 6.21 (canonical) The unique cycle that contains a single positive edge is a *canonical cycle*. The set of all canonical cycles is the *canonical basis*.

We will use this basis for computation. In Chapter 7, we will modify the persistence algorithm to compute canonical cycles and their spanning surfaces. In Chapter 10, we look at data structures and algorithms for computing the linking number of a filtration.

Part Two

Algorithms

7

The Persistence Algorithms

In this chapter, we look at algorithms for computing persistence. We begin by reviewing an algorithm for computing Betti numbers by Delfinado and Edelsbrunner (1995) in Section 7.1. This algorithm works over subspaces of $\mathbb{S}^3$, which do not have torsion. We utilize this algorithm for marking simplices as positive or negative (recall Definition 6.3.) We also show how the algorithm may be used to speed up the computation of persistence. In Section 7.2, we develop the persistence algorithm over $\mathbb{Z}_2$ coefficients for subcomplexes of any triangulation of $\mathbb{S}^3$.

To compute persistence over arbitrary fields, we need the alternate point of view described in Section 6.1.5. Using this view, we extend and generalize the persistence algorithm to arbitrary dimensions and ground fields in Section 7.3. We do so by deriving the algorithm from the classic reduction scheme, illustrating that the algorithm derives its simple structure from the properties of the underlying algebraic structures. While no simple description exists over nonfields, we may still be interested in computing a single homology group over an arbitrary PID. We give an algorithm in Section 7.4 for this purpose.

7.1 Marking Algorithm

In the first two sections of this chapter, we assume that the input spaces are three-dimensional and torsion-free, as discussed in section 4.2.3. Consequently, we use $\mathbb{Z}_2$ coefficients for computation. Recall from Section 4.3 that using these coefficients greatly simplifies homology: The homology groups are vector spaces, a k-chain is simply the list of simplices with coefficients 1, each simplex is its own inverse, and the group operation is *symmetric difference*, as shown in Figure 7.1. The only nonzero Betti numbers to be computed are β_0, β_1, and β_2.

We also need a filtration ordering of the simplices (Definition 2.44). We use

125

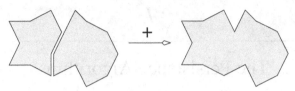

Fig. 7.1. Symmetric difference in dimensions one and two. We add two 1-cycles to get a new 1-cycle. We add the surfaces that the cycles bound to get a spanning surface for the new 1-cycle.

this total ordering to construct a filtration, where one, and only one, simplex is added at each time step, that is, $K^i = \{\sigma^j \mid 0 \leq j \leq i\}$, for $0 \leq i < m$. We use this filtration for developing the persistence algorithm, as it simplifies discussion: Simplex σ^i is added at time i, so its index is also its birth index. Figure 7.2 displays a small filtration of a complex with 18 simplices. This filtration will be the primary example we will use for illustrations in this and the next chapters. The filtration is small enough to be examined and understood in detail. This filtration is also the smallest example with a structural property that makes computing persistence difficult for 1-cycles. A good exercise is to see the logic behind the pairs of simplices representing cycles, using the visualization of the k-triangles in Figure 7.5.

The total ordering of simplices in a filtration permits a simple incremental algorithm for computing Betti numbers of all complexes in a filtration (Delfinado and Edelsbrunner, 1995). Before running the algorithm, the Betti number variables are set to the Betti numbers of the empty complex, that is, $\beta_0 = \beta_1 = \beta_2 = 0$. The algorithm is shown in Figure 7.3. The function returns a list of three integers, denoted $\texttt{integer}^3$. But how do we decide whether a $(k+1)$-simplex σ^i belongs to a $(k+1)$-cycle in K^i? For $k+1 = 0$, this is trivial because every vertex belongs to a 0-cycle. For edges, we maintain the connected components of the complex, each represented by its vertex set. An edge belongs to a 1-cycle iff its two endpoints belong to the same component. Triangles and tetrahedra are treated similarly, using the symmetry provided by complementarity, duality, and time-reversal. We use these algorithms to mark the simplices as positive or negative. Let $\mathrm{pos}_k = \mathrm{pos}_k^l$ and $\mathrm{neg}_k = \mathrm{neg}_k^l$ be the number of positive and negative k-simplices in K^l. The correctness of the incremental algorithm implies

$$\beta_k = \mathrm{pos}_k - \mathrm{neg}_{k+1}, \tag{7.1}$$

for $0 \leq k \leq 2$. In words, the Betti number β_k is the number of k-simplices that create k-cycles minus the number of $(k+1)$-simplices that destroy k-cycles.

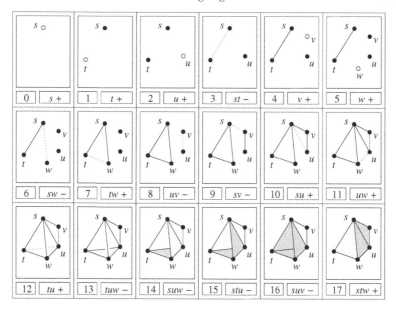

Fig. 7.2. A small filtration of a tetrahedron with a flap. The lightly shaded simplex is added at time time *i*. The simplices are named and marked according to persistence.

```
integer³ BETTI-NUMBERS () {
    for i = 0 to m − 1 {
        k = dim σⁱ − 1;
        if σⁱ belongs to a (k + 1)-cycle in Kⁱ
            β_{k+1} = β_{k+1} + 1;
        else
            β_k = β_k − 1;
    }
    return (β₀, β₁, β₂);
}
```

Fig. 7.3. The function returns the Betti numbers of the last complex in the filtration.

Observe that Equation (7.1) is just a different way of writing

$$\operatorname{rank} \mathsf{H}_k \quad = \quad \operatorname{rank} \mathsf{Z}_k - \operatorname{rank} \mathsf{B}_k, \tag{7.2}$$

which follows from Corollary 3.3. We also saw this equation in the proof of the Euler-Poincaré Theorem (Theorem 4.5, Equation (4.10)). All Betti numbers are nonnegative so $\operatorname{pos}_k \geq \operatorname{neg}_{k+1}$ for all *l*. We will see in the next section that there exists a pairing between positive *k*-simplices and negative $(k+1)$-

simplices. This pairing is the key to understanding the persistence of non-bounding cycles in homology groups.

7.2 Algorithm for $\mathbb{Z}_2$

In this section, we develop and present the persistence algorithm for $\mathbb{Z}_2$ coefficients (Edelsbrunner et al., 2002). We begin with an abstract algorithm for computing persistence. After showing its correctness, we complete the scheme by describing a data structure and an algorithm for computing the persistence pairings. We then extend the algorithm to compute a canonical basis for cycles and analyze the running time of the algorithm.

7.2.1 Abstract Algorithm

The persistence computation takes the form of finding the pairs of simplices responsible for the creation and destruction of cycles. Once we have this pairing, computing the persistent Betti numbers is trivial. Throughout this section, we assume that the simplices have been marked using the algorithm from the last section. The persistence algorithm may be extended to also mark simplices. We will need this modification for computing persistence in arbitrary dimensions, where the incremental algorithm of Delfinado and Edelsbrunner (1995) is no longer viable. In three dimensions, however, the incremental algorithm is fast, and we will use it for marking simplices.

Algorithm. To measure the life-time of a nonbounding cycle, we find when the cycle's homology class is created by a positive simplex and destroyed by a negative simplex. To detect these events, we maintain a basis for H_k implicitly through simplex representatives. Initially, the basis for H_k is empty. For each positive k-simplex σ^i, we first find a nonbounding k-cycle c^i that contains σ^i, but no other positive k-simplices. This is precisely a canonical cycle (Definition 6.21).

Theorem 7.1 *Canonical cycles exist.*

Proof We use induction, as follows: Start with an arbitrary k-cycle that contains σ^i and remove other positive k-simplices by adding their corresponding k-cycles. This method succeeds because each added cycle contains only one positive k-simplex by the inductive assumption. $\square$

```
list³ PAIR-SIMPLICES () {
    L₀ = L₁ = L₂ = ∅;
    for j = 0 to m − 1 {
        k = dim σʲ − 1;
        if σʲ is negative {
(*)         d = ∂_{k+1}(σʲ);  i = y(d);
            L_k = L_k ∪ {(σⁱ,σʲ)};
        }
    }
    return (L₀,L₁,L₂);
}
```

Fig. 7.4. The function returns three lists of paired simplices in the filtration.

After finding c^i, we add the homology class of c^i as a new element to the basis of H_k. In short, the class $c^i + \mathsf{B}_k$ is represented by c^i, and c^i, in turn, is represented by σ^i. For each negative $(k+1)$-simplex σ^j, we find its corresponding positive k-simplex σ^i and remove the homology class of σ^i from the basis. A general homology class of K^i is a sum of basis classes,

$$
\begin{aligned}
d + \mathsf{B}_k &= \sum (c^g + \mathsf{B}_k) \\
&= \mathsf{B}_k + \sum c^g.
\end{aligned}
$$

The chains d and $\sum c^g$ are homologous, that is, they belong to the same homology class. Each c^g is represented by a positive k-simplex σ^g, $g < j$, that is not yet paired by the algorithm. The collection of positive k-simplices $\Gamma = \Gamma(d)$ is uniquely determined by d. The youngest simplex in Γ is the one with the largest index, and we denote this index as $y(d)$. The algorithm, as shown in Figure 7.4, identifies σ^j as the destroyer of the cycle class, created by σ_i. We document this by appending (σ^i, σ^j) to the list L_k.

Correctness. Assume for now that the algorithm just presented is correct. This means that $\beta_k^{l,p}$ is the number of k-triangles that contain point (l, p), as in Figure 7.5. Then, the persistent Betti numbers are nonincreasing along vertical lines in the index-persistence plane. The same is true for lines in the diagonal direction and for all lines between the vertical and the diagonal directions. This gives us the following corollary.

Corollary 7.1 (Monotonicity Corollary) $\beta_k^{l,p} \leq \beta_k^{l',p'}$ *whenever* $p' \leq p$ *and* $l \leq l' \leq l + (p - p')$.

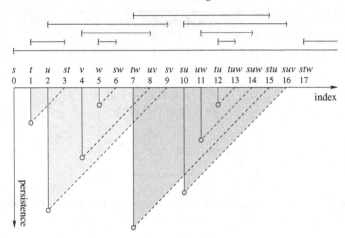

Fig. 7.5. The k-intervals and k-triangles for the filtration in Figure 7.2.

To prove the abstract algorithm's correctness, we show that the pairs it produces are consistent with the persistent Betti numbers defined by the persistence formulation (Equation (6.1)). In other words, the visualization in Figure 7.5 is valid.

Theorem 7.2 (k-**triangle**) $\beta_k^{l,p}$ *is the number of k-triangles containing (l, p) in the index-persistence plane.*

Proof The proof proceeds by induction over p. For $p = 0$, the number of k-triangles that contain $(l, 0)$ is equal to the number of k-intervals $[i, j)$ that contain l. This is equal to the number of left endpoints minus the number of right endpoints that are smaller than or equal to l. Equivalently, it is the number of positive k-simplices σ^i with $i \leq l$ minus the number of negative $(k+1)$-simplices σ^j with $j \leq l$. But this is just a restatement of Equation (7.1), which establishes the basis of the induction.

Consider (l, p) with $p > 0$ and assume inductively that the claim holds for $(l, p-1)$. The relevant simplex for the step from $(l, p-1)$ to (l, p) is σ^{l+p}. The persistent kth Betti number can either stay the same or decrease by 1. It will decrease only if σ^{l+p} is a negative $(k+1)$-simplex, or equivalently, $(l+p, 0)$ is the upper right corner of a k-triangle. Indeed, no other k-triangle can possibly separate $(l, p-1)$ and (l, p). This proves the claim if σ^{l+p} is a positive $(k+1)$-simplex or a simplex of dimension different from $k+1$. Now suppose that σ^{l+p} is a negative $(k+1)$-simplex and define the k-cycle $d = \partial_{k+1}(\sigma^{l+p})$. There are two cases, as shown in Figure 7.6.

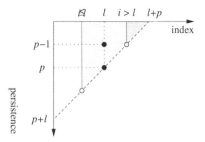

Fig. 7.6. The light k-triangle corresponds to Case 1 and the dark one to Case 2.

1. Assume there is a k-cycle c in K^l homologous to d, that is, $c \in d + B_k^{l+p-1}$. Then, c bounds neither in K^l nor in K^{l+p-1}, but it bounds in K^{l+p}. It follows that $\beta_k^{l,p} = \beta_k^{l,p-1} - 1$. We need to show that the pair (σ^i, σ^{l+p}) constructed by the algorithm satisfies $i \leq l$, because only in this case does the k-triangle of σ^{l+p} separate $(l, p-1)$ from (l, p). Recall that σ^i is the youngest positive k-simplex in $\Gamma(d)$. To reach a contradiction suppose $i > l$. Then c is a nonbounding k-cycle also in K^i, and because it is homologous to d, we have $\sigma^i \in c$. But this contradicts $c \subseteq K^l$ as $\sigma^i \notin K^l$.

2. Assume there is no k-cycle in K^l homologous to d. Then $Z_k^l \cap B_k^{l+p-1} = Z_k^l \cap B_k^{l+p}$, and hence $\beta_k^{l,p} = \beta_k^{l,p-1}$. We need to show that the pair (σ^i, σ^{l+p}) constructed by the algorithm satisfies $i > l$, because only in this case does the k-triangle of σ^{l+p} not separate $(l, p-1)$ from (l, p). Our assumption above implies that at least one of the positive k-simplices in $\Gamma(d)$ was added after σ^l. Hence $i = y(d) > l$.

The theorem follows. □

7.2.2 Cycle Search

Having proven the correctness of the abstract algorithm, we complete its description by specifying how to implement line (*) of the function PAIR-SIMPLICES. We need to compute the index i of the youngest positive k-simplex in $\Gamma(d)$, where $d = \partial_{k+1}(\sigma^j)$. We refer to this computation as a *cycle search* for σ^j. We will first describe the data structure, then explain cycle search, prove its correctness, and analyze its running time.

Data structure. We use a linear array $T[0..m-1]$, which acts similar to a hash table (Cormen et al., 1994). Initially, T is empty. A pair (σ^i, σ^j) identified

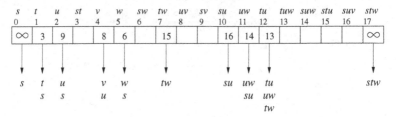

Fig. 7.7. Hash table after running the algorithm on the filtration of Figure 7.2.

by the algorithm is stored in $T[i]$ together with a list of positive simplices Λ^i defining the cycle created by σ^i and destroyed by σ^j. The simplices in that list are not necessarily the same as the ones in $\Gamma(d)$. All we guarantee is that d is homologous to the sum of cycles represented by the simplices in the list and that the list contains the youngest simplex in $\Gamma(d)$, which is σ^i as above. The correctness proof following the algorithm will show that this property is sufficient for our purposes. The data structure is illustrated in Figure 7.7 for the filtration in Figure 7.2 at the end of the persistence computation. Each simplex in the filtration has a slot in the hash table, but information is stored only in the slots of the positive simplices. This information consists of the index j of the matching negative simplex and a list of positive simplices defining a cycle. Some cycles exist beyond the end of the filtration, in which case we use ∞ as a substitute for j.

Algorithm. Suppose the algorithm arrives at index j in the filtration, and assume σ^j is a negative $(k+1)$-simplex. Recall that $\Gamma(d)$ is the set of positive k-simplices that represent the homology class of $d = \partial\sigma^j$ in H_k^{j-1}. We search for the youngest k-simplex in $\Gamma(d)$ by successively probing slots in T until we find the right one. Specifically, we start with a set Λ equal to the set of positive k-simplices in d, which is necessarily nonempty, and we let $i = \max(\Lambda)$ be the index of the youngest member of Λ. We will see later that if $T[i]$ is unoccupied, then $i = y(d)$. We can therefore end the search and store j and Λ in $T[i]$. If $T[i]$ is occupied, it contains a collection Λ^i representing a permanently stored k-cycle. At this moment, the stored k-cycle is already a k-boundary. We add Λ and Λ^i to get a new Λ representing a k-cycle, homologous to the old one, and therefore also homologous to d. The function YOUNGEST in Figure 7.8 performs a cycle search for simplex σ^j.

A *collision* is the event of probing an occupied slot of T. It triggers the addition of Λ and Λ^i, which means we take the symmetric difference of the two collections. For example, the first collision for the filtration of Figure 7.2

```
integer YOUNGEST (simplex σʲ) {
    Λ = {σ ∈ ∂_{k+1}(σʲ) | σ positive};
    while (true) {
        i = max(Λ);
        if T[i] is unoccupied {
            store j and Λ in T[i];
            break;
        }
        Λ = Λ + Λⁱ;
    }
    return i;
}
```

Fig. 7.8. The function returns the index of the youngest basis cycle used in the description of the boundary of σ^j.

occurs for the negative edge sv. Initially, we have $\Lambda = \{s, v\}$ and i equal to 4, the index of v. $T[4]$ is occupied and stores $\Lambda^4 = \{u, v\}$. The sum of the two 0-cycles is $\Lambda + \Lambda^4 = \{s, u\}$, which is the new set Λ. We now have $i = 2$, the index of u. This time, $T[2]$ is unoccupied and we store the index of sv and the new set Λ in that slot.

Correctness. We will first show that cycle search always halts and then that it halts with the correct simplex. Consider a collision at $T[i]$. The list Λ^i stored in $T[i]$ contains σ^i and possibly other positive k-simplices, all older than σ^i. After adding Λ and Λ^i we get a new list Λ. This list is necessarily nonempty, as otherwise d would bound. Furthermore, all simplices in Λ are strictly older than σ^i. Therefore, the new i is smaller than the old one, which implies that the search proceeds strictly from right to left in T. It necessarily ends at an unoccupied slot $T[g]$ of the hash table, for all other possibilities lead to contradictions.

It takes more effort to prove that $T[g]$ is the correct slot or, in other words, that $g = y(d)$, where $d = \partial_{k+1}(\sigma^j)$ is the boundary of the negative $(k+1)$-simplex that triggered the search. Let e be the cycle defined by Λ^g. Since e is obtained from d through adding bounding cycles, we know that e and d are homologous in K^{j-1}. A *collision-free* cycle is one where the youngest positive simplex corresponds to an unoccupied slot in the hash table. Cycle search ends whenever it reaches a collision-free cycle. For example, e is collision-free because its youngest positive simplex is σ^g and $T[g]$ is unoccupied before e arrives.

Theorem 7.3 (collision) *Let e be a collision-free k-cycle in K^{j-1} homologous to d. Then, the index of the youngest positive simplex in e is $i = y(d)$.*

Proof Let σ^g be the youngest positive simplex in e and f be the sum of the basis cycles, homologous to d. By definition, f's youngest positive simplex is σ^i, where $i = y(d)$. This implies that there are no cycles homologous to d in K^{i-1} or earlier complexes; therefore $g \geq i$. We show $g \leq i$ by contradiction. If $g > i$, then $e = f + c$, where c bounds in K^{j-1}. $\sigma^g \notin f$ implies $\sigma^g \in c$, and as σ^g is the youngest in e, it is also the youngest in c. By assumption, $T[g]$ is unoccupied as e is collision-free. In other words, the cycle created by σ^g is still a nonbounding cycle in K^{j-1}. Hence this cycle cannot be c. Also, the cycle cannot belong to c's homology class at the time c becomes a boundary. It follows that the negative $(k+1)$-simplex that converts c into a boundary pairs with a positive k-simplex in c that is younger than σ^g, a contradiction. Hence $g = i$. $\qquad\square$

The cycle search continues until it finds a collision-free cycle e homologous to d, and the collision theorem implies that e has the correct youngest positive simplex. This proves the correctness of the cycle search, and we may now substitute $i = \text{YOUNGEST}(\sigma^j)$ for line (*) in function PAIR-SIMPLICES.

7.2.3 Analysis

Let us now examine the running time of the cycle search algorithm. Let $d = \partial_{k+1}(\sigma^j)$ and let σ^i be the youngest positive k-simplex in $\Gamma(d)$. The persistence of the cycle created by σ^i and destroyed by σ^j is $p_i = j - i - 1$. The search for σ^i proceeds from right to left starting at $T[j]$ and ending at $T[i]$. The number of collisions is at most the number of positive k-simplices strictly between σ^i and σ^j, which is less than p_i. A collision happens at $T[g]$ only if σ^g already forms a pair, which implies its k-interval $[g, h)$ is contained inside $[i, j)$. We use the nesting property to prove by induction that the k-cycle defined by Λ^i is the sum of fewer than p_i boundaries of $(k+1)$-simplices. Hence, Λ^i contains fewer than $(k+2)p_i$ k-simplices, and similarly Λ^g contains fewer than $(k+2)p_g < (k+2)p_i$ k-simplices. A collision requires adding the two lists and finding the youngest in the new list. We do this by merging, which keeps the lists sorted by age. A single collision takes time at most $O(p_i)$, and the entire search for σ^i takes time at most $O(p_i^2)$. The total algorithm runs in time at most $O(\sum p_i^2)$, which is at most $O(m^3)$. As we will see in Chapter 12, the algorithm is quite fast in practice, as both the average number of collisions and the average length of the simplex lists are small constants.

The running time of cycle search can be improved to almost constant for dimensions $k = 0$ and $k = 2$ using a *union-find* data structure representing a system of disjoint sets and supporting *union* and *find* operations (Cormen et al., 1994). For $k = 0$, each set is the vertex set of a connected component. Each set has exactly one yet unpaired vertex, namely the oldest one in the component. We modify standard union-find implementations in such a way that this vertex represents the set. Given a vertex, the find operation returns the representative of the set that contains this vertex. Given an edge whose endpoints lie in different sets, the union operation merges the two sets into one. At the same time, it pairs the edge with the younger of the two representatives and retains the older one as the representative of the merged set.

In this modified algorithm, a cycle search is replaced by two find operations possibly followed by a union operation. If we use *union by rank* and *path compression* for find, the amortized time per operation is $O(A^{-1}(m))$, where $A^{-1}(m)$ is the notoriously slowly growing inverse of the Ackermann function (Cormen et al., 1994). We may use symmetry to accelerate the cycle search for 2-cycles using the union-find data structure for a system of sets of tetrahedra (Delfinado and Edelsbrunner, 1995). We cannot achieve the same acceleration for 1-cycles using this method, however, as there can be multiple unpaired positive edges at any time. The additional complication seems to require the more cautious and therefore slower algorithm described above.

7.2.4 Canonization

The persistence algorithm halts when it finds the matching positive simplex σ^i for a negative simplex σ^j, often generating a cycle z with several positive simplices. We have shown that even though this cycle is not canonical, the algorithm computes the correct persistence pairs. In order to compute linking numbers, however, we need to convert z into a canonical cycle. We do so by eliminating all positive simplices in z except for σ^i. We call this process *canonization* (Edelsbrunner and Zomorodian, 2003). To canonize a cycle, we add cycles associated with unnecessary positive simplices to z successively, until z is composed of σ^i and some negative simplices, as shown in Figure 7.9 for 1-cycles. Canonization amounts to replacing one homology basis element with a linear combination of other elements in order to reach the unique canonical basis, defined in Section 6.3.3. A cycle undergoing canonization changes homology classes, but the rank of the basis never changes.

For each canonical 1-cycle, we also need a spanning surface in order to compute linking numbers. Again, we may compute such "surfaces" for cycles of all dimensions by simply maintaining the spanning surfaces while computing

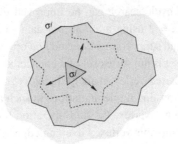

Fig. 7.9. Canonization of 1-cycles. Starting from the boundary of the negative triangle σ^j, the persistence algorithm finds a matching positive edge σ^i by finding the dashed 1-cycle. We modify this 1-cycle further to find the solid canonical 1-cycle and a spanning surface.

the cycles. For a 0-cycle, the spanning manifold is a connected path of edges. For a 2-cycle, the spanning manifold is the set of tetrahedra that fill the void. We generalize this concept by the following definition.

Definition 7.1 (spanning manifold) A *spanning manifold* for a k-cycle is a set of simplices whose sum has the cycle as its boundary.

Recall that, initially, a cycle representative is the boundary of a negative simplex σ^j. We use σ^j as the initial spanning manifold for z. Every time we add a cycle y to z in the persistence algorithm, we also add the surface y bounds to the z's surface. We continue this process through canonization to produce both canonical cycles and their spanning manifolds. Here, we are using a crucial property of α-complex filtrations: The final complex is always the Delaunay complex of the set of weighted points and does not contain any 1-cycles. Therefore, all 1-cycles are eventually turned to boundaries and have spanning manifolds.

7.3 Algorithm for Fields

In this section, we devise an algorithm for computing persistent homology over an arbitrary field (Zomorodian and Carlsson, 2004). Given the theoretical development of Section 6.1.5, our approach is rather simple: We simplify the standard reduction algorithm using the properties of the persistence module. Our arguments give an algorithm for computing the $\mathcal{P}$-intervals for a filtered complex directly over the field F, without the need for constructing the persistence module. The algorithm is, in fact, a generalized version of the cycle search algorithm shown in the previous section.

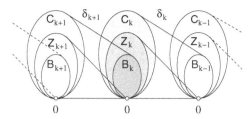

Fig. 7.10. A chain complex with its internals: chain, cycle, and boundary groups, and their images under the boundary operators.

7.3.1 Reduction

The standard method for computing homology is the reduction algorithm. We describe this method for integer coefficients as it is the more familiar ring. The method extends to modules over arbitrary PIDs, however.

Recall the chain complex and its related groups, as shown in Figure 7.10 for a complex in an arbitrary dimension. As C_k is free, the oriented k-simplices form the *standard basis* for it. We represent the boundary operator $\partial_k : C_k \to C_{k-1}$ relative to the standard bases of the chain groups as an integer matrix M_k with entries in $\{-1, 0, 1\}$. The matrix M_k is called the *standard matrix representation* of ∂_k. It has m_k columns and m_{k-1} rows (the number of k- and $(k-1)$-simplices, respectively.) The null-space of M_k corresponds to Z_k and its range-space to B_{k-1}, as manifested in Figure 7.10. The *reduction algorithm* derives alternate bases for the chain groups, relative to which the matrix for ∂_k is diagonal. The algorithm utilizes the following *elementary row operations* on M_k:

1. exchange row i and row j;
2. multiply row i by -1;
3. replace row i by (row i) + q(row j), where q is an integer and $j \neq i$.

The algorithm also uses *elementary column operations* that are similarly defined. Each column (row) operation corresponds to a change in the basis for C_k (C_{k-1}). For example, if e_i and e_j are the ith and jth basis elements for C_k, respectively, a column operation of type (3) amounts to replacing e_i with $e_i + qe_j$. A similar row operation on basis elements $\hat{e}_i$ and $\hat{e}_j$ for C_{k-1}, however, replaces $\hat{e}_j$ by $\hat{e}_j - q\hat{e}_i$. We shall make use of this fact in Section 7.3.3. The algorithm systematically modifies the bases of C_k and C_{k-1} using elemen-

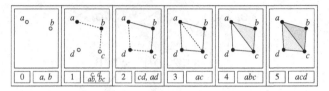

Fig. 7.11. A filtered complex with newly added simplices highlighted.

tary operations to reduce M_k to its *(Smith) normal form*:

$$
\tilde{M}_k \;=\; \left[
\begin{array}{ccc|c}
b_1 & & 0 & \\
 & \ddots & & 0 \\
0 & & b_{l_k} & \\
\hline
 & 0 & & 0
\end{array}
\right],
$$

where $l_k = \mathrm{rank}\, M_k = \mathrm{rank}\, \tilde{M}_k$, $b^i \geq 1$, and $b_i | b_{i+1}$ for all $1 \leq i < l_k$. The algorithm can also compute corresponding bases $\{e_j\}$ and $\{\hat{e}_i\}$ for C_k and C_{k-1}, respectively, although this is unnecessary if a decomposition is all that is needed. Computing the normal form in all dimensions, we get a full characterization of H_k:

  (i) The torsion coefficients of H_{k-1} (d_i in Equation (3.1)) are precisely the diagonal entries b_i greater than 1.
 (ii) $\{e_i \mid l_k + 1 \leq i \leq m_k\}$ is a basis for Z_k. Therefore, $\mathrm{rank}\, Z_k = m_k - l_k$.
(iii) $\{b_i \hat{e}_i \mid 1 \leq i \leq l_k\}$ is a basis for B_{k-1}. Equivalently, $\mathrm{rank}\, B_k = \mathrm{rank}\, M_{k+1} = l_{k+1}$.

Combining (ii) and (iii), we have

$$
\beta_k \;=\; \mathrm{rank}\, Z_k - \mathrm{rank}\, B_k = m_k - l_k - l_{k+1}. \tag{7.3}
$$

Example 7.1 We illustrate the reduction method using the filtration in Figure 7.11. We use a smaller filtration than the one we used in the previous section so the matrices are smaller. However, this example is more general as we allow multiple simplices to be added at the same time. For this complex, the standard matrix representation of ∂_1 is

$$
M_1 \;=\;
\begin{array}{c|ccccc}
 & ab & bc & cd & ad & ac \\
\hline
a & -1 & 0 & 0 & -1 & -1 \\
b & 1 & -1 & 0 & 0 & 0 \\
c & 0 & 1 & -1 & 0 & 1 \\
d & 0 & 0 & 1 & 1 & 0 \\
\end{array},
$$

where we show the bases within the matrix. Reducing the matrix, we get the normal form

$$
\tilde{M}_1 \;=\;
\begin{array}{c|ccccc}
 & cd & bc & ab & z_1 & z_2 \\
\hline
d-c & 1 & 0 & 0 & 0 & 0 \\
c-b & 0 & 1 & 0 & 0 & 0 \\
b-a & 0 & 0 & 1 & 0 & 0 \\
a & 0 & 0 & 0 & 0 & 0 \\
\end{array},
$$

where $z_1 = ad - bc - cd - ab$ and $z_2 = ac - bc - ab$ form a basis for Z_1 and $\{d-c, c-b, b-a\}$ is a basis for B_0.

We may use a similar procedure to compute homology over graded PIDs. A *homogeneous basis* is a basis of homogeneous elements. We begin by representing ∂_k relative to the standard basis of C_k (which is homogeneous) and a homogeneous basis for Z_{k-1}. Reducing to normal form, we read off the description provided by the direct sum (Equation (3.2)) using the new basis $\{\hat{e}_j\}$ for Z_{k-1}:

(i) Zero row i contributes a free term with shift $\alpha_i = \deg \hat{e}_i$.

(ii) Row with diagonal term b_i contributes a torsional term with homogeneous $d_j = b_j$ and shift $\gamma_j = \deg \hat{e}_j$.

The reduction algorithm requires $O(m^3)$ elementary operations, where m is the number of simplices in K. The operations, however, must be performed in exact integer arithmetic. This is problematic in practice, as the entries of the intermediate matrices may become extremely large.

7.3.2 Derivation

We use the small filtration in Figure 7.11 as a running example and compute over $\mathbb{R}$, although any field will do. The persistence module corresponds to a $\mathbb{R}[t]$-module by the correspondence established in Theorem 3.19. Table 7.1 reviews the degrees of the simplices of our filtration as homogeneous elements of this module.

Throughout this section, we use $\{e_j\}$ and $\{\hat{e}_i\}$ to represent homogeneous

Table 7.1. *Degree of simplices of filtration in Figure 7.11*

a	b	c	d	ab	bc	cd	ad	ac	abc	acd
0	0	1	1	1	1	1	2	2	3	5

bases for C_k and C_{k-1}, respectively. Relative to homogeneous bases, any representation M_k of ∂_k has the following basic property:

$$\deg \hat{e}_i + \deg M_k(i,j) = \deg e_j, \tag{7.4}$$

where $M_k(i,j)$ denotes the element at location (i,j). We get

$$
M_1 =
\begin{bmatrix}
 & ab & bc & cd & ad & ac \\
\hline
d & 0 & 0 & t & t & 0 \\
c & 0 & 1 & t & 0 & t^2 \\
b & t & t & 0 & 0 & 0 \\
a & t & 0 & 0 & t^2 & t^3
\end{bmatrix}, \tag{7.5}
$$

for ∂_1 in our example. The reader may verify Equation (7.4) using this example for intuition, e.g., $M_1(4,4) = t^2$ as $\deg ad - \deg a = 2 - 0 = 2$, according to Table 7.1.

Clearly, the standard bases for chain groups are homogeneous. We need to represent $\partial_k : C_k \to C_{k-1}$ relative to the standard basis for C_k and a homogeneous basis for Z_{k-1}. We then reduce the matrix and read off the description of H_k according to our discussion in Section 7.3.1. We compute these representations inductively in dimension. The base case is trivial. As $\partial_0 \equiv 0$, $Z_0 = C_0$ and the standard basis may be used for representing ∂_1. Now, assume we have a matrix representation M_k of ∂_k relative to the standard basis $\{e_j\}$ for C_k and a homogeneous basis $\{\hat{e}_i\}$ for Z_{k-1}. For induction, we need to compute a homogeneous basis for Z_k and represent ∂_{k+1} relative to C_{k+1} and the computed basis. We begin by sorting basis $\hat{e}_i$ in reverse degree order, as already done in the matrix in Equation (7.5). We next transform M_k into the *column-echelon form* $\tilde{M}_k$, a lower staircase form shown in Figure 7.12 (Uhlig, 2002). The steps have variable height, all landings have width equal to 1, and nonzero elements may only occur beneath the staircase. A boxed value in the figure is a *pivot* and a row (column) with a pivot is called a *pivot row (column)*. From linear algebra, we know that rank M_k = rank B_{k-1} is the number of pivots in an echelon form. The basis elements corresponding to nonpivot columns form the desired

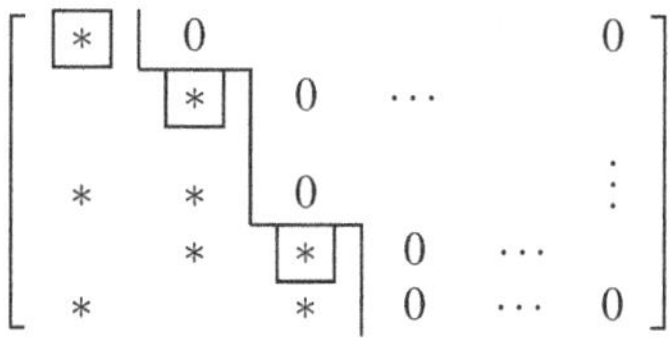

$$
\begin{bmatrix}
\boxed{*} & 0 & & & 0 \\
 & \boxed{*} & 0 & \cdots & \\
* & * & 0 & & \vdots \\
 & * & \boxed{*} & 0 & \cdots \\
* & & * & 0 & \cdots & 0
\end{bmatrix}
$$

Fig. 7.12. The column-echelon form. An $*$ indicates a nonzero values and the pivots are boxed.

basis for Z_k. In our example, we have

$$
\tilde{M}_1 =
\begin{bmatrix}
 & cd & bc & ab & z_1 & z_2 \\
\hline
d & \boxed{t} & 0 & 0 & 0 & 0 \\
c & t & \boxed{1} & 0 & 0 & 0 \\
b & 0 & t & \boxed{t} & 0 & 0 \\
a & 0 & 0 & t & 0 & 0
\end{bmatrix},
\tag{7.6}
$$

where $z_1 = ad - cd - t \cdot bc - t \cdot ab$ and $z_2 = ac - t^2 \cdot bc - t^2 \cdot ab$ form a homogeneous basis for Z_1.

The procedure that arrives at the echelon form is Gaussian elimination on the columns, utilizing elementary column operations of types (1, 3) only. Starting with the left-most column, we eliminate nonzero entries occurring in pivot rows in order of increasing row. To eliminate an entry, we use an elementary column operation of type (3) that maintains the homogeneity of the basis and matrix elements. We continue until we either arrive at a zero column or we find a new pivot. If needed, we then perform a column exchange (type (1)) to reorder the columns appropriately.

Theorem 7.4 (echelon form) *The pivots in column-echelon form are the same as the diagonal elements in normal form. Moreover, the degree of the basis elements on pivot rows is the same in both forms.*

Proof Because of our sort, the degree of row basis elements $\hat{e}_i$ is monotonically decreasing from the top row down. Within each fixed column j, $\deg e_j$ is a constant c. By Equation (7.4), $\deg M_k(i, j) = c - \deg \hat{e}_i$. Therefore, the degree of the elements in each column is monotonically increasing with row. We may eliminate nonzero elements below pivots using row operations that do not change the pivot elements or the degrees of the row basis elements. We then place the matrix in diagonal form with row and column swaps. $\qquad\square$

The theorem states that if we are only interested in the degree of the basis

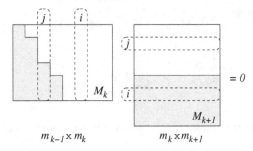

Fig. 7.13. As $\partial_k \partial_{k+1} = \emptyset$, $M_k M_{k+1} = 0$, and this is unchanged by elementary operations. When M_k is reduced to echelon form $\tilde{M}_k$ by column operations, the corresponding row operations zero out rows in M_{k+1} that correspond to pivot columns in $\tilde{M}_k$.

elements, we may read them off from the echelon form directly. That is, we may use the following corollary of the standard structure theorem to obtain the description.

Corollary 7.2 *Let $\tilde{M}_k$ be the column-echelon form for ∂_k relative to bases $\{e_j\}$ and $\{\hat{e}_i\}$ for C_k and Z_{k-1}, respectively. If row i has pivot $\tilde{M}_k(i,j) = t^n$, it contributes $\Sigma^{\deg \hat{e}_i} F[t]/t^n$ to the description of H_{k-1}. Otherwise, it contributes $\Sigma^{\deg \hat{e}_i} F[t]$. Equivalently, we get $(\deg \hat{e}_i, \deg \hat{e}_i + n)$ and $(\deg \hat{e}_i, \infty)$, respectively, as $\mathcal{P}$-intervals for H_{k-1}.*

In our example, $\tilde{M}_1(1,1) = t$ in Equation (7.6). As $\deg d = 1$, the element contributes $\Sigma^1 \mathbb{R}[t]/(t)$ or the $\mathcal{P}$-interval (1,2) to the description of H_0.

We now wish to represent ∂_{k+1} in terms of the basis we computed for Z_k. We begin with the standard matrix representation M_{k+1} of ∂_{k+1}. As $\partial_k \partial_{k+1} = \emptyset$, $M_k M_{k+1} = 0$, as shown in Figure 7.13. Furthermore, this relationship is unchanged by elementary operations. Since the domain of ∂_k is the codomain of ∂_{k+1}, the elementary column operations we used to transform M_k into echelon form $\tilde{M}_k$ give corresponding row operations on M_{k+1}. These row operations zero out rows in M_{k+1} that correspond to nonzero pivot columns in $\tilde{M}_k$ and give a representation of ∂_{k+1} relative to the basis we just computed for Z_k. This is precisely what we are after. We can get it, however, with hardly any work.

Theorem 7.5 (basis change) *To represent ∂_{k+1} relative to the standard basis for C_{k+1} and the basis computed for Z_k, simply delete rows in M_{k+1} that correspond to pivot columns in $\tilde{M}_k$.*

Proof We only used elementary column operations of types (1,3) in our variant of Gaussian elimination. Only the latter changes values in the matrix.

Suppose we replace column i by (column i) + q(column j) in order to eliminate an element in a pivot row j, as shown in Figure 7.13. This operation amounts to replacing column basis element e_i by $e_i + qe_j$ in M_k. To effect the same replacement in the row basis for ∂_{k+1}, we need to replace row j with (row j) − q(row i). But row j is eventually zeroed-out, as shown in Figure 7.13, and rows i is never changed by any such operation. ☐

Therefore, we have no need for row operations. We simply eliminate rows corresponding to pivot columns one dimension lower to get the desired representation for ∂_{k+1} in terms of the basis for Z_k. This completes the induction. In our example, the standard matrix representation for ∂_2 is

$$
M_2 \;=\; \begin{bmatrix}
 & abc & acd \\ \hline
ac & t & t^2 \\
ad & 0 & t^3 \\
cd & 0 & t^3 \\
bc & t^3 & 0 \\
ab & t^3 & 0
\end{bmatrix}.
$$

To get a representation in terms of C_2 and the basis (z_1, z_2) for Z_1 we computed earlier, we simply eliminate the bottom three rows. These rows are associated with pivots in $\tilde{M}_1$, according to Equation (7.6). We get

$$
\check{M}_2 \;=\; \begin{bmatrix}
 & abc & acd \\ \hline
z_2 & t & t^2 \\
z_1 & 0 & t^3
\end{bmatrix},
$$

where we have also replaced ad and ac with the corresponding basis elements $z_1 = ad - bc - cd - ab$ and $z_2 = ac - bc - ab$.

7.3.3 Algorithm

Our discussion gives us an algorithm for computing $\mathcal{P}$-intervals of an $F[t]$-module over field F. It turns out, however, that we can simulate the algorithm over the field itself, without the need for computing the $F[t]$-module. Rather, we use two significant observations from the derivation of the algorithm. First, Theorem 7.4 guarantees that if we eliminate pivots in the order of decreasing degree, we may read off the entire description from the echelon form and do not need to reduce to normal form. And second, Theorem 7.5 tells us that by simply noting the pivot columns in each dimension and eliminating the corresponding rows in the next dimension, we get the required basis change.

Therefore, we only need column operations throughout our procedure and

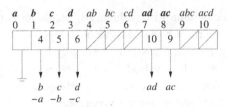

Fig. 7.14. Data structure after running the algorithm on the filtration in Figure 7.11. Marked simplices are in bold italic.

there is no need for a matrix representation. We represent the boundary operators as a set of boundary chains corresponding to the columns of the matrix. Within this representation, column exchanges (type 1) have no meaning, and the only operation we need is of type 3. Our data structure is an array T with a slot for each simplex in the filtration, as shown in Figure 7.14 for our example. Each simplex gets a slot in the table. For indexing, we need a full ordering of the simplices, so we complete the partial order defined by the degree of a simplex by sorting simplices according to dimension, breaking all remaining ties arbitrarily (we did this implicitly in the matrix representation). We also need the ability to *mark* simplices to indicate nonpivot columns. Rather than computing homology in each dimension independently, we compute homology in all dimensions incrementally and concurrently. The algorithm, as shown in Figure 7.15, stores the list of $\mathcal{P}$-intervals for H_k in L_k. When simplex σ^j is added, we check via the procedure REMOVEPIVOTROWS to see whether its boundary chain d corresponds to a zero or pivot column. If the chain is empty, it corresponds to a zero column and we mark σ^j: Its column is a basis element for Z_k, and the corresponding row should not be eliminated in the next dimension. Otherwise, the chain corresponds to a pivot column and the term with the maximum index $i = \text{maxindex}\, d$ is the pivot, according the procedure described for the $F[t]$-module. We store index j and chain d representing the column in $T[i]$. Applying Corollary 7.2, we get the $\mathcal{P}$-interval $(\deg \sigma^i, \deg \sigma^j)$. We continue until we exhaust the filtration. We then perform another pass through the filtration in search of infinite $\mathcal{P}$-intervals: marked simplices whose slot is empty.

We give the function REMOVEPIVOTROWS in Figure 7.16. Initially, the function computes the boundary chain d for the simplex. It then applies Theorem 7.5, eliminating all terms involving unmarked simplices to get a representation in terms of the basis for Z_{k-1}. The rest of the procedure is Gaussian elimination in the order of decreasing degree, as dictated by our discussion for the $F[t]$-module. The term with the maximum index $i = \max d$ is a potential

```
COMPUTEINTERVALS (K) {
    for k = 0 to dim(K) L_k = ∅;
    for j = 0 to m − 1 {
        d = REMOVEPIVOTROWS (σ^j);
        if (d = ∅) Mark σ^j;
        else {
            i = maxindex d; k = dim σ^j;
            Store j and d in T[i];
            L_k = L_k ∪ {(deg σ^i, deg σ^j)}
        }
    }
    for j = 0 to m − 1 {
        if σ^j is marked and T[j] is empty {
            k = dim σ^j; L_k = L_k ∪ {(deg σ^j, ∞)}
        }
    }
}
```

Fig. 7.15. Algorithm COMPUTEINTERVALS processes a complex of m simplices. It stores the sets of $\mathcal{P}$-intervals in dimension k in L_k.

```
chain REMOVEPIVOTROWS (σ) {
    k = dim σ; d = ∂_k σ;
    Remove unmarked terms in d;
    while (d ≠ ∅) {
        i = maxindex d;
        if T[i] is empty, break;
        Let q be the coefficient of σ^i in T[i];
        d = d − q^{−1} T[i];
    }
    return d;
}
```

Fig. 7.16. Algorithm REMOVEPIVOTROWS first eliminates rows not marked (not corresponding to the basis for Z_{k-1}) and then eliminates terms in pivot rows.

pivot. If $T[i]$ is nonempty, a pivot already exists in that row, and we use the inverse of its coefficient to eliminate the row from our chain. Otherwise, we have found a pivot and our chain is a pivot column. For our example filtration in Figure 7.14, the marked 0-simplices $\{a, b, c, d\}$ and 1-simplices $\{ad, ac\}$ generate the $\mathcal{P}$-intervals $L_0 = \{(0, \infty), (0, 1), (1, 1), (1, 2)\}$ and $L_1 = \{(2, 4), (3, 5)\}$, respectively.

7.3.4 Discussion

From our derivation, it is clear that the algorithm has the same running time as Gaussian elimination over fields. That is, it takes $O(m^3)$ in the worst case, where m is the number of simplices in the filtration. The algorithm is very simple, however, and represents the matrices efficiently. Having derived the algorithm from the reduction scheme, we find the algorithm to have the same structure as the persistence algorithm for $\mathbb{Z}_2$ coefficients. It is different in two aspects:

1. It does its own marking, so it is independent of the Delfinado-Edelsbrunner algorithm. Therefore, the algorithm is no longer restricted to subcomplexes of a triangulation of $\mathbb{S}^3$, but can compute over arbitrary complexes in any dimension.
2. It allows for arbitrary fields as coefficients. This allows us to detect low-order torsion by computing over different rings.

Most significantly, the approach in this section places the persistence algorithm within the classical framework of algebraic topology.

7.4 Algorithm for PIDs

The correspondence we established in Section 6.1.5 eliminated any hope for a simple classification of persistent groups over rings that are not fields. Nevertheless, we may still be interested in their computation. In this section, we give an algorithm to compute the persistent homology groups $H_k^{i,p}$ of a filtered complex K for a fixed i and p. The algorithm we provide computes persistent homology over any PID D of coefficients by utilizing a reduction algorithm over that ring.

To compute the persistent group, we need to obtain a description of the numerator and denominator of the quotient group in Equation (6.1). We already know how to characterize the numerator. We simply reduce the standard matrix representation M_k^i of ∂_k^i using the reduction algorithm. The denominator, $\mathsf{B}_k^{i,p} = \mathsf{B}_k^{i+p} \cap \mathsf{Z}_k^i$, plays the role of the boundary group in Equation (6.1). Therefore, instead of reducing matrix M_{k+1}^i, we need to reduce an alternate matrix $M_{k+1}^{i,p}$ that describes this boundary group. We obtain this matrix as follows:

(1) We reduce matrix M_k^i to its normal form and obtain a basis $\{z^j\}$ for Z_k^i, using fact (ii) in Section 7.3.1. We may merge this computation with that of the numerator.

(2) We reduce matrix M_{k+1}^{i+p} to its normal form and obtain a basis $\{b^l\}$ for B_k^{i+p} using fact (iii) in Section 7.3.1.

(3) Let $N = [\{b^l\}\ \{z^j\}] = [B\ Z]$, that is, the columns of matrix N consist of the basis elements from the bases we just computed, and B and Z are the respective submatrices defined by the bases. We next reduce N to normal form to find a basis $\{u^q\}$ for its null-space. As before, we obtain this basis using fact (ii). Each $u^q = [\alpha^q\ \zeta^q]$, where α^q, ζ^q are vectors of coefficients of $\{b^l\}, \{z^j\}$, respectively. Note that $Nu^q = B\alpha^q + Z\zeta^q = 0$ by definition. In other words, element $B\alpha^q = -Z\zeta^q$ belongs to the span of both bases. Therefore, both $\{B\alpha^q\}$ and $\{Z\zeta^q\}$ are bases for $\mathsf{B}_k^{i,p} = \mathsf{B}_k^{i+p} \cap \mathsf{Z}_k^i$. We form a matrix $M_{k+1}^{i,p}$ from either.

We now reduce $M_{k+1}^{i,p}$ to normal form and read off the torsion coefficients and the rank of $\mathsf{B}_k^{i,p}$. It is clear from the procedure that we are computing the persistent groups correctly, giving us the following.

Theorem 7.6 *For coefficients in any PID, persistent homology groups are computable in the order of time and space of computing homology groups.*

8

Topological Simplification

In Chapter 6, we motivated the definition of persistence by the need for intelligent methods for topological simplification. In this chapter, we look at algorithms for simplifying a space topologically, using persistence as a measure. We begin by reviewing prior work and formalizing a notion of topological simplification within the framework of filtrations in Section 8.1. We then look at a simple algorithm for computing persistent Betti numbers, which motivates the reordering algorithms for simplification in Section 8.2. There are conflicts, however, between the goals established for simplification. We formalize these conflicts, and discuss their resolution or diminution in Section 8.3. To view the entire persistent history of a filtration, we develop color maps in Section 8.4. We end this chapter with visualizations of simplified complexes.

8.1 Motivation

Topological issues arise in surface reconstruction and mesh optimization. Surface reconstruction is, by itself, a topological question, but it is often addressed with geometric methods. Consequently, fast ad-hoc heuristics for surface reconstruction usually give rise to defective surfaces, requiring hole-filling or filtering as a post-processing step (Curless and Levoy, 1996; Turk and Levoy, 1994). Furthermore, surface modification methods such as decimation, refinement, thickening, and smoothing may cause changes in the surface's topology. We gave an example of this connection in the discussion in Section 1.2.3 in relation to surface decimation.

8.1.1 Prior Work

Topological questions have been mostly marginalized in the past. In the computer graphics community, for example, where appearance is the paramount issue, the topological changes caused by a geometric simplification algorithm are often touted as a feature of the algorithm (Garland and Heckbert, 1997; Hoppe et al., 1993; Popović and Hoppe, 1997; Schroeder et al., 1992). Dey et al. (1999) describe a topology-preserving decimation operation that disallows topological changes all together. In general, however, geometrical concerns override topological ones, and there is little control or understanding of the resulting topological changes.

There has been little work, moreover, in the area of topological simplification. Rossignac and Borrel (1993) use a global grid and simplify the topology within grid elements. He et al. (1996) use low-pass filters for volume grid data sets. Their work does not apply, however, to polygonal objects, unless they are voxelized. El-Sana and Varshney (1998) approach simplification using α-shape inspired ideas and convolution. Wood and Guskov (2001) eliminate small tunnels by growing regions on a surface. None of the work considers the problem using a theoretical foundation or a well-defined *topological* measure.

8.1.2 Approach and Goals

In this book, I advocate the approach of using persistence within the framework of filtrations. The topological complexity of a filtration is reflected in its Betti numbers. Consequently, I consider *topological simplification* to be a process that decreases a space's Betti numbers. If we view a filtration as a history of a growing complex, simplification is a process that does not allow short-lived cycles to ever exist. Simply put, a cycle cannot be born unless it has a long life, and persistence controls the prerequisite life-time for existence. There are two goals in the simplification process:

1. elimination of nonpersistent cycles,
2. and maintenance of the filtration.

As stated, it is not clear whether any conflicts exist between achieving the above two goals.

The simplification process reorders the simplices in the filtration to eliminate nonpersistent cycles. It is the entire history of a growing complex that is being simplified, however, and not a single complex. Some may argue, therefore, that no simplification has taken place: The same simplices exist as before in the filtration, but in a new order. This argument is based on notions from geometric simplification, where simplices are removed and new ones are introduced in a single complex. The argument is not valid, however, as the two simplification processes are not analogous. The filtrations in this book exist in a geometric context, and the order of simplices has meaning. For example,

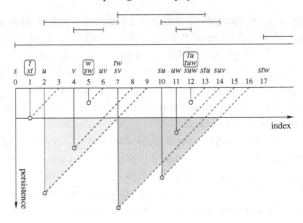

Fig. 8.1. The k-triangles that intersect the new axis at $p = 2$ have persistence 2 or larger. The simplex pairs representing cycles of persistence less than 2 are boxed.

a topologically simplified filtration of a Morse complex specifies a sequence of geometric modifications to the Morse complex. In other words, there is a level of indirection between topological simplification and the meaning of that simplification.

8.2 Reordering Algorithms

In this section, we present two reordering algorithms for simplification. These algorithms are successful in simplifying a filtration in most cases. Conflicts occur, however, between the goals of simplifying and maintaining a filtration. We will discuss such conflicts in the next section and provide algorithms for simplification in the presence of conflicts.

8.2.1 Persistent Betti Number Algorithm

We get inspiration for simplification methods through an algorithm for computing persistent Betti numbers. By the k-triangle theorem (Theorem 7.2 in Section 7.2.1), the p-persistent kth Betti number of K^l is the number $\beta_k^{l,p}$ of k-triangles that contain the point (l, p) in the index-persistence plane. To compute these numbers for a fixed p, we intersect the k-triangles with a horizontal line at p. Figure 8.1 illustrates this operation by modifying Figure 7.5, the k-triangles of our example filtration. The algorithm for p-persistent Betti numbers is similar to the function BETTI-NUMBERS given in Figure 7.3. We go through the filtration from left to right and increase β_k^p whenever we encounter

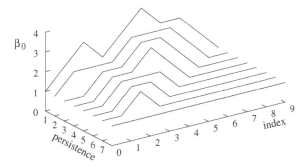

Fig. 8.2. Persistent 0-th Betti numbers of the first ten complexes in the filtration of Figure 7.2 and for persistence up to 7.

the left endpoint of a k-interval longer than p. Similarly, we decrease β_k^p whenever there is a right endpoint of a k-interval longer than p, p positions ahead of us. Figure 8.2 shows the results of the algorithm applied to our example filtration for $k = 0$.

8.2.2 Migration

The intersection of the k-triangles and the horizontal line at p is a collection of half-open intervals. We interpret these intervals as k-intervals of a simplified version of the original filtration. Our goal is to reorder the filtration so that this interpretation is valid, that is, we wish to obtain a new filtration whose Betti numbers are the p-persistent Betti numbers of the original filtration.

Definition 8.1 (persistent complexes) Let $\{K^l\}$ be a filtration. $K^{l,p}$ is the l-th complex in a reordered filtration, where cycles with persistence less than p are eliminated. We call $K^{l,p}$ a *p-persistent complex*.

The algorithm for reordering is clear from Figure 8.1. For each pair (σ^i, σ^j), we move σ^j to the left, closer or all the way to σ^i. The new position of σ^j is $\max\{i, j - p\}$. If $j - p \leq i$, then σ^i and σ^j no longer form an interval as they both occupy the same index in the new filtration.

There is a complication in the reordering algorithm that occurs whenever a negative simplex attempts to move past one of its faces. To maintain the filtration ordering, we must move the face along with its coface. For example, if we increase p to 4 in Figure 8.1, then stu will move to index 11 past its face tu at index 12. Moving a face along with a simplex will not change any Betti numbers if the face represents a cycle whose persistence is less than p. At the time

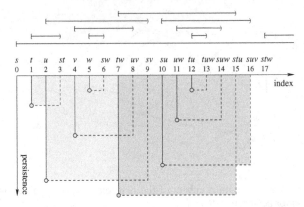

Fig. 8.3. Alternative visualization of the result of the function PAIR-SIMPLICES in Section 7.2.1. The squares of s and stw are unbounded and not shown. The light squares represent 0-cycles and the dark squares represent 1-cycles.

we move it, the face is already co-located with its matching negative simplex, and the two cancel each other's contributions. We may then grab the pair and move it with the simplex, moving the pair (tu, tuw) with stu in our example. For any moving simplex, however, we must also move all the necessary faces and their matching negative simplices recursively. There is trouble if the face of a moving negative simplex represents a cycle whose persistence is at least p. For instance, when stu encounters the edge su, the triangle suv that is paired with su has not yet reached su. There is a conflict between our two goals of maintaining a filtration and reordering so the new Betti numbers are the old p-persistent Betti numbers. We will postpone discussion on conflicts until the next section.

8.2.3 Lazy Migration

Our motivation for formulating persistent homology in Equation (6.1) was to eliminate cycles with low persistence. As a consequence of the formulation, the life-time of *every* cycle is reduced regardless of its persistence, leading to the creation of k-triangles. A possibly more intuitive goal would be to eliminate cycles with low persistence without changing the life-time of cycles with high persistence. In other words, we replace k-triangles by k-*squares* as illustrated in Figure 8.3. We may also define square Betti numbers, analogs to Betti numbers, for a filtration.

Definition 8.2 (square Betti numbers) The *p-persistent kth square Betti num-*

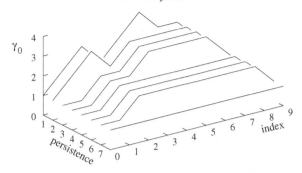

Fig. 8.4. Numbers γ_0 for the first ten complexes in the filtration of Figure 7.2.

ber $\gamma_k^{l,p}$ *of* K^l is the number of k-squares that contain the point (l, p) in the index-persistence plane.

Figure 8.4 illustrates how these numbers change as we increase persistence from $p = 0$ to 7. Note that we can easily read off persistent cycles from the graph. We may also simplify complexes using $\gamma_k^{l,p}$ by only collapsing k-intervals of length at most p, leaving other k-intervals unchanged.

8.2.4 Others

Naturally, we do not have to stop with squares. We may replace the k-triangles with any shape we wish, provided the shapes are meaningful. For example, irregular shapes correspond to adaptive reordering, where we eliminate cycles selectively. We may also reorder to the right instead of the left, moving the positive simplex toward the negative simplex and getting k-triangles that are the other half of k-squares. This reordering has meaning: Reordering to the right corresponds to reordering the dual of our complex to the left. Persistence pairs give us power over the topology of space. We may use this power to simplify spaces differently, according to the application at hand.

8.3 Conflicts

In the last section, we saw that conflicts could exist between our two objectives in simplification. In this section, we formalize and analyze the notion of conflicts. We then discuss two approaches for dealing with conflicts: resolution and diminution.

Fig. 8.5. Basic conflict configuration.

8.3.1 Definition

We begin by formalizing conflicts.

Definition 8.3 (conflict) A *conflict* occurs whenever there are pairs (σ^i, σ^j) and (σ^g, σ^h) with $g < i < h < j$, where σ^i is a face of σ^h, as shown in Figure 8.5.

There are $\binom{4}{2}$ possible types of conflicts, each identified by the pair $(\dim \sigma^i, \dim \sigma^h)$ of the dimensions of the main participants.

Definition 8.4 (conflict type) A conflict between simplex pairs (σ^i, σ^j) and (σ^g, σ^h) has *type* $(\dim \sigma^i, \dim \sigma^h)$.

For example, the pairs (su, suv) and (tw, stu) in Figure 8.1 constitute a conflict of type $(1, 2)$ and show that conflicts do occur. They are, however, rather rare, as the experiments in Section 12.4 will demonstrate. This rarity stems partially from the following fact.

Theorem 8.1 (conflict) *All conflicts have type* $(1, 2)$.

Proof Suppose a conflict exists in pairs (σ^i, σ^j) and (σ^g, σ^h), where σ^i is a vertex. When σ^h enters the filtration, it belongs to the same component as σ^g, since σ^h completes a chain whose boundary includes σ^g. Vertex σ^i, one of the vertices of σ^h, is unpaired and therefore represents the component of σ^h and σ^g. Recall that any component is represented by its oldest vertex, which implies that σ^i is older than all the vertices of σ^g. By the filtration property, σ^i is older than σ^g, i.e., $i < g$, which contradicts the assumption that (σ^i, σ^j) and (σ^g, σ^h) form a conflict. This proves there are no conflicts of types $(0, 1)$, $(0, 2)$, $(0, 3)$. By complementarity and duality, there are no conflicts of types $(1, 3)$ and $(2, 3)$. □

Difficulties in reordering may also arise indirectly because of the recursive nature of any reordering algorithm. For example, moving a negative triangle may require moving one of its edges. This edge holds on to its matching triangle, which in turn grabs its needed faces. Some of these faces may be unpaired.

To capture this situation, we define recursive conflicts and call other conflicts *basic*.

Definition 8.5 (recursive conflicts) A *recursive conflict* is a positive simplex that is moved by a reordering process, when it is not co-located with its matching negative simplex.

Note that the simplices in a basic conflict include a simplex that is a recursive conflict. We may easily extend the conflict theorem for recursive conflicts.

Theorem 8.2 (recursive conflict) *All recursive conflicts are edges.*

Proof We have a situation as in Figure 8.5, except that σ^i is not necessarily a face of σ^h. However, the moving simplices all belong to the same component as σ^h: This is true for a face by definition, for a matching negative simplex by the reason given in the proof above, and for all moving simplices by transitivity. The theorem follows. □

Basic and recursive conflicts exist in practice but are rather rare, as shown in Section 12.4. When conflicts occur, we view filtration maintenance as inviolable and approximate our secondary goal, that of achieving the correct Betti numbers. We may do so via two approaches:

(i) Resolution: We eliminate conflicts by refining the complex.
(ii) Diminution: We allow conflicts to exist and minimize their effects through appropriate reordering algorithms.

In approach (i), we realize our goal of a reordered filtration with Betti numbers equivalent to the p-persistent Betti numbers of the original filtration. The reordered filtration, however, is refined. In approach (ii), we approximate our goal of the reordered filtration but maintain the same complex.

8.3.2 Resolution

We may resolve a conflict by subdivision. Suppose pairs (σ^i, σ^j) and (σ^g, σ^h) form a conflict. Then, σ^i, σ^g are edges; σ^j, σ^h are triangles; and σ^i is a face of σ^h. Let $\sigma^i = bc$ and $\sigma^h = abc$ as drawn in Figure 8.6. We resolve the conflict by starring from the midpoint x of edge bc, subdividing all simplices that share bc as a common face. We replace each subdivided k-simplex by one $(k-1)$-simplex and two k-simplices. For computing persistence, the order of the three new simplices is important. As shown in Figure 8.6, the order of the edges bx, cx within the new filter is the opposite of the triangles acx, abx.

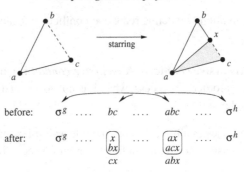

Fig. 8.6. The conflict exists between moving abc toward σ^g and keeping bc ahead of abc. We subdivide edge bc and order the new simplices to resolve the conflict.

The persistence algorithm produces new pairs (x, bx) and (ax, acx) that have no effect on Betti numbers. After acx enters, the complex is homotopy equivalent to the old complex just before abc enters. The edge cx replaces bc and the triangle abx replaces abc in the filter. Consequently, the algorithm produces pairs (σ^g, abx) and (cx, σ^h). As cx is not a face of abx, we have removed the conflict and preserved the Betti numbers of a refined filtration.

8.3.3 Diminution

Often times, simplices have structural meaning in a filtration, and conflicts signal properties of the structure the simplices describe. We may not wish to tamper with this structure through subdivision, as such action may not have any meaning within our filtration. For example, in α complex filtrations, simplices are ordered according to a particular growth model. The ordering of the new simplices specified by subdivision in Figure 8.6 might not have a corresponding set of balls that would generate the filtration under the growth model.

We may attempt to reduce the effect of conflicts on Betti numbers without eliminating the conflicts. Recall that a simplex pair (σ^i, σ^j) defines a k-cycle that may be visualized by a k-triangle, as in Figure 8.1. Whenever σ^i occurs in a conflict, we allow it to be dragged to a new location. This clearly changes the Betti numbers of the reordered filtration, so they no longer match the p-persistent Betti numbers of the original filtration. If we just follow the reordering algorithms from the last section, however, we may never destroy a cycle, as in Figure 8.7(a). On the other hand, we may modify the reordering algorithms to allow σ^j to reach σ^i through the various schemes displayed graphically in Figure 8.7(b–e). For example, we also allow σ^j to move faster during reordering, whenever σ^i is moved. This method creates a pseudo-triangle with the

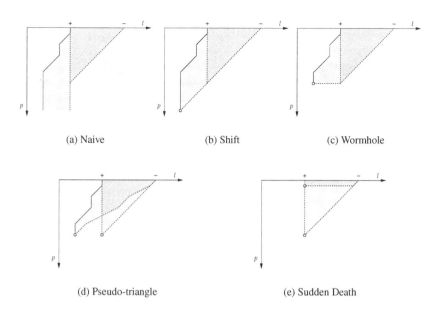

Fig. 8.7. Reordering algorithms and regions of influence. We show the k-triangle in each case for comparison. The regions are transparent filled polygons, and darker regions correspond to areas of overlap.

same area as the cycle's k-triangle, as shown in Figure 8.7(d). Therefore, this algorithm allows each k-cycle to have the same effect on Betti numbers as it would in the absence of conflicts, but at different times. As such, it seems to be the ideal algorithm for reordering in the presence of conflicts.

8.4 Topology Maps

Before presenting the experiments, we introduce a powerful tool for visualizing the topology of a space. We have already seen that persistence is correctly visualized as k-triangles in the index-persistence plane, as in Figure 8.1. In general, we may only view the triangles in each dimension separately. For example, we may look at the persistent Betti numbers of data set *FAU* as surfaces in three dimensions, as shown in Figure 8.8. If the only nonzero Betti numbers are β_0, β_1, and β_2, we may use color to assemble a single image presenting all the values at once. The space of all colors is three-dimensional and may be parametrized by a three-dimensional coordinate system (Foley et al., 1996). There are many such coordinate systems called *color models*. We use the *CMY* color model, as described in Figure 8.9. This color model is appropriate as it is

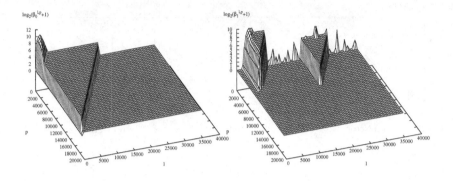

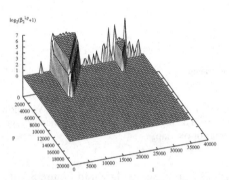

Fig. 8.8. Graphs of $\log_2(\beta_k^{l,p} + 1)$ for $k = 0, 1, 2$, respectively, for zeolite *FAU*. The graphs are sampled onto an 80 by 80 grid.

subtractive, starting from white and ending with black. We use shades of cyan, magenta, and yellow for representing values of β_0, β_1, and β_2, respectively. Given this system, we can now visualize the complete topological content of a space in a single image. We call these images *topology maps*. Given a topology map, we can immediately observe the salient topological features of the associated space.

Example 8.1 (topology map of *FAU*) Figure 8.10 displays the topology maps of *FAU*, corresponding to its Betti and square Betti numbers. The map of *FAU* has six regions, clearly delineated by color. There is a seventh dark cyan region in the top left corner, describing the arrival of all the vertices. We perceive that persistent components are formed in the large cyan triangle: The vertices arrive, are connected into structures with tunnels (creating 1-cycles in the blue triangle), completed into voids (creating 2-cycles in the green region), and finally filled up with tetrahedra. In the second stage, these components are connected to form a single structure with tunnels (magenta triangle) and form voids again (yellow triangle), which are again filled.

Each point of a topology map (l, p) corresponds to a p-persistent complex $K^{l,p}$. Consequently, these maps provide us with an powerful navigational tool for software design. I use these maps in my topology visualization program, *CView*, which I will describe in Chapter 11.

We end this chapter with a few visualizations of persistent complexes. We claimed earlier that topology maps were useful for displaying the entire topological content of a space. We substantiate these structural predictions in Example 8.1 by showing persistent complexes from the various regions of the topology map of *FAU* in Figure 8.11. The Betti numbers of the complexes are listed underneath them. We may also use the persistent algorithm to view cycles and their manifolds in each complex. Figure 8.12 displays the eight voids of a persistent complex for zeolite *KFI*. We will see more cycles and manifolds in Chapter 10, when discussing the linking number algorithm.

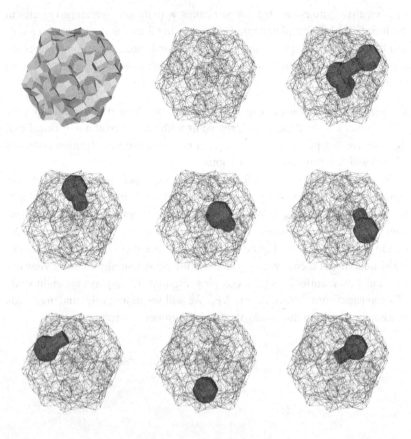

Fig. 8.12. $K^{24893,8137}$ of the filtration (top left corner) for zeolite *KFI* has $\beta_2 = 8$. The eight (noncanonical) voids are displayed inside the exterior edges of the complex.

9

The Morse-Smale Complex Algorithm

In Chapter 6, we presented an approach for constructing hierarchical Morse-Smale complexes for 2-manifolds with an associated function. The approach utilized Simulation of Differentiability (SoD) to construct a Morse-Smale complex in two stages. In this chapter, we complete this description by specifying algorithms for the two stages of SoD: computing quasi Morse-Smale complex (QMS complex) and locally transforming this complex to the Morse-Smale complex (MS complex). Figure 9.1 places the algorithms in this chapter within the context of the approach taken.

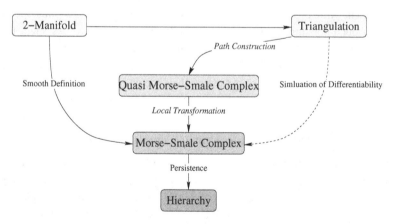

Fig. 9.1. Approach for constructing hierarchical Morse-Smale complexes. This chapter includes algorithms for the italicized steps.

9.1 Motivation

Physical simulation problems often start with a space and measurements over this space. If the measurements are scalar values, they are usually called *height functions*. The functions can be arbitrary, however, and do not necessarily measure height. In two dimensions, familiar examples include the intensity values of an image and the elevation of a terrain, as parametrized by longitude and latitude. Images are the input of the field of *computer vision*, where researchers seek to understand the features of the image and eliminate the noise. Terrains are used in *geographic information systems (GIS)* for modeling natural phenomena and planning urban developments. In three dimensions, we have volume information, such as intensities produced by *magnetic resonance imaging (MRI)*, atmospheric measurements over the surface of Earth, and the electron density over a crystallized molecule. Once again, the primary goal is the derivation of structures that enhance our understanding of these measurements.

Consider a geographic landscape modeled as a height function $h: D \to \mathbb{R}$ over a two-dimensional domain D. This landscape is often visualized by a discrete set of iso-lines $h^{-1}(c)$ for constant height values c. A *contour tree* partially captures the topology of these iso-lines, and it has been constructed for the fast generation of iso-lines in the past (de Berg and van Kreveld, 1993; van Kreveld et al., 1997). Recently, Carr et al. (2000) gave a simple and elegant algorithm for computing contour trees in all dimensions. If h is differentiable, we may define the gradient field consisting of vectors in the direction of the steepest ascent. Researchers in visualization have studied this vector field for some time (Bajaj et al., 1998; de Leeuw and van Liere, 1999; Tricoche et al., 2000). The Morse-Smale complex captures the characteristics of this vector field by decomposing the manifold into cells of uniform flow. As such, the Morse-Smale complex represents a full analysis of the behavior of the vector field. Moreover, the Morse-Smale complex is a richer structure than the contour tree, and we may extract the tree from the complex when needed.

9.2 The Quasi Morse-Smale Complex Algorithm

Given a triangulation K of a compact 2-manifold without boundary and a PL function h, our goal is to compute the MS complex for a simulated unfolding of h. In this section, we take the first step of computing a QMS complex of h (see Section 6.2 for definitions). We limit ourselves to curves following the edges of K. While the resulting complex is numerically inaccurate, our focus is on capturing the structure of the MS complex, and this limitation gives us a fast algorithm. Recall that the QMS complex Q will have the critical points of h as vertices and monotonic noncrossing paths as arcs. To resolve the merging and forking of paths, we formulate a three-stage algorithm. In each stage, we compute a complex whose arcs are noncrossing monotonic paths, guaranteeing this property for the final complex.

9.2.1 Complex with Junctions

In the first stage, we draw paths by following edges in the triangulation. Eventually, these paths become the arcs of the QMS complex, in turn defining the 2-cells implicitly. Recall that we can classify the vertices using persistence. Having classified them, we compute the wedges of their lower and upper stars, and identify the steepest edge in each wedge. We then start $k + 1$ ascending and $k + 1$ descending paths from every k-fold saddle. Each path begins in its own wedge and follows a sequence of steepest edges until it hits

    (a) a minimum or a maximum,

    (b) a previously traced path at a regular point, or

    (c) another saddle,

at which point the path ends. Case (a) corresponds to the generic case for smooth height functions, Case (b) corresponds to a merging or forking, and Case (c) is the PL counterpart of a nontransversal intersection between a stable and an unstable 1-manifold. In Case (b), the regular point is special, so we call it a junction.

Definition 9.1 (junction) A *junction* is a regular point where paths merge or fork.

The key idea in this stage is to temporarily upgrade junctions to the status of critical points, allowing them to be vertices of the complex being constructed. Whenever Case (b) occurs, we either create a new junction by splitting a previously traced path or we increase the degree of a junction that has already been created. Case (c) is the PL counterpart of a nontransversal intersection between a stable and an unstable 1-manifold.

For my implementations, I utilize a quad edge data structure (Guibas and Stolfi, 1985) to store the complex defined by the paths. The vertices of the complex are the critical points and junctions, and the arcs are the pairwise edge-disjoint paths connecting these vertices. I also use the data structure to simulate the infinitesimal separation of the paths combinatorially.

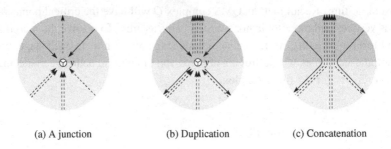

(a) A junction   (b) Duplication   (c) Concatenation

Fig. 9.2. Paths ending at a junction (a) are extended by duplication (b) and concatenation (c).

9.2.2 Extending Paths

In the second stage of the algorithm, we extend paths to remove junctions and reduce the number of arcs per k-fold saddle to $2(k + 1)$. The latter action corresponds to eliminating nontransversal intersections. Whenever we extend a path, we route it along and infinitesimally close to an already existing path. Again, this action is done combinatorially using the data structure: The actual paths are geometrically the same for now. In extending paths, we may create new paths ending at other junctions and saddles. Consequently, we wish to process the vertices in a sequence that prevents cyclic dependencies. We classify a path at a vertex as ascending or descending, relative to the original saddle. Since ascending and descending paths are extended in opposite directions, we need two orderings, touching every vertex twice. It is convenient to first duplicate ascending paths in the order of increasing height and then duplicate descending paths in the order of decreasing height. Then, all paths are concatenated for extension. We discuss the routing procedures for junctions and saddles next. In the figures that follow, we orient paths in the direction they emanate from a saddle. The solid paths are ascending stable manifolds, and the dashed paths are descending unstable manifolds.

Junctions. Figure 9.2(a) displays a neighborhood of a junction y. Consider the junction y in Figure 9.2 on the left. By definition, y is a regular point with lower and upper stars consisting of one wedge each. The first time we encounter y, the path is traced right through the point. In each additional encounter, the path ends at y, as y is now a junction. If the first path is ascending, then one ascending path leaves y into the upper star, all other ascending paths approach y from the lower star and all descending paths approach y from the upper star. We show this case in Figure 9.2. Some of the paths may already have duplicates

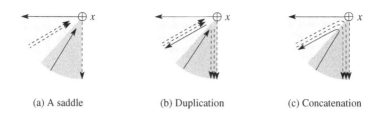

| (a) A saddle | (b) Duplication | (c) Concatenation |

Fig. 9.3. Paths that end at a saddle (a) are extended by duplication (b) and concatenation (c).

because of other path extensions. We duplicate paths for all junctions using our two orderings. Note that the new paths, shown in Figure 9.2(b), may include duplicates spawned by junctions that occur before this vertex in an ordering. Finally, we concatenate the resulting paths in pairs without creating crossings, as shown in Figure 9.2(c).

Saddles. We next resolve Case (c), paths that have another saddle as an end point. Consider the saddle x in Figure 9.3. We look at path extensions only within one of the sectors between two cyclically contiguous steepest edges. Within this sector, there may be ascending paths approaching x from within the overlapping wedge of the lower star, and descending paths approaching x from within the overlapping wedge of the upper star, as shown in Figure 9.3(a). After path duplications (b), we concatenate the paths in pairs (c). Again, we can concatenate without creating crossings. At the end of this process, our complex has critical points as vertices and monotonic noncrossing paths from saddles to minima or maxima as arcs.

Unfolding multiple saddles. In the third and last stage of the algorithm, we unfold every k-fold saddle into k simple saddles. We saw in Section 6.12 that such saddles may be unfolded by duplicating the saddle and paths ending at the saddle. At this point, we have already eliminated Case (c) from above, so we only have to consider the $k + 1$ ascending and $k + 1$ descending paths that originate at the k-fold saddle. In each of the $k - 1$ steps, we duplicate the saddle, one ascending path, and a nonadjacent descending path. In the end, we have k saddles and $2(k + 1) + 2(k - 1) = 4k$ paths, or four per saddle. Figure 9.4 illustrates the operation by showing a possible unfolding of a 3-fold saddle. The unfolding procedure does not create any path crossings in the previous complex, which had no crossings.

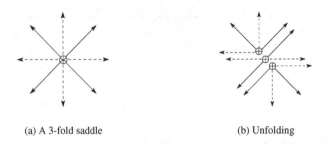

(a) A 3-fold saddle   (b) Unfolding

Fig. 9.4. A 3-fold (monkey) saddle (a) is unfolded into three simple saddles (b).

Lemma 9.1 (quasi Morse-Smale complex) *The algorithm computes a quasi Morse-Smale for K.*

Proof Let Q be the complex constructed by the algorithm. The vertices of Q are the unfolded critical points of K, so they are minima, saddles, and maxima. The paths are noncrossing, and stage two guarantees that the paths go from saddles to minima or maxima. Therefore, Q is splitable. Moreover, the vertices on the boundary of any region of Q alternate between saddles and other critical points. The Quadrangle Lemma implies Q is a quadrangulation. Therefore, Q is a splitable quadrangulation, or a QMS complex.   □

9.3 Local Transformations

Having computed the QMS complex, we now seek to transform it to the MS complex. Recall that the QMS complex has the combinatorial form of the MS complex, but its structure and geometry are different. To compute the MS complex, we allow numerical tests to trigger local transformations that maintain the form of the QMS complex. In this section, we will first describe these transformations, and then describe the numerical condition that triggers them.

9.3.1 Handle Slide

The local transformation we use is a *handle slide*, and it transforms one QMS complex into another. The two quadrangulations differ only in their decompositions of a single octagon. In the first quadrangulation, the octagon consists of a quadrangle *abcd* together with two adjacent quadrangles *baDC* and *dcBA*, as shown in Figure 9.5. Let a and c be the two saddles of the quadrangle in the

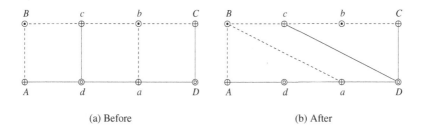

(a) Before   (b) After

Fig. 9.5. A handle slide. The octagon is the union of a row of three quadrangles.

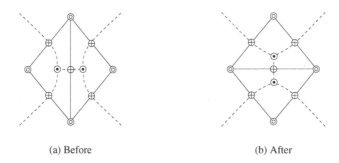

(a) Before   (b) After

Fig. 9.6. Edge-flip shown in superimposition of solid triangulation with its dashed dual diagram. The maxima before and after the flip should be at the same location but are moved for clarity of the illustration.

middle. We perform a slide by drawing an ascending path from a to B replacing ab, and a descending path from c to D replacing cd. After the slide, the octagon is decomposed into quadrangles $DcBa$ in the middle and $cDCb, aBAd$ on its two sides.

It is possible to think of the better-known *edge-flip* in a two-dimensional triangulation as the composition of two octagon slides. To explain this, Figure 9.6 superimposes a triangulation with its dual diagram, making sure that only corresponding edges cross. The vertices of the triangulation correspond to minima, the vertices of the dual diagram to maxima, and the crossing points to saddles. When we flip an edge in the triangulation, we also reconnect the five edges in the dual diagram that correspond to the five edges of the two triangles sharing the flipped edge. The result of the edge-flip is thus the same as that of two octagon slides, one for the lower left three quadrangles and the other for the upper right three quadrangles in Figure 9.6.

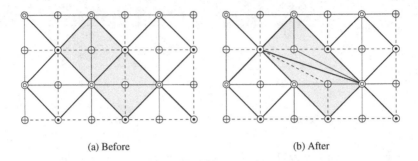

(a) Before   (b) After

Fig. 9.7. The associated quadrangulation (thick edges) superimposed on an MS complex, before and after a handle slide. The handle slide corresponds to a diagonal slide inside the shaded hexagon in the coarser quadrangulation.

We may also relate a handle slide in an MS complex to a *diagonal slide* in an associated quadrangulation (Negami, 1999). The quadrangulation has only the maxima and minima of the terrain as vertices. We connect the maximum and minimum of each quadrangle in the MS complex via an edge to construct the quadrangulation, as shown for an example in Figure 9.7. A handle slide in the MS complex alters the structure of the quadrangulation within the shaded hexagon, consisting of two adjacent cells in the quadrangulation. The diagonal of the hexagon *slides* clockwise and connects the next pair of opposite vertices of the hexagon.

9.3.2 Steepest Ascent

To decide when to apply a handle slide to an octagon, we need a numerical test. Our test will consist of checking whether a path starting from a saddle will reach the same critical endpoint, if it were computed by following the direction of locally steepest ascent. In other words, we check to see if the path yields the same combinatorial structure. Such paths may go along an edge or pass through a triangle of K. There are three cases as shown in Figure 9.8. In the interior of a triangle, that steepest direction is unique and orthogonal to the level lines. In the interior of an edge, there may be one or two locally steepest directions. At a vertex there may be as many locally steepest directions as there are triangles in the star.

We may compute the steepest direction numerically with small error, but errors accumulate as the path traverses triangles. Alternatively, we can compute the steepest direction exactly with constant bit-length arithmetic operations,

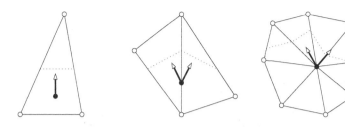

Fig. 9.8. The three cases of locally steepest ascent. The directions are orthogonal to the dotted level lines.

but the bit-length needed for the points along the path grows as it traverses more triangles. This phenomenon justifies the SoD approach to constructing an MS complex. In this approach the computed complex has the same combinatorial form as the MS complex, and it is numerically as accurate as the local rerouting operations used to control handle slides.

9.4 Algorithm

Having described the local transformation and the numerical test that triggers it, we now present an algorithm for transforming the QMS complex to the MS complex in this section. The algorithm applies handle slides to octagons in the order of decreasing height. Here, the *height* of an octagon is the height of the lower saddle of the middle quadrangle. This saddle is either a or c for the octagon in Figure 9.5. Without loss of generally, let us assume here that it is a. When we consider a, we may also assume that the arcs connecting higher critical points are already correct. The iso-line at the height of a decomposes the manifold into an *upper* and a *lower region*. Let Γ be the possibly pinched component of the upper region that contains a. There are two cases, as shown in Figure 9.9. In case (a), the higher critical points in Γ and their connecting arcs bound one annulus, which is pinched at a. In case (b), they bound two annuli, one on each side of a. The ascending path emanating from a is rerouted within these annuli.

Let ab be the interior path of the octagon with height $h(a)$, and let p be the maximum we hit by rerouting the path. If p is the first maximum after b along the arc boundary of the annulus, we may use a single handle slide to replace ab by ap, as we do for the upper new path in Figure 9.9(a). Note that the slide is possible only because ap crosses no arc ending at b. Any such arc would have

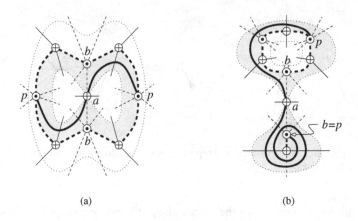

(a)   (b)

Fig. 9.9. The two cases in the algorithm. The iso-line is dotted, the annuli are shaded, the arcs bounding the annuli are bold dashed, and the new paths emanating from a are bold solid.

to be changed first, which we do by recursive application of the algorithm, as for the lower new path in Figure 9.9(a).

It is also possible that p is more than one position removed from b, as for the upper new path in Figure 9.9(b). In this case we perform several slides for a, the first connecting a to the first maximum after b in the direction of p. Each such slide may require recursive slides to clear the way, as before. Finally, it is possible that the new path from a to p winds around the arc boundary of the annulus several times, as does the lower new path in Figure 9.9(b). The algorithm is the same as before.

The winding case shows that the number of slides cannot be bounded from above in terms of the number of critical points. Instead, consider the crossings between arcs of the initial QMS and the final MS complexes, and note that the number of slides is at most some constant times the number of such crossings.

10

The Linking Number Algorithm

In Chapter 6, we discussed a topological invariant called the linking number and extended this invariant to simplicial complexes. In this chapter, we provide data structures and algorithms for computing the linking numbers of a filtration, using the canonical cycles and manifolds generated by the persistence algorithm. After motivating this computation, we describe the data structures and algorithms. We end this chapter by discussing an alternate definition of the linking number that may be helpful in understanding the topology of molecular structures.

10.1 Motivation

In the 1980s, it was shown that DNA, the molecular structure of the genetic code of all living organisms, can become knotted during replication (Adams, 1994). This finding initiated interest in knot theory among biologists and chemists for the detection, synthesis, and analysis of knotted molecules (Flapan, 2000). The impetus for this research is that molecules with nontrivial topological attributes often display exotic chemistry. Such attributes have been observed in currently known proteins. Taylor recently discovered a figure-of-eight knot in the structure of a plant protein by examining 3,440 proteins using a computer program (Taylor, 2000). Moreover, chemical self-assembly units are being used to create *catenanes*, chains of interlocking molecular rings, and *rotaxanes*, cyclic molecules threaded by linear molecules. Researchers are building nano-scale chemical switches and logic gates with these structures (Bissell et al., 1994; Collier et al., 1999). Eventually, chemical computer memory systems could be built from these building blocks.

171

10.1.1 Prior work

Catenanes and rotaxanes are examples of nontrivial structural tanglings. The focus of this chapter is on computing the linking number, the link invariant defined in Section 6.3. Haken (1961) showed that important knotting and linking problems are decidable in his seminal work on normal surfaces. His approach, as reformulated by Jaco and Tollefson (1995), forms the basis of many current knot detection algorithms. Hass et al. (1999) showed that these algorithms take exponential time in the number of crossings in a knot diagram. They also placed both the UNKNOTTING PROBLEM and the SPLITTING PROBLEM in NP, the latter problem being the focus of this chapter. Generally, other approaches to knot problems have unknown complexity bounds and are assumed to take at least exponential time. As such, the state of the art in knot detection only allows for very small data sets.

10.1.2 Approach

The approach in this chapter is to model molecules by filtrations of α-complexes, and detect potential tanglings by computing the linking numbers of the filtration. The linking numbers constitute a signature function for the filtration. This combinatorial approach makes the same fundamental assumption as in Chapter 2 that α-complex filtrations capture the topology of a molecular structure. Given a filtration, we will use the spanning surface definition of the linking number for its computation. Consequently, we need data structures for the efficient enumeration of co-existing pairs of cycles in different components. We also need an algorithm to compute the linking number of a pair of such cycles.

10.2 Algorithm

In this section, we present data structures and algorithms for computing the linking numbers of the complexes in a filtration. As we only use canonical 1-cycles for this computation, we will refer to them simply as cycles. Assume we have a filtration $K^1, K^2, \ldots, K^m$ as input. As simplices are added, the complex undergoes topological changes that affect the linking number: New components are created and merged together, and new nonbounding cycles are created and eventually destroyed. A basis cycle z with persistence interval $[i, j)$ may only affect the linking numbers of complexes $K^i, K^{i+1}, \ldots, K^{j-1}$ in the filtration. Consequently, we only need to consider basis cycles z' that exist during some subinterval $[u, v) \subseteq [i, j)$ in a different component than z's.

```
for each p-linked pair z_p, z_q with interval [u, v) {
    Compute λ = |λ(z_p, z_q)|;
    Output (λ, [u, v));
}
```

Fig. 10.1. Linking number algorithm.

Definition 10.1 (potentially linked) A pair of canonical cycles z, z' in different components, whose persistence intervals have a nonempty intersection $[u, v)$, are *potentially linked (p-linked)*. The interval $[u, v)$ is the *p-linking interval* for this p-linked pair of cycles.

Focusing on p-linked pairs, we get an algorithm with three phases. In the first phase, we compute all p-linked pairs of cycles. In the second phase, as shown in Figure 10.1, we compute the linking numbers of such pairs. The third and final phase is trivial. We simply aggregate the contributions from the pairs to find the linking number signature for the filtration.

Two cycles z_p, z_q with persistence intervals $[i_p, j_p), [i_q, j_q)$ co-exist during $[r, s) = [i_p, j_p) \cap [i_q, j_q)$. We need to know if these cycles also belong to different components during some subinterval $[u, v) \subseteq [r, s)$. Let $t_{p,q}$ be the minimum index in the filtration when z_p and z_q are in the same component. Then, $[u, v) = [r, s) \cap [0, t_{p,q})$. The cycles z_p, z_q are p-linked during $[u, v) \neq \emptyset$. In the remainder of this section, we first develop a data structure for computing $t_{p,q}$ for any pair of cycles z_p, z_q. We then use this data structure to efficiently enumerate all pairs of p-linked cycles. Finally, we examine an algorithm for computing $\lambda(z_p, z_q)$ for a p-linked pair of cycles z_p, z_q.

10.2.1 Component Tree

To compute $t_{p,q}$, we need to have a history of the changes to the set of components in a filtration. There are two types of simplices that can change this set. Vertices create components and are therefore all positive. Negative edges connect components. To record these changes, we construct a binary tree called a *component tree* by maintaining a union-find data structure for components (Cormen et al., 1994). The leaves of the component tree are the vertices of the filtration. When a negative edge connects two components, we create an internal node for the component tree and connect the new node to the nodes representing these components, as shown in Figure 10.2. The component tree has size $O(n)$ for n vertices. We construct it in time $O(nA^{-1}(n))$, where $A^{-1}(n)$ is the inverse of the Ackermann's function, encountered earlier in Section 7.2.3.

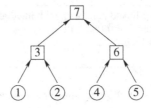

Fig. 10.2. The component tree has the complex vertices as leaves and negative edges as internal nodes. During construction, the tree exists as a forest.

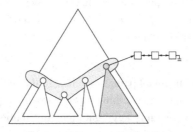

Fig. 10.3. The augmented union-find data structure places root nodes in the shaded circular doubly linked list. Each root node stores all active canonical cycles in that component in a doubly linked list, as shown for the darker component.

Having constructed the component tree, we find the time the two vertices w, x are in the same component by finding their lowest common ancestor (lca) in this tree. We may utilize the optimal method by Harel and Tarjan (1984) to find the lca's with $O(n)$ preprocessing time and $O(1)$ query time. Their method uses bit operations. If such operations are not allowed, we may alternatively use the method of van Leeuwen (1976) with the same preprocessing time and $O(\log \log n)$ query time.

10.2.2 Enumeration

Having constructed the component tree, we use a modified union-find data structure to enumerate all pairs of p-linked cycles. We augment the data structure to allow for a quick listing of all existing canonical cycles in each component in K^i. Our augmentation takes two forms: We put the roots of the disjoint trees, representing components, into a circular doubly linked list. We also store all existing cycles in each component in a doubly linked list at the root node of the component, as shown in Figure 10.3. When components merge, the root x_1 of one component becomes the parent of the root x_2 of the other component. We concatenate the lists stored at the x_1, x_2, store the resulting list at x_1, and

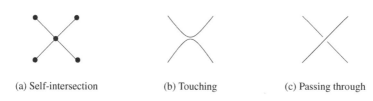

(a) Self-intersection   (b) Touching   (c) Passing through

Fig. 10.4. A surface self-intersection viewed from its side (a). We cannot resolve it as the surface touching (b) or passing through itself (c).

eliminate x_2 from the circular list in $O(1)$ time. When cycle z_p is created at time i, we first find z_p's component in time $O(A^{-1}(n))$, using find operations. Then, we store z_p at the root of the component and keep a pointer to z_p with simplex σ_j, which destroys z_p. This implies that we may delete z_p from the data structure at time j in constant time.

The algorithm to enumerate p-linked cycles is incremental. We add and delete cycles using the above operations from the union-find forest, as the cycles are created and deleted in the filtration. When a cycle z_p is created at time i, we output all p-linked pairs in which z_p participates. We start at the root that now stores z_p and walk around the circular list of roots. At each root x, we query the component tree we constructed in the last subsection to find the time t when the component of x merges with that of z_p. Note that $t = t_{p,q}$ for all cycles z_q stored at x. Consequently, we can compute the p-linking interval for each pair z_p, z_q, as described at the beginning of this section. If the filtration contains P p-linked pairs, our algorithm takes time $O(mA^{-1}(n) + P)$, as there are at most m cycles in the filtration.

10.2.3 Orientation

In Section 7.2.4, we showed how one may compute spanning surfaces s_p, s_q for cycles z_p, z_q, respectively. To compute the linking number using our lemma, we need to orient either the pair s_p, z_q or z_p, s_q. Orienting a cycle is trivial: We orient one edge and walk around to orient the cycle. If either surface has no self-intersections, we may easily attempt to orient it by choosing an orientation for an arbitrary triangle on the surface and spreading that orientation throughout. The procedure either orients the surface or classifies it as nonorientable. We currently do not have an algorithm for orienting surfaces with self-intersections. The main difficulty is distinguishing between two cases for a self-intersection: a surface touching itself and passing through itself, as shown in Figure 10.4.

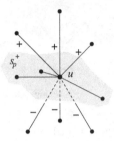

Fig. 10.5. Edges $uv \in \mathrm{St}\,u, u \in s_p, v \notin s_p$ are marked $+$ or $-$ depending on where they end relative to the oriented Seifert surface s_p.

10.2.4 Computing λ

I now give an algorithm to compute $\lambda(z_p, z_q)$ for a pair of p-linked cycles z_p, z_q, completing the description of the algorithm in Figure 10.1. I assume that s_p, z_q are already oriented for the remainder of this subsection. We begin by subdividing the complex via a *barycentric subdivision*, connecting the centroid of each triangle to its vertices and midpoints of its edges and subdividing the triangles and tetrahedra accordingly. This subdivision guarantees that no edge uv will have both ends on a Seifert surface unless it is entirely contained in that surface. This approach mimics the construction of regular neighborhoods for complexes (Giblin, 1981). For a vertex $u \in s_p$, the edge property guaranteed by subdivision enables us to mark each edge $uv \in \mathrm{St}\,u, v \notin s_p$ as positive or negative, depending on the location of v with respect to s_p. Figure 10.5 illustrates this marking for a vertex. After marking the edges, we walk once around z_q, starting at a vertex not on s_p. If such a vertex does not exist, then $\lambda(z_p, z_q) = 0$. Otherwise, we create a string $S_{p,q}$ of $+$ and $-$ characters by noting the marking of edges during our walk. $S_{p,q}$ has even length as we start and end our walk on a vertex not on s_p, and each intersection of z_q with s_p produces a pair of characters, as shown in Figure 10.6. If $S_{p,q}$ is the empty string, z_q never intersects s_p and $\lambda(z_p, z_q) = 0$. Otherwise, z_q passes through s_p for pairs $+-$ and $-+$, corresponding to z_q piercing the positive or negative side of s_p, respectively. Scanning $S_{p,q}$ from left to right in pairs, we add $+1$ for each occurrence of $-+$, -1 for each $+-$, and 0 for each $++$ or $--$. Applying the Seifert surface theorem (Theorem 6.6 in Section 6.3.2), we see that this sum is $\lambda(z_p, z_q)$.

10.2.5 Computing λ mod 2

If neither of the spanning surfaces s_p, s_q of the two cycles z_p, z_q is Seifert, we may still compute $\lambda(z_p, z_q)$ mod 2 by a modified algorithm, provided one sur-

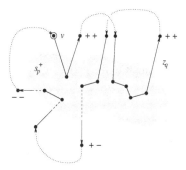

Fig. 10.6. Starting at v, we walk on z_q according to its orientation. Segments of z_q that intersect s_p are shown, along with their contribution to $S_{p,q} =$ "$+ + + + + - - - -$". We get $\lambda(z_p, z_q) = -1$.

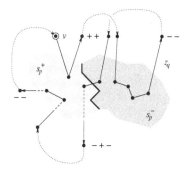

Fig. 10.7. The bold flip curve is the border of s_p^+ and s_p^-, the portions of s_p that are oriented differently. $S_{p,q} =$ "$+ + - - - + - - -$", so, counting all $+$'s, we get $\lambda(z_p, z_q) \bmod 2 = 3 \bmod 2 = 1$.

face, say s_p, has no self-intersections. We choose an orientation on s_p locally and extend it until all the stars of the original vertices are oriented. This orientation will not be consistent globally, resulting in pairs of adjacent vertices in s_p with opposite orientations. We call the implicit boundary between vertices with opposite orientations a *flip curve*, as shown in bold in Figure 10.7. When a cycle segment crosses the flip curve, the orientation changes. Therefore, in addition to noting marked edges, we add a $+$ to the string $S_{p,q}$ every time we cross a flip line. To compute $\lambda(z_p, z_q) \bmod 2$, we only count $+$'s in $S_{p,q}$ and take the parity as our answer.

If s_p is orientable, there are no flip curves on it. The contribution of cycle segments to the string is the same as before: $+-$ or $-+$ for segments that pass through s_p, and $++$ and $--$ for segments that do not. By counting $+$'s, only segments that pass through s_p change the parity of the sum for λ. Therefore, the algorithm computes λ mod 2 correctly for orientable surfaces. For the orientable surface in Figure 10.6, for instance, we get $\lambda(z_p, z_q)$ mod 2 = 5 mod 2 = 1, which is equivalent to the parity of the answer computed by the previous algorithm.

Discussion. One remaining question is that of orienting surfaces with self-intersections. Using the current methods, we may obtain a lower bound signature for λ by computing a mixed sum: We compute λ and λ mod 2 whenever we can to obtain the approximation. It is also possible to develop other methods, including those based on the projection definition of the linking number. Regardless of the approach taken, pairs of potentially linked cycles must be first detected and enumerated. The algorithms and data structures in this chapter provide the tools for such enumeration.

We end this chapter with visualizations of complexes, their cycles, and spanning surfaces in Figure 10.8.

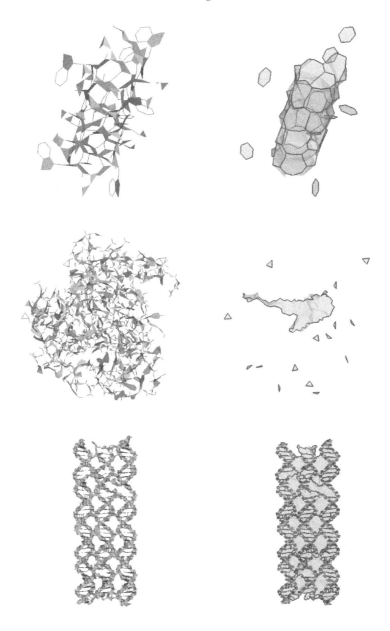

Fig. 10.8. Complex K^{1123} of the filtration for data set *1grm* (top) has 1 component and 34 basis cycles. Complex K^{8168} of *1hck* has 2 components and 17 cycles. Complex K^{90000} of *TAO* (bottom) has 1 component and 237 cycles. In each case, the spanning surfaces are rendered transparently.

Part Three

Applications

11

Software

I devote this chapter to a brief description of the implementation of some of the algorithms in Part Two. After discussing the programming methodology, I give an overview of the organization of the code and sketch some of the fundamental data structures. Finally, I introduce a software program, *CView*, for viewing persistent simplicial complexes, homology cycles and their manifolds, and Morse complexes of grid data.

11.1 Methodology

Computer science solves problems by translating them into the language of very fast machines. We could claim that fast programs are the primary goal of this field. Fast software enables a user to quickly scrutinize a problem, observe patterns, gather data, and conjecture. There are two components to fast software: efficient data structures and algorithms, grounded in theory, and lean implementations, tailored to computer architectures. Knuth observes that "the best theory is inspired by practice, and the best practice is inspired by theory (Knuth, 1996)." I apply this observation not only to my work in general, but also to implementations in particular. The theory of practice in computer science has provided numerous abstractions to tackle the complexity of programming, from high-level languages, compilers, and interpreters, to the recent advent of "patterns." Most of these abstractions, however, depend on extra levels of indirection, consume memory for the services they provide, and yield bloated and slow programs. We can only realize the goal of fast software by selective use of the theory of programming, constructing enough scaffolding to manage complexity without sacrificing performance.

Consequently, I use ideas from *Object-Oriented Programming (OOP)* (Meyer, 2000) and construct *Abstract Data Types (ADTs)* (Roberts, 1997). Rather than implementing in an OOP language, I use the ANSI C program-

183

ming language, which gives me great control over the design of a program, yielding fast and lean programs. I simulate classes by using function pointers and break walls of abstractions when it boosts performance. The code, however, is still divided into about 30, mostly independent, reentrant, functional modules.

My design philosophy is also deeply affected by the UNIX approach to having many utility programs instead of a large monolith. The interactive program *CView* simply wraps a graphical interface on the utility programs using the scripting language `tcl` and its interface library `tk`.

11.2 Organization

Having described the programming methodology, I give a brief description of the organization of the code and the associated tools in this section.

11.2.1 Libraries and Packages

I use a number of existing libraries and program packages. To generate alpha-shape filtrations, I utilize the `alf` library by Ernst Mücke. This library is robust and relatively fast. Unfortunately, the code modules in the library are neither independent nor reentrant, as globals abound. In addition, obfuscating macros, as well as abuse of obscure features of C, make the code unreadable and ANSI noncompliant. To limit these effects, my code interacts with the `alf` library through a a single module, `alphashape`, which provides the interface that my filtration module requires. My implementation of the quad edge data structure follows Lischinski (1994) but is also affected by the original implementation by Stolfi (Guibas and Stolfi, 1985).

11.2.2 New Code

In addition to using the existing libraries, I have written around 23,000 lines of C and `tcl` for this project. About 15,000 lines are organized into 27 modules and 4 header-only files. Table 11.1 lists and describes the modules. The header files define the boolean type, the simplex and Morse data structures, and combine the linear algebra routines for convenience. Each module is tested independently, using an additional 3,500 lines of C.

Table 11.1. *Code modules. The modules are grouped according to topic.*
Each program, however, utilizes modules from all groups.

PERSISTENCE	`filtration`	filtration ADT
	`alphashape`	alpha-shape filtration
	`grid`	grid filtration
	`unionfind`	union-find with representatives
	`cycles`	cycle search, cycles and manifolds
	`pbetti`	reordering algorithms and Betti numbers
MORSE COMPLEX	`quadedge`	quad-edge data structure
	`manifolds`	cell structure for Morse complexes
	`paths`	using manifolds for Morse complexes
LINKING NUMBER	`ufnc`	union find with no path compression
	`auguf`	augmented union find
	`linknr`	λ computation
	`scan`	interval scanning
LINEAR ALGEBRA	`vector`	3 and 4 dimensional vectors
	`matrix`	3 by 3 and 4 by 4 matrices
	`quaternion`	quaternion routines
CVIEW	`cview`	new `tcl/tk` routines
	`complex`	simplicial complex routines
	`light`	lighting
	`camera`	scene and camera
	`color`	colors
	`trackball`	trackball interface
UTILITY	`collision`	collision/list length data gathering
	`histogram`	histogram ADT
	`utility`	memory allocation utilities
	`timer`	small timer ADT
	`times`	timing data gathering module

11.2.3 Tools

The modular code design allows me to easily craft programs for code development, testing, timing, quantitative analysis, and automatic data generation. Table 11.2 describes 25 of the tools I have developed to this day, using about 2,700 lines of C. The group of ESSENTIAL tools is used by *CView* for the computation of persistent complexes and quasi Morse complexes.

Table 11.2. *Tools and their descriptions*

ESSENTIAL	mkcyc	writes cycles and manifolds in .cyc
	mgf	writes grid filtration in .gf file
	mkpath	writes paths in .path file
	mkprs	writes persistence in .prs file
	terrain	topological maps, as in Figure 8.10
PRESENTATION	bettigraph	graphs, as in Figure 8.8
	funpgm	function images, as in Figure 12.9(a)
	gridpgm	grid images as in Figure 12.9(b–e)
	morsegraph	graphs of number of critical points
	ppmdiff	difference images in Figure 12.8
UTILITIES	canonize	canonization data in Table 12.9
	conflict	conflict data in Table 12.13
	drawufnc	PSTricks drawings of ufnc trees
	gengrid	random grids
	gensurf	synthetic surfaces
	morse	number of criticals in Table 12.15
	pers	persistence data in Table 12.8
	reorder	reordering data in Table 12.13
	simplexnum	simplex numbers, as in Table 12.1
EXPERIMENTAL	filterlength	experiment on filtrations
	findtunnel	experiment on data set *1grm*
	phistogram	persistence histograms
	printfilter	ASCII filtration table
	scatterplot	persistence experiment
	trace	persistence experiment

11.3 Development

My programming environment is comprised of GNU tools on a UNIX operating system, currently *Solaris 8*. I utilize gcc with the ansi and pedantic options for strict ANSI compliance. I also use gdb for debugging and gprof for profiling. Each module has its own version control system using RCS, as it is developed and tested independently. Once a module is ready, I archive it using ar and ship it to a shared library directory, where it is linked with all current programs.

11.3.1 Testing

I have found that the best testing method for this project is the brute force method. Whenever a filtration is modified (such as by reordering), it is thoroughly tested. Similarly, when a quasi Morse complex is computed, it is fully

```
Filter:
        4 Vertex       (4+, 0-)
        6 Edge         (3+, 3-)
        4 Triangle     (1+, 3-)
        1 Tetrahedron  (0+, 1-)
-----------------------------------------------------------------------
   Index   Number TIndex        Type   What      Link # Link Index Faces
-----------------------------------------------------------------------
       0        0      1       Vertex  (++)  Not Linked
       1        1      2       Vertex  (++)         4      4
       2        2      3       Vertex  (++)         5      5
       3        3      4       Vertex  (++)         7      7
       4        4      8         Edge  (--)         1      1 (0 1)
       5        5      3         Edge  (--)         2      2 (1 2)
       6        6      2         Edge  (++)        10     10 (2 0)
       7        7     10         Edge  (--)         3      3 (3 2)
       8        8      6         Edge  (++)        11     11 (3 0)
       9        9      7         Edge  (++)        12     12 (1 3)
      10       10      2     Triangle  (--)         6      6 (4 5 6)
      11       11      3     Triangle  (--)         8      8 (8 7 6)
      12       12      4     Triangle  (--)         9      9 (9 5 7)
      13       13      1     Triangle  (++)        14     14 (4 9 8)
      14       14      1  Tetrahedron  (--)        13     13 (13 10 11 12)
```

Fig. 11.1. Output of `printfilter` for a tetrahedron data set. The program gives the number of positive and negative simplices of each type and lists the simplices in the filtration ordering. Each simplex has a unique cumulative index, as well as a unique index for its type.

tested for structural integrity. I eliminate these tests from the final optimized modules through C preprocessor directives.

Another powerful tool for testing is the `printfilter` tool I developed early in the project. I show the output of `printfilter` for a small data set containing the vertices of a tetrahedron in Figure 11.1. By simply printing two filtrations and comparing the text using the standard UNIX utility, `diff`, I was able to quickly find discrepancies and identify the problematic simplices. I could then localize the problem within `gdb` and eliminate the bug. This method enabled fast implementation and verification of the reordering algorithms. Finally, because of the nature of the pairing algorithm, it is hard for an implementation to be incorrect if it pairs simplices for a large data set without encountering problems. Therefore, an easy method for testing implementations of the pairing algorithm was by simply using large data sets as input.

11.3.2 Optimization

I compile all modules with the `O3` and `funroll-loops` optimization options of `gcc`. My testing paradigm allows me to completely redesign and reimplement modules within the project. Each time, I use data from the previous implementation to verify the new code. I give a case study for persistence computation in this section.

Figure 11.2 displays graphs of the running times of two different implementations of the persistence algorithm. These timings were done on my previous

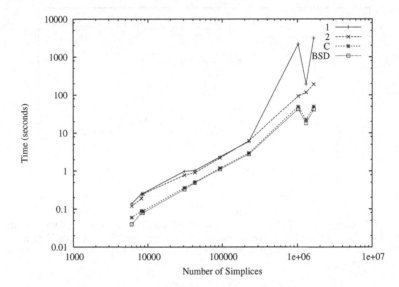

Fig. 11.2. Running time in seconds for computing persistence without union-find. Implementations (1) and (2) are linked with mapmalloc, and (C) and (BSD) are linked with malloc and bsdmalloc, respectively.

desktop computer, a Micron PC with a 233 MHz Pentium II processor and 128 MB RAM, running *Solaris 8*. As the graphs illustrate, the first implementation (1) is relatively fast. For large data sets, however, the memory consumption generates page faults and impairs the performance. For the second implementation, I reduced the size of the simplex data structure from 24 bytes to 16 bytes and recomputed information that I no longer store. I also eliminated dynamic memory allocation during the operation of symmetric difference, where lists representing cycles are merged. Instead, I computed an upper bound on the size of the lists and allocated several temporary arrays. The resulting implementation (2) is up to 26 times faster, as it consumes less memory and exhibits better cache coherency.

Both implementations use the mapmalloc memory allocation library, which is also used by the alpha-shapes software. Mücke seems to favor this library because of the additional functionality it provides. My approach is to minimize dynamic memory allocation with simple customized memory managers within each module. As such, I do not require intelligent memory allocators. I experimented with alternate libraries: the standard C malloc and the BSD UNIX bsdmalloc memory allocation libraries. Both libraries boost the performance of the persistence algorithm by another factor of three, as shown

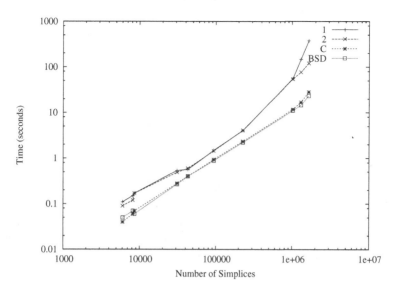

Fig. 11.3. Running time in seconds for computing persistence with union-find. Implementations (1) and (2) are linked with `mapmalloc`, and (C) and (BSD) are linked `malloc` and `bsdmalloc`, respectively.

in Figure 11.2. In total, the fastest implementation is up to 135 times faster than the initial implementation. If we do not need descriptions of homology cycles and their manifolds, we may use union-find for computing persistence pairs. The fastest implementation is up to 16 times faster than my initial implementation, as shown in Figure 11.3.

My other ventures in optimization were not as successful as that of the persistence algorithm. An alternate implementation of the filtration ADT that encapsulated the data better by using a list ADT was 100 times slower than my current implementation. I also implemented what I considered to be a clever algorithm for finding the least common ancestor in a union-find tree. But the implementation ran twice as slow as the simple two-traversal scheme. The basic lesson learned here is that caches play a significant role in the performance of algorithms. The processor-memory performance gap has widened in recent years (Hennessy and Patterson, 1989), making it even more critical to supply the processor with the data it needs from fast local caches. Cache-coherent algorithms perform much faster than sophisticated algorithms that exhibit random memory access.

```
typedef struct _simplexT {
  struct _simplexT *next;
  int cIndex;
  int link;
  int filterloc;
} simplexT;
```

Fig. 11.4. The simplex data structure

11.3.3 Portability

All the code presented in this chapter is portable. By ensuring strict compliance with ANSI C, the libraries can easily be recompiled on other platforms. The packages I use, such as OpenGL and tcl/tk, are all platform independent. I have already compiled the programs on two different platforms successfully without any difficulties or code changes.

11.4 Data Structures

In this section, I briefly discuss the fundamental data structures used in my implementations. In Chapter 2, I introduced filtrations as the primary input to all the algorithms in this thesis. Naturally, the fundamental data structures store filtrations of simplices. Throughout this section, I assume slight familiarity with the C language. The language is quite intuitive, however, to a reader who is familiar with any programming language.

11.4.1 Filter

The primary data structure is filterT, and it stores both the filtration ordering and the filtration. Initially, we called a filtration ordering a *filter*. We then realized that the name was not appropriate for the mathematical setting, as "filter" already had an alternate meaning. I still use it for the implementations, however, out of habit and convenience. To describe a filter, we must know what a simplex is. Figure 11.4 displays the declaration of the structure for a simplex. Before describing a simplex, let us first look at the filterT data structure, as declared in Figure 11.5 A filter is like a virtual class, implemented in C, with concrete classes of filtrations derived from it. A filter concerns itself only with the pairing and reordering of the simplices. Topological and geo-metrical functionalities are pushed down to the derived "classes" through the topology pointer, function pointers not given in the figure, and the cIndex field of simplices. A simplex also stores the index of its persistence match in

```
typedef enum {kAlphaShapeFilter, kGridFilter}
    filterType;

typedef struct _filterT {
    simplexT **structured;
    simplexT **simplices;
    simplexT *simplexArray;
    int filterLen;
    int numSimplices;
    /* Topology */
    void *topology;
    /* Topology Function Pointers*/
    /* Geometry Functionality */
    filterType type;
} filterT;
```

Fig. 11.5. An excerpt of the filtration data structure filterT.

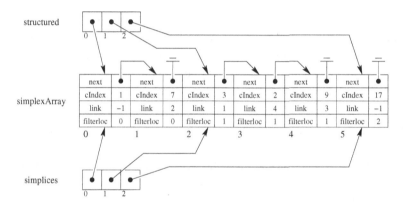

Fig. 11.6. A diagram of filterT for a small filtration.

its link field and its own current location in the filtration in its filterloc field.

This design is very flexible, allowing different topological and geometric representations for the filtered complex. The simplices are stored in the three arrays: structured, simplices, and simplexArray. Figure 11.6 shows the filter for a small filtration. The filtration diagrammed has six simplices, so numSimplices is six. The first two simplices arrive at time 0, the next three at time 1, and the last at time 2. So, the filtration has filterLen equal to 3. The *structured* filtration is laid flat in simplexArray, according to the filtration ordering. Note that, as of now, the next pointers of the simplices in `simplexArray` are redundant, as the information they contain is implicit in their order in the array and the pointers in `structured`. The `next` pointers will be necessary for reordering the filtration, however. Also, if only a single simplex enters at a time, `structured` is not necessary, so it is not used.

A reordering algorithm changes the `next` pointers, as well as the pointers in `simplices` to derive a reordered filtration. The algorithm always recovers the initial filtration before reordering. The recovery is through accessing `structured`, or assuming that a single simplex enters at each time slot whenever `structured` is `NULL`.

Topology To compute persistence, `filterT` requires some topological functionality from the derived ADTs. Recall from Section 7.2.1 that the persistence algorithm searches for the youngest simplex in a list of positive simplices Γ. Initially, Γ is a subset of the boundary of a negative simplex. To compute Γ, we need a routine that gives us the faces of a simplex. We also need both the faces and cofaces of a simplex for the union-find algorithm. To identify simplices, the derived ADTs must assign a unique index to each simplex and store it in the `cIndex` (connectivity index) field. Each derived ADT will use its own scheme to compute this index.

Geometry To visualize persistent complexes, `filterT` also requires some geometric functionality from the derived ADTs. There are two main routines: an initialization procedure and a routine to draw a simplex. This design has the drawback that rendering code is included in each derived ADT. However, the design allows each type of filtration to optimize simplex rendering.

11.4.2 Alphashape

The `alphashape` filtration provides topological and geometric primitives for `filterT` by using Mücke's `alf` library. The module encapsulates the *edge-facet* data structure and the filtration, as represented by the *master list*. The simplices store an index into the master list in the `cIndex` field. The module utilizes edge-facet primitives to quickly compute the faces and cofaces of a simplex, when required.

To render simplices efficiently, `alphashape` takes advantage of the *Vertex Array* functionality in `OpenGL` (Woo et al., 1997). The coordinates of vertices are stored in a single array in the `alf` library. In its initialization routine, the module activates the array through a `glVertexPointer` call and computes the triangle normals. To draw a simplex, the module first computes the simplex's vertices using the edge-facet data structure and then renders the simplex through glArrayElement calls. This is the most efficient rendering method for rendering simplices for the module data structures.

11.4.3 Grid

The grid module provides topological and geometric primitives for gridded terrains. The module takes advantage of the uniform connectivity in grid structures and does not store triangulated grids explicitly. Rather, it uses a scheme to assign unique indices to simplices, which they store in their cIndex fields. The indexing scheme for a triangulated grid is rather simple, but the additional vertex at negative infinity complicates matters by introducing special cases at the boundary of the grid. The resulting complexity doubles the code size. In hindsight, it is not obvious to me whether the savings in memory are worth the additional code complexity and development time.

To render a simplex, the module creates the implicit simplices on the fly, through glVertex3fv calls to OpenGL. Once again, the method represents an efficient rendering method for the module.

11.4.4 Other Filtrations

It should be clear that the flexible design of the filterT data structure allows for other topologies to be represented easily. In particular, I am interested in computing Morse complexes for *triangulated irregular networks (TINs)* which are often used to represent terrains. I am also interested in exploiting other implementations of alpha-shapes that might offer better performance than Mücke's implementation. Regardless of the representation, the uniform interface of filterT allows for new filtration types to be plugged in. Then, we can compute persistence and reorder the filtration with the pbetti module, and visualize the complexes with *CView*.

11.5 *CView*

In this section, I introduce a software program for viewing persistent complexes and quasi Morse complexes called *CView* (pronounced "See View") for *complex viewer*. I use the graphics library OpenGL (Woo et al., 1997) for rendering simplices. To call OpenGL routines within tcl, I employ Brian Paul and Ben Bederson's widget, Togl (Paul and Bederson, 2003). I am indebted

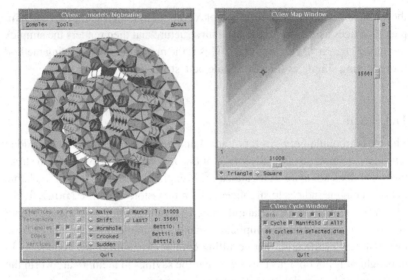

Fig. 11.7. The *CView* main, map, and cycle windows, visualizing *bearing*.

to Brian Curless for sharing with me his code for `plyview`, from which I learned a great deal.

CView is a `tcl/tk` script with extra commands for manipulating complexes. The user may write additional scripts in `tcl` for generating data, images, and movies. Figure 11.7 shows the three main windows of *CView*.

11.5.1 Main Window

The main window of *CView* includes a menu bar, a canvas, four panels, and a quit button. The menu bar consists of three menus: Complex, Tools, and About. The Complex menu allows the user to load any type of supported filtration by data set name. The Tools menu enables the user to activate and deactivate the cycle window, toggle rendering the bounding box for the object, or reset the view point. The About menu simply invokes a message box with information about the program.

Currently, the user may load an alpha-shape or a grid filtration. *CView* then checks for the required files and generates them if needed:

1. Filtration: If there is no filtration file for the data set, *CView* generates and stores the filtration using utilities. For alpha-shape data sets, *CView* employs `delcx` and `mkalf` (utilities from the alpha-shapes software). For grid filtrations, *CView* utilizes `mkgf`.

2. Persistence and Cycles: If persistence and cycle files do not exist, or the filtration was just generated, *CView* uses mkcyc to compute and store this information. mkcyc has an option to also store persistence information.

3. Topological Maps: If the triangle and square topological maps are not available, or the filtration was just generated, *CView* uses terrain to generate these images.

Having generated the required information using the utility programs, *CView* loads a complex and uses a run-time library to generate display lists for fast rendering. I have taken great care to only regenerate display lists when needed. However, all reordering, Betti number computation, and display list generation is done on the fly. The object is rendered in the large canvas area that dominates the main window. The user may zoom, translate, or rotate the object using the mouse.

Panels. There are four panels in the main window for user selection and data presentation:

- **Simplices:** This panel allows the user to select the rendered simplices. Simplices are divided into three groups: singular, regular, and interior (Edelsbrunner and Mücke, 1994). A simplex is *interior* if it is not on the boundary of the complex. Otherwise, it is *singular*, when none of its cofaces are present in the complex, or *regular*. The program renders singular simplices and regular triangles by default, as these are the only simplices that may be observed.

- **Reordering:** The user may select the method of reordering from this panel. The pseudo-triangle reordering algorithm is the default method, because of the study in Section 12.4.1.

- **Miscellaneous:** The user may elect to see positive and negative simplices in sea-green and magenta, respectively, using the "Mark?" checkbox. The user may also select the last simplices added to be rendered in orange using the "Last?" checkbox. The latter option is useful to view the effect of reordering on a filtration, as in Figure 11.8(a).

- **Data:** This panel gives information about the current complex. It lists the current complex index l and persistence p, along with the Betti number $\beta^{l,p}$ or $\gamma^{l,p}$, depending on which topological map is selected in the map window.

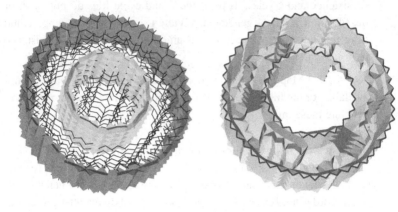

(a) All the darker simplices have just ar-   (b) A noncanonical 1-cycle and its mani-
rived into the complex   fold

Fig. 11.8. Complex $K^{4025,70852}$ of *bearing*.

11.5.2 Map Window

The map window is the primary navigation tool in *CView*. It displays either the
triangle or the square topological map, corresponding to the Betti and square
Betti numbers of the filtration. The user may use the radio buttons at the bottom
of the window to switch between the maps. The user may also select new
values for index l and persistence p by clicking on the map or, alternatively, by
using the scrollbars or even directly inputting the values in the shell window.
CView displays a cross-hair at the current point (l, p) on the topological map.

11.5.3 Cycle Window

The cycle window is available through the Tools menu from the main window. It allows visualization of cycles and their associated manifolds in any
dimension. The manifolds are visualized as transparent paths, membranes, or
volumes, as shown in Figure 11.8(b). Currently, *CView* visualizes noncanonical cycles, as they are much smaller than canonical cycles (see Table 12.9 for
details). It is easy to add canonization, and I plan to add it as an option in the
interface. The user may either view a single cycle by using the scrollbar or all
cycles by using the "All?" checkbox. Naturally, the scrollbar is disabled when
the "All?" checkbox is selected.

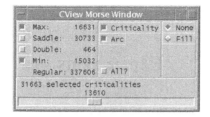

Fig. 11.9. *CView* Morse window.

11.5.4 Morse Window

Whenever a grid filtration is loaded into the program, *CView* computes the quasi Morse complex and opens an additional window containing information and control interface for the complex, as shown in Figure 11.9. The window has three panels and a scrollbar:

- **Data:** This panel lists the number of Morse critical and regular points and allows for user selection for visualization.
- **Visualization:** This panel enables the user to select visualization of critical points and arcs. It also contains an "All?" button, similar to the one in the *CView* cycle window.
- **Simplification:** This is an experimental panel for simplifying the surface using persistence.

The Morse window showcases the flexibility of *CView*. As *CView* is a script, it is easy to make modifications to the program and add features. The interested user may design her own interfaces for the intended application. I plan to include more `tcl` commands for manipulating complexes in the near future.

12

Experiments

In this chapter, we examine the feasibility of the algorithms in Part Two of this book using the implementations described in the last chapter. To make our experiments meaningful, we use real-world data from a variety of different sources, in a variety of different sizes. We time each algorithm to examine its running time behavior in practice. We also gather statistics on significant structural information contained in the data, such as number of conflicts or collisions in the persistence algorithm.

We begin by introducing the three-dimensional data for α-complex filtrations in Section 12.1. This is the data we use for timings and experiments on the persistent algorithm for $\mathbb{Z}_2$ coefficients in Section 12.2, topological simplification in Section 12.4, and the linking number algorithm in Section 12.6. We introduce alternate data for the persistence algorithm for fields in Section 12.3 as well as the Morse-Smale complex algorithm in Section 12.5. When appropriate, we also discuss additional implementation details not included in the last chapter.

12.1 Three-Dimensional Data

In Chapter 1, we motivated the study of topological spaces through a few diverse examples. It is appropriate, therefore, that the experimental data be from disparate sources. We use data that range in scale from nanometers to centimeters. The data will include proteins and inorganic molecules, resolved molecular structures, designed synthetic molecules, acquired samples from real world objects, and sampled mathematical functions. All data, however, will be treated using the unified approach described in Chapter 2: The data are weighted or unweighted points, generating α-complex filtrations for the study of the spaces they describe.

Table 12.1. *Proteins data sets, identified with their PDB ID code. In order, the proteins are: gramicidin A, sperm whale myoglobin, human CDC25b, HIV-1 protease, and human cyclin-dependent kinase.*

PDB ID	0	# k-simplices		3	total
		1	2		
1grm	318	2,322	3,978	1,973	8,591
1mbn	1,216	9,251	16,005	7,969	34,441
1qb0	1,417	10,743	18,586	9,259	40,005
1hiv	1,532	11,563	19,991	9,959	43,045
1hck	2,370	17,976	31,135	15,528	67,009

12.1.1 Proteins

Proteins are the fundamental building blocks and functional units of life forms. A protein is a linear heteropolymer macromolecule composed of amino acids. These amino acid *residues* connect by peptide bonds to form the *backbone* for the protein. The rest of a residue hangs off the backbone, forming a *side chain*. A protein generally folds into a globular structure because of the interaction between the many forces on the backbone and side chains, including electrostatics, van der Waals forces, hydrogen bonds between different residues, hydrophobic forces, and entropy (Creighton, 1984). A protein functions through its shape, and consequently there is significant interest in discovering the properties of their shapes. Table 12.1 lists the proteins we explore in this book, along with the size of their Delaunay triangulations. The proteins are taken from the Protein Data Bank (Berman et al., 2000; RCSB, 2003), but we have modified them by removing water molecules and ligands. There is considerable ambiguity in assigning radii to atoms. We use Jie Liang's pdb2alf to convert the proteins to weighted balls and the input to alpha-shapes. Finally, a PDB file may have multiple models in the same file, and we use only one model in each case.

We may visualize a protein with balls, representing atoms, and sticks, representing covalent bonds. In Figure 12.1(a), the pentagonal and hexagonal rings of Tryptophan (an amino acid) are clearly visible as side chains of Gramicidin A. However, researchers have developed alternate visualization techniques for displaying the structure of proteins. The primary secondary structures exhibited by proteins are helices called α-*helices* and sheet-like structures called β-*sheets*. In Figure 12.1(b), we see the eight α-helices of the sperm whale myoglobin as its secondary structure. The symmetric structure of the two chains

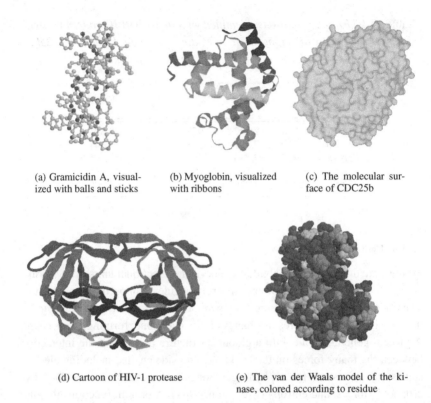

(a) Gramicidin A, visual-   (b) Myoglobin, visualized   (c) The molecular sur-
ized with balls and sticks   with ribbons   face of CDC25b

(d) Cartoon of HIV-1 protease   (e) The van der Waals model of the ki-
                                          nase, colored according to residue

Fig. 12.1. Proteins in Table 12.1, visualized using the Protein Explorer (Martz, 2001).

of HIV-1 protease is manifest in its *cartoon* drawing in (d), where the arrows
orient the secondary structures. We may also also visualize the globular structure of proteins using the molecular surface (c) or the van der Waals model (e),
as before. These protein secondary structures, in turn, form tertiary and qua-
ternary structures, which are used by researchers to devise human-defined or
algorithmic classifications of proteins (Holm and Sander, 1995; Murzin et al.,
1995; Orengo et al., 1997) and construct hierarchies (CATH, 2003; FSSP,
2003; SCOP, 2003).

12.1.2 Zeolites

Zeolites are three-dimensional, microporous, crystalline solids. They occur
as natural minerals, but most are produced synthetically for commercial pur-

Table 12.2. *Zeolites, identified by their three-letter codes.*

	\# k-simplices				total
	0	1	2	3	
SOD	324	2,253	3,772	1,842	8191
LTA	1,296	8,471	14,168	6,992	30,927
FAU	1,296	9,588	16,420	8,127	35,431
KFI	1,296	9,760	16,788	8,323	36,167
BOG	1,296	11,401	20,098	9,992	42,787

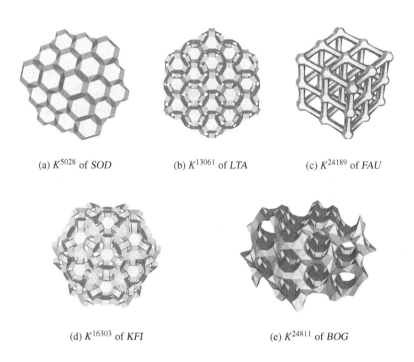

(a) K^{5028} of *SOD*   (b) K^{13061} of *LTA*   (c) K^{24189} of *FAU*

(d) K^{16303} of *KFI*   (e) K^{24811} of *BOG*

Fig. 12.2. Zeolites in Table 12.2. A single complex in the filtration for a zeolite is rendered.

poses (Zeolyst International, 2003). Zeolites contain regular frameworks of aluminum and silicone atoms, bound together through shared oxygens atoms. Outside this framework, zeolites have cavities and channels that can host cations (positively charged ions), water, or other molecules. Consequently, zeolites are very effective desiccants and can hold up to 25% of their weight in water. Zeolites can also be shape-selective catalysts through their different pore and channel sizes, and are used as such for petroleum refining and synthetic fuel and petrochemical production. The highest volume use for zeolites is, however, in detergents and water softeners, where they exchange sodium ions for calcium and magnesium ions present in the water.

The topology of a zeolite clearly determines its function, so zeolites provide ideal spaces for explorations using the algorithms in this book. Table 12.2 lists the zeolites we have selected as data because of their topological properties. Zeolites are identified with mnemonic three-letter codes (IZA Structure Comission, 2003). Figure 12.2 displays specific complexes from the filtrations of the zeolites.

12.1.3 Surfaces

Surfaces constitute another type of space that we explore in this book. Real-life objects are often sampled using input devices, such as a laser scanner. The surfaces are then reconstructed using acquired and estimated connectivity information (Curless and Levoy, 1996; Turk and Levoy, 1994). Recently, there was a flurry of theoretical activity in this area by computational geometers, starting with the Crust algorithm of Amenta and Bern (1999). Most surfaces examine enclose large voids, and we may look for these voids as part of our examination. Table 12.3 lists the surfaces we will use for my experiments. The data set *torus* is synthetically generated by Ernst Mücke. The other surfaces are from *The Stanford 3D Scanning Repository* (Stanford Graphics Laboratory, 2003). The surfaces are rather large, generating a lot of simplices in the full Delaunay triangulation. So, we decimate them to the size given in the table. We then discard the connectivity information and retain the coordinates as points. Figure 12.3 displays renderings of the surfaces in Table 12.3.

12.1.4 Miscellaneous

In addition to the spaces already described, we use the data sets listed in Table 12.4 for experiments. The data sets are as follows:

- *hopf* contains contains points regularly sampled along two linked circles. The resulting filtration contains a complex that is a *Hopf link*.
- *möbius* contains regularly sampled points along the boundary of a Möbius strip, which is a nonorientable 2-manifold with a single connected boundary,
- *bearing* is a nano-bearing, constructed from atoms, which we received from Ralph Merkle.

Table 12.3. *Surface data. The numbers in the names of the Buddha and dragon data sets indicate the decimation percentage.*

| | # k-simplices | | | | total |
	0	1	2	3	
torus	256	1,706	2,760	1,309	6,031
bunny	34,834	274,701	478,236	238,368	1,026,139
buddha10	54,262	438,134	766,893	383,020	1,642,309
dragon1	4,443	32,111	55,232	27,563	119,349
dragon10	43,714	348,645	609,345	304,413	1,306,117
dragon20	87,170	704,806	1,234,422	616,785	2,643,183

(a) Torus   (b) Bunny

(c) Buddha   (d) Dragon

Fig. 12.3. Original surfaces used to generate data sets in Table 12.3. We used Brian Curless's `plyview` for visualization.

Table 12.4. *Miscellaneous data.*

	# k-simplices				total
	0	1	2	3	
hopf	100	1,752	3,240	1,587	6,679
möbius	100	2,809	5,331	2,621	10,861
bearing	2,881	24,993	44,042	21,929	93,845
TAO	7,774	60,675	105,710	52,808	226,967
bone	42,311	346,664	608,445	304,091	1,301,511

- *TAO* is a molecular tile composed of crossover DNA strands, which we received from Thomas LaBean (LaBean et al., 2000). It is used for DNA-based computation.
- *bone* is a sampled iso-surface of a cube of microscopic human bone. The volume data were provided by Françoise Peyrin from CNRS CREATIS in Lyon, and were issued from Synchrotron Radiation Microtomography from the ID19 beamline at ESRF in Grenoble. Dominique Attali generated the iso-surface that we sampled.

While *bone* is a surface data set, it does not have the characteristics of surfaces introduced in the last section, as it does not enclose large volumes. We show renderings of these data sets in Figure 12.4.

12.2 Algorithm for $\mathbb{Z}_2$

Having described the three-dimensional data, we now begin examining the persistence algorithm over $\mathbb{Z}_2$ coefficients. While the algorithm has $O(m^3)$ running time, we show that it is extremely fast in practice.

12.2.1 Timings

We only time and present the portion of the software that is directly related to computing persistence. In particular, we do not time the construction of the Delaunay complex or the α-shape filtration. All timings in this section were done on a Sun Ultra-10 with a 440 MHz UltraSPARC IIi processor and 256 megabyte RAM, running *Solaris 8*. Table 12.5 distinguishes four steps in the computation: marking simplices as positive or negative, and adding k-cycles for $k = 0, 1, 2$. Recall that the computation of persistence can be accelerated for $k = 0, 2$ by using a union-find data structure. As the times show, this improvement subsumes adding 0- and 2-cycles in the marking process, shrinking

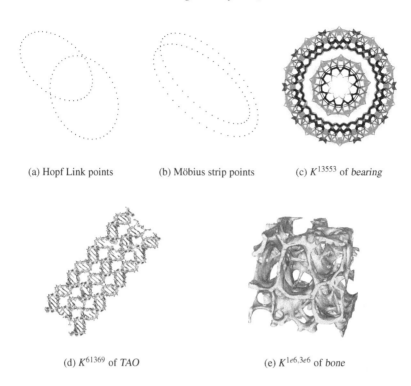

(a) Hopf Link points   (b) Möbius strip points   (c) K^{13553} of *bearing*

(d) K^{61369} of *TAO*   (e) $K^{1e6.3e6}$ of *bone*

Fig. 12.4. Miscellaneous data used.

the time for these to steps to essentially nothing. Figure 12.5 graphs the total time for the persistence algorithm, with and without the union-find speedup, against the number of simplices in a filtration. The graph shows that the computation time is essentially linear in the number of simplices in the filtration. This is substantially faster than the cubic dependence proved in Section 7.2.3. Of course, we need to distinguish worst-case analysis from average running time. After accelerating with union-find, the slowest portion of the algorithm adds 1-cycles, which is still $O(m^3)$ in the worst case.

12.2.2 Statistics

The cubic upper bound in Section 7.2.3 followed from the observation that the k-cycle created by σ^i goes through fewer than p_i collisions, and the length of its list built up during these collisions is less than $(k+2)p_i$. We may explain the linear running time in Figure 12.5 by showing that the average number of col-

Table 12.5. *Running time in seconds for computing persistence pairs for the data sets, sorted by their size.*

| | size | mark | add k-cycles | | | total | |
			0	1	2	w/o UF	w UF
torus	6,031	0.02	0.00	0.01	0.01	0.04	0.02
hopf	6,679	0.02	0.00	0.03	0.00	0.05	0.05
SOD	8,191	0.02	0.01	0.02	0.00	0.05	0.05
1grm	8,591	0.03	0.00	0.02	0.01	0.06	0.04
möbius	10,861	0.04	0.00	0.04	0.00	0.08	0.07
LTA	30,927	0.10	0.01	0.08	0.02	0.21	0.17
1mbn	34,441	0.11	0.01	0.10	0.02	0.24	0.21
FAU	35,431	0.12	0.01	0.10	0.02	0.25	0.22
KFI	36,167	0.11	0.01	0.09	0.02	0.23	0.21
1qb0	40,005	0.14	0.01	0.11	0.03	0.29	0.25
BOG	42,787	0.14	0.01	0.12	0.02	0.29	0.25
1hiv	43,045	0.14	0.01	0.12	0.03	0.30	0.27
1hck	66,993	0.24	0.01	0.19	0.05	0.49	0.43
bearing	93,845	0.35	0.02	0.28	0.07	0.72	0.62
dragon1	119,349	0.43	0.03	0.35	0.12	0.93	0.78
TAO	226,967	0.87	0.06	0.73	0.19	1.85	1.59
bunny	1,026,139	4.44	0.31	3.71	8.63	17.09	8.16
bone	1,301,511	6.04	0.40	4.77	1.33	12.54	10.81
dragon10	1,306,117	5.76	0.41	4.68	11.86	22.71	10.44
buddha10	1,642,309	7.64	0.53	6.53	4.64	19.34	14.11
dragon20	2,643,183	12.32	0.91	10.42	51.75	75.40	22.47

lisions and the average list length are both nearly constant, and much smaller than the trivial upper bound of the length of the filtration. Tables 12.6 and 12.7 provide strong evidence for this argument. Table 12.7 does not include 0-cycles, as every 0-cycle is represented by a list of length 2. Also, the algorithm only needs to track the positive simplices, so the negative simplices are not stored in the cycle lists, giving us memory and time savings. While the maximum number of collisions and list lengths can get quite high, the averages are generally small numbers. In other words, the algorithm performs linearly on all the data presented here. Recall that the number of collisions and the length of lists is bounded from above by the persistence of cycles. Table 12.8 shows that the average persistence is considerably larger than the average number of collisions and list length, however.

Finally, Table 12.9 shows that canonical cycles and their spanning manifolds are up to two orders of magnitude larger than the cycles in the noncanonical basis computed by the persistence algorithm. We will only use canonization

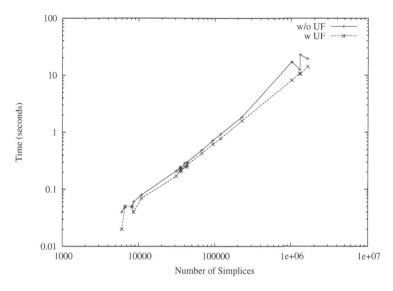

Fig. 12.5. Graph of total computation time from Table 12.5, with and without union-find.

when we need the full description of canonical cycles. For example, we will need canonical 1-cycles for computing the linking number. For this description, the persistence algorithm must also store the negative simplices for the cycle lists, increasing its memory usage and decreasing its performance. The much larger canonical cycles consume a lot of storage, slowing down the algorithm even further. We do not generate statistics for the five largest datasets as their memory requirements eclipsed the computer's memory by a few fold, reducing the program to thrashing.

12.2.3 Discussion

The discrepancy between the worst-case time analysis and the experimental results is naturally puzzling. Either the analysis is not tight or the input is not representative of the space of all inputs. We know that the latter is certainly the case: All the filtrations explored are simplicial complexes, but the persistence algorithm will work on any abstract simplicial complex, even those that are not geometrically realizable in $\mathbb{R}^3$. The relationship between the algorithm and the reduction scheme discussed in Section 7.3, however, seems to imply that the worst-case analysis is tight, as the normal form algorithm has time complexity $O(m^3)$. The results of this section show, however, that the persistence algo-

Table 12.6. *Maximum and average number of collisions.*

	0-cycles		1-cycles		2-cycles	
	max	avg	max	avg	max	avg
torus	18	0.73	29	0.32	21	0.59
hopf	25	0.49	50	0.06	2	0.00
SOD	9	0.97	18	0.41	44	0.64
1grm	12	0.53	31	0.19	91	0.13
möbius	80	0.95	49	0.05	0	0.00
LTA	12	0.96	26	0.37	72	0.56
1mbn	15	0.85	85	0.27	58	0.14
FAU	10	0.94	20	0.29	93	0.44
KFI	11	0.98	22	0.38	66	0.65
1qb0	15	0.86	73	0.26	47	0.17
BOG	16	0.91	32	0.51	37	0.40
1hiv	29	0.92	113	0.27	55	0.18
1hck	46	0.85	125	0.27	72	0.17
bearing	65	0.91	198	0.39	66	0.38
dragon1	25	0.88	60	0.14	2,837	0.16
TAO	13	0.61	207	0.32	26	0.19
bunny	182	0.96	306	0.28	53,869	0.23
bone	21	0.99	589	0.26	1462	0.15
dragon10	19	0.96	1,559	0.22	77,328	0.29
buddha10	20	1.01	1,073	0.19	33,325	0.14
dragon20	23	0.95	1,610	0.22	173,321	0.31

rithm is fast and efficient in practice. We may use the persistence algorithm as a computational tool for discovering the topology of spaces.

12.3 Algorithm for Fields

In this section, we discuss experiments using an implementation of the persistence algorithm for arbitrary fields. We look at two scenarios where the $\mathbb{Z}_2$ algorithm would not be applicable, but where this algorithm succeeds in providing information about a topological space.

12.3.1 Implementation

We have implemented the field algorithm for $\mathbb{Z}_p$ for p a prime and $\mathbb{Q}$ coefficients. Our implementation is in C and utilizes GNU MP, a multi-precision library, for exact computation (Granlund, 2003). We have a separate implementation for coefficients in $\mathbb{Z}_2$ as the computation is greatly simplified in this field. This implementation is exactly like the algorithm for $\mathbb{Z}_2$ discussed in the

Table 12.7. *Maximum and average length of cycle lists, over all lists (avg), and all final stored lists (avgf). Only the positive simplices are stored in the lists.*

	1-cycles			2-cycles		
	max	avg	avgf	max	avg	avgf
torus	18	2.58	2.39	10	2.74	1.94
hopf	2	2.00	2.00	3	1.94	1.94
SOD	28	2.80	2.33	22	3.76	2.03
1grm	10	2.46	2.22	104	4.75	2.07
möbius	2	1.99	2.00	1	1.96	1.96
LTA	93	3.37	2.53	28	6.07	1.97
1mbn	98	4.31	2.35	63	2.72	2.06
FAU	27	2.57	2.31	89	4.76	2.01
KFI	76	2.66	2.40	65	3.41	2.12
1qb0	171	5.24	2.44	39	2.81	2.07
BOG	55	4.08	2.51	24	2.93	2.05
1hiv	214	6.00	2.51	73	2.82	2.07
1hck	233	6.07	2.43	48	2.81	2.07
bearing	116	3.34	2.29	87	3.64	2.14
dragon1	156	3.06	2.41	666	46.49	2.05
TAO	119	3.85	2.21	15	2.26	2.02
bunny	419	2.91	2.34	12,478	1,426.26	2.05
bone	1,724	9.44	2.50	526	8.20	2.07
dragon10	2,849	13.33	2.44	10,712	1,541.47	2.05
buddha10	4,993	19.65	2.47	7,492	374.67	2.04
dragon20	5,973	36.17	2.46	21,293	3,326.70	2.04

Table 12.8. *Maximum and average persistence of cycles.*

	0-cycles		1-cycles		2-cycles	
	max	avg	max	avg	max	avg
torus	804	354.20	4,090	166.42	2,519	63.01
hopf	198	98.03	727	36.93	304	24.76
SOD	740	326.50	2,035	124.46	4,666	64.83
1grm	640	320.36	5,767	55.35	634	4.47
möbius	194	98.00	1,497	2.97	107	0.94
LTA	3,460	1,473.01	11,972	783.52	12,935	126.77
1mbn	2,784	654.60	20,573	402.59	5,115	56.95
FAU	18,604	1,699.46	8,263	390.40	8,218	71.75
KFI	3,033	1,342.35	21,867	664.98	8,988	284.68
1qb0	3,020	760.64	24,486	520.66	9,057	95.78
BOG	3,236	1,333.88	30,966	757.01	6,612	194.54
1hiv	8,377	834.70	30,249	584.29	9,965	114.95
1hck	9,574	1,296.33	45,285	906.12	14,159	151.04
bearing	12,760	3,029.22	84,911	3,498.73	26,959	990.82
dragon1	55,079	19,089.71	40,733	391.80	23,174	14.13
TAO	16,256	7,902.83	193,418	2,706.18	42,507	462.17
bunny	215,610	35,804.36	448,848	9,408.45	361,638	4.31
bone	452,958	59,383.77	1,087,293	5,264.04	234,117	393.92
dragon10	410,674	91,370.23	845,865	4,678.24	577,447	16.34
buddha10	913,353	95,620.32	1,209,948	3,828.92	366,388	45.22
dragon20	848,329	164,768.17	1,830,518	8,059.36	1,260,004	15.56

Table 12.9. *Time in seconds for canonizing 1-cycles and 2-cycles, along with the average cycle length and spanning manifold size, before and after canonization.*

		1-cycles					2-cycles			
	time	cycle len		manifold size		time	cycle len		manifold size	
		before	after	before	after		before	after	before	after
torus	0.01	4.36	11.34	1.55	45.85	0.01	6.85	34.68	2.94	36.56
hopf	0.02	4.06	52.03	1.06	62.57	0.01	5.00	14.37	1.00	10.44
SOD	0.02	4.89	15.86	2.18	41.25	0.01	6.36	18.48	2.28	16.16
1grm	0.02	4.26	14.05	1.38	51.38	0.01	5.24	18.52	1.17	15.87
möbius	0.03	4.14	28.97	1.14	62.10	0.01	5.00	17.42	1.00	24.42
LTA	0.16	4.91	24.94	1.98	111.64	0.05	5.84	24.44	1.63	18.79
1mbn	0.19	4.44	48.68	1.55	115.73	0.05	5.24	19.79	1.16	16.69
FAU	0.13	4.39	25.70	1.40	78.60	0.06	5.59	26.62	1.57	27.88
KFI	0.13	4.67	27.88	1.69	66.79	0.05	6.31	19.91	1.93	17.12
1qb0	0.28	4.50	60.56	1.63	141.52	0.05	5.29	20.24	1.20	16.71
BOG	0.23	5.67	25.68	3.21	112.71	0.07	5.78	22.43	1.51	22.56
1hiv	0.30	4.50	57.21	1.64	124.55	0.06	5.31	20.74	1.22	17.36
1hck	0.57	4.49	68.71	1.63	166.61	0.11	5.29	24.29	1.20	22.72
bearing	1.95	4.78	56.98	2.53	583.15	0.17	5.81	22.87	1.67	26.68
dragon1	1.01	4.21	43.23	1.25	226.23	0.55	5.17	48.40	1.19	66.81
TAO	1.69	4.46	40.94	1.81	160.72	0.35	5.31	22.35	1.21	21.24

Fig. 12.6. A wire-frame visualization of dataset K, an immersed triangulated Klein bottle with 4000 triangles.

last section, when we do not use the union-find speedup. We use a 2.2 GHz Pentium 4 Dell PC with 1 GB RAM running *Red Hat Linux 7.3* for computing the timings in this section.

12.3.2 Framework and Data

We have implemented a general framework for computing persistence complexes from Morse functions defined over manifolds of arbitrary dimension.

Our framework takes a tuple (K, f) as input and produces a persistence complex $\mathcal{C}(K, f)$ as output. K is a d-dimensional simplicial complex that triangulates an underlying manifold. And $f: \text{vert}\, K \rightarrow \mathbb{R}$ is a discrete function over the vertices of K that we extend linearly over the remaining simplices of K. The function f acts as the Morse function over the manifold, but it need not be Morse for our purposes, as we perform symbolic perturbation to eliminate the degeneracies. Frequently, our complex is augmented with a map $\varphi: K \rightarrow \mathbb{R}^d$ that immerses or embeds the manifold in Euclidean space. Our algorithm does not require φ for computation, but φ is often provided as a discrete map over the vertices of K and is extended linearly as before. For example, Figure 12.6 displays a triangulated Klein bottle immersed in $\mathbb{R}^3$.

To generate the dataset K, we sampled the following parametrization. Let $r = 4(1 - \cos(u))/2$. Then,

$$x = \begin{cases} 6\cos(u)(1 + \sin(u)) + r\cos(u)\cos(v), & \text{if } u < \pi \\ 6\cos(u)(1 + \sin(u)) + r\cos(v + \pi), & \text{otherwise} \end{cases}$$

$$y = \begin{cases} 16\sin(u) + r\sin(u)\cos(v), & \text{if } u < \pi \\ 16\sin(u), & \text{otherwise} \end{cases}$$

$$z = r\sin(v).$$

The underlying space for the other two data sets is the four-dimensional space-time manifold. For each data set, we triangulate the convex hull of the samples to get a triangulation. Each resulting complex, listed in Table 12.10, is homeomorphic to a four-dimensional ball and has $\chi = 1$. Data set E contains the potential around electrostatic charges at each vertex. Data set J records the supersonic flow velocity of a jet engine. We use these values as Morse functions to generate the filtrations. We then compute persistence over $\mathbb{Z}_2$ coefficients to get the Betti numbers. For each data set, Table 12.10 gives the number s_k of k-simplices, as well as the Euler characteristic $\chi = \sum_k (-1)^k s_k$. We use the Morse function to compute the excursion set filtration for each data set. Table 12.11 gives information on the resulting filtrations.

12.3.3 Field Coefficients

With the generalized algorithm, we may compute the homology of the Klein bottle over different coefficient fields. Here, we are interested only in the Betti numbers of the final complex in the filtration for illustrative purposes. The nonorientability of this surface is visible in Figure 12.6. The change in triangle orientation at the parametrization boundary leads to a rendering artifact where two sets of triangles are front-facing. In homology, the nonorientabil-

Table 12.10. *Data sets.* K *is the Klein bottle, shown in Figure 12.6.* E *is the potential around electrostatic charges.* J *is supersonic jet flow.*

| | number s_k of k-simplices | | | | | χ |
	0	1	2	3	4	
K	2,000	6,000	4,000	0	0	0
E	3,095	52,285	177,067	212,327	84,451	1
J	17,862	297,372	1,010,203	1,217,319	486,627	1

Table 12.11. *Filtrations. The number of simplices in the filtration* $|K| = \sum_i s_i$, *the length of the filtration (number of distinct values of function f), time to compute the filtration, and time to compute persistence over $\mathbb{Z}_2$ coefficients.*

	$|K|$	len	filt (s)	pers (s)
K	12,000	1,020	0.03	< 0.01
E	529,225	3,013	3.17	5.00
J	3,029,383	256	24.13	50.23

ity manifests itself as a torsional 1-cycle c where $2c$ is a boundary (indeed, it bounds the surface itself.) The homology groups over $\mathbb{Z}$ are

$$H_0(K) = \mathbb{Z},$$
$$H_1(K) = \mathbb{Z} \times \mathbb{Z}_2,$$
$$H_2(K) = \{0\}.$$

Note that $\beta_1 = \text{rank}\, H_1 = 1$. We now use the "height function" as our Morse function, $f = z$, to generate the filtration in Table 12.11. We then compute the homology of data set K with field coefficients using our algorithm, as shown in Table 12.12.

Over $\mathbb{Z}_2$, we get $\beta_1 = 2$ as homology is unable to recognize the torsional boundary $2c$ with coefficients 0 and 1. Instead, it observes an additional class of homology 1-cycles. By the Euler-Poincaré relation, $\chi = \sum_i \beta_i$, so we also get a class of 2-cycles to compensate for the increase in β_1. Therefore, $\mathbb{Z}_2$ homology misidentifies the Klein bottle as the torus. Over any other field, however, homology turns the torsional cycle into a boundary, as the inverse of 2 exists. In other words, while we cannot observe torsion in computing homology over fields, we can deduce its existence by comparing our results

Table 12.12. *Field coefficients. The Betti numbers of K computed over field F and time for the persistence algorithm. We use a separate implementation for $\mathbb{Z}_2$ coefficients.*

F	β_0	β_1	β_2	time (s)
$\mathbb{Z}_2$	1	2	1	0.01
$\mathbb{Z}_3$	1	1	0	0.23
$\mathbb{Z}_5$	1	1	0	0.23
$\mathbb{Z}_{3203}$	1	1	0	0.23
$\mathbb{Q}$	1	1	0	0.50

over different coefficient sets. Similarly, we can compare sets of $\mathcal{P}$-intervals from different computations to discover torsion in a persistence complex.

Note that our algorithm's performance for this data set is about the same over arbitrary finite fields, as the coefficients do not get large. The computation over $\mathbb{Q}$ takes about twice as much time and space, since each rational is represented as two integers in GNU MP.

12.3.4 Higher Dimensions

We now examine the performance of this algorithm in higher dimensions using the large-scale time-varying data. Again, we give the filtration sizes and timings in Table 12.11. Figure 12.7(a) displays β_2 for data set J. We observe a large number of two-dimensional cycles (voids), as the co-dimension is 2. Persistence allows us to do to decompose this graph into the set of $\mathcal{P}$-intervals. Although there are 730,692 $\mathcal{P}$-intervals in dimension 2, most are empty as the topological attribute is created and destroyed at the same function level. We draw the 502 nonempty $\mathcal{P}$-intervals in Figure 12.7(b). Note that the $\mathcal{P}$-intervals represent a compact and general *shape descriptor* for arbitrary spaces.

For the large data sets, we do not compute persistence over alternate fields as the computation requires in excess of 2 GB of memory. In the case of finite fields $\mathbb{Z}_p$, we may restrict the prime p to be less than the maximum size of an integer. This is a reasonable restriction, as on most modern machines with 32-bit integers, it implies $p < 2^{32}$. Given this restriction, any coefficient will be less than p and representable as a 4-byte integer. The GNU MP exact integer format, on the other hand, requires at least 16 bytes for representing any integer.

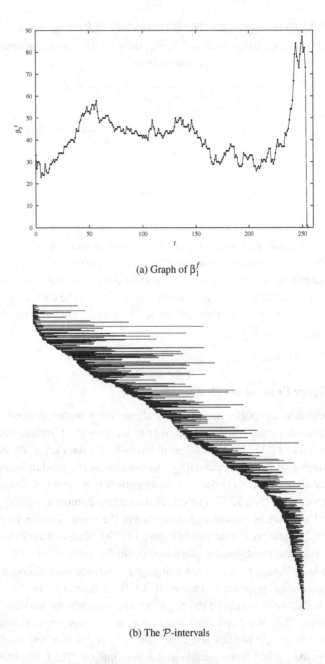

(a) Graph of β_1^f

(b) The $\mathcal{P}$-intervals

Fig. 12.7. The data set J defines function f, the flow velocity, over the four-dimensional space-time manifold. We show the graph of f (top) and the 502 nonempty $\mathcal{P}$-intervals in dimension 2. The amalgamation of these intervals gives the graph.

12.4 Topological Simplification

In this section, we first present a case study of the five reordering algorithms described in Chapter 8 and illustrated in Figure 8.7. We then provide experimental evidence of the utility of the algorithms, as well as the rarity of basic and recursive conflicts. We end this chapter with visualizations of persistent complexes.

12.4.1 A Case Study

In this brief picturesque study, we show the effect of the reordering algorithms in the presence of conflicts. Figure 12.8(a) displays the k-triangles of the data set *SOD*. This zeolite does not contain any basic conflicts, but it does have 26 recursive conflicts. We are interested in the tip of the region of large overlapping 1-triangles, shown in Figure 12.8(b). The rest of the figures in (c–l) show how this area changes with the different reordering algorithms in Figure 8.7. Note that the differences for the pseudo-triangle algorithm cancel, as each cycle is given its due influence, given its persistence. Consequently, we will use this algorithm as the default method for simplification.

12.4.2 Timings and Statistics

We have implemented all of the reordering algorithms for experimentation. The algorithms have the basic structure and therefore take about the same time. So, we only give the time taken for the Pseudo-triangle algorithm in Table 12.13. All timings were done on a Sun Ultra-10 with a 440 MHz Ultra-SPARC IIi processor and 256 megabyte RAM, running *Solaris 8*. Here, each complex is reordered with p equal to the size of the filtration. Generally, the reordering algorithms encounter the same number of conflicts, so we only list the number of basic and recursive conflicts for the pseudo-triangle algorithm in Table 12.13. The time taken for reordering correlates very well with the size of the filtration, as all algorithms make a single pass through the filter. A simplex may move multiple times during reordering, however, because of the recursive nature of the algorithms. The number of recursive conflicts is one indication of the complexity of the reordering. The table shows that the data sets with a large number of recursive conflicts, namely *BOG*, *bearing*, *TAO*, and *bone*, all have large reordering times.

216   12 Experiments

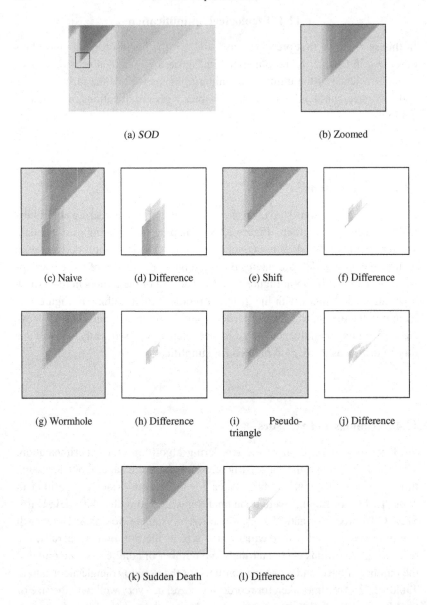

(a) *SOD*   (b) Zoomed

(c) Naive   (d) Difference   (e) Shift   (f) Difference

(g) Wormhole   (h) Difference   (i)   Pseudo-   (j) Difference
                                triangle

(k) Sudden Death   (l) Difference

Fig. 12.8. Reordering algorithms on *SOD*. (a) displays the k-triangles of *SOD* with the region of interest boxed and zoomed in (b). (c–l) show the results of each reordering algorithm and the image difference between these results and (b). The difference between images is shown in shades of gray. I have increased the saturation by 25% for better viewing.

Table 12.13. *Time in seconds for the pseudo-triangle reordering algorithm, as well as the number of basic and recursive conflicts.*

	time	# conflicts basic	recursive
torus	0.03	297	1,938
hopf	0.04	0	1
SOD	0.17	0	26
1grm	0.05	0	0
möbius	0.07	0	1
LTA	0.38	0	22
1mbn	0.34	0	9
FAU	0.28	1	2
KFI	0.52	0	20
1qb0	0.39	2	15
BOG	1.81	0	132
1hiv	0.52	1	21
1hck	0.83	0	15
bearing	3.34	22	219
dragon1	0.96	0	1
TAO	3.26	0	212
bunny	12.40	0	0
bone	51.82	1	188
dragon10	15.77	0	1
buddha10	18.47	0	10
dragon20	36.40	0	2

12.4.3 Discussion

The timings show that the reordering algorithms are fast and feasible. The data also confirm the rarity of conflicts. Conflicts are structural in nature and may be used as an additional measure of complexity of the connectivity of a space. They arise when a topologically complicated region of space is coarsely triangulated. This is the case for both small triangulations like the data set *torus* and large triangulations of complex spaces like the data set *bone*. As we saw earlier, conflicts may be eliminated by refining a complex. Fine triangulations of topologically simple spaces, such as *bunny* or the *dragon* family, generally have few, if any, conflicts.

12.5 The Morse-Smale Complex Algorithm

In this section, we present experimental results to support the practical viability of the Morse-complex algorithm presented in Chapter 9. I have only

Table 12.14. *The four data sets. The second column gives the latitude and longitude coordinates (in degrees) for the upper-left and lower-right corners of the terrain. The south and west coordinates are negative.*

	coordinates	grid size	filt. length	# simplices
Sine	n/a	100×100	10,001	59,996
Iran	(42, 42), (23, 65)	277×229	63,434	380,594
Himalayas	(46, 66), (24, 105)	469×265	124,286	745,706
Andes	(15, –87), (–58, –55)	385×877	337,646	2,025,866
North America	(55, –127), (13, –61)	793×505	400,466	2,402,786

implemented the algorithms for constructing QMS complexes and computing the persistence of the critical points. My implementation for the former uses a different algorithm than the one presented in this chapter. The algorithm uses edge tags to reroute paths using a single pass through the critical points.

12.5.1 Data

We use four rectangle sections of rectilinear 5-minute gridded elevation data of Earth (National Geophysical Data Center, 1988) and one synthetic data sampled from $h(x, y) = \sin x + \sin y$ for input. Table 12.14 gives the names and sizes of the data sets. Each data set is a height function $h : \mathbb{Z}^2 \to \mathbb{R}$, assigning a height value $h(x, y)$ to each point of its domain. Consequently, we may view the data sets as gray-scale images, mapping heights to pixel intensities, as in Figure 12.9. In each case, we compactify the domain of the function, a gridded rectangle, into a sphere by adding a dummy vertex at height minus infinity. We then triangulate the resulting mesh by adding diagonals to the square cells. As a result, the 2-manifold that we use for experimentation is always $\mathbb{S}^2$. The filtration is generated by a manifold sweep, as described in Section 2.5. Therefore, each filtration has length equivalent to the number of vertices in the manifold, which is one more than the size of the grid (because of the dummy vertex). For example, *Sine* has a filtration of $100 \times 100 + 1 = 10{,}001$ complexes.

12.5.2 Timings and Statistics

We first compute a filtration of the sphere triangulation by a manifold sweep. We then use the persistence algorithm to compute and classify the critical

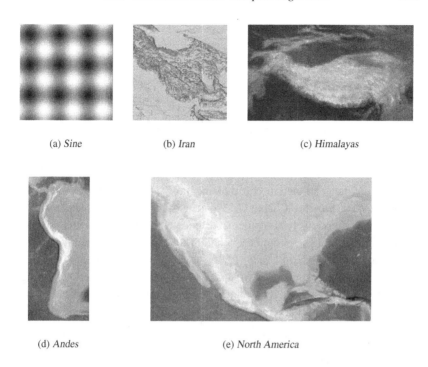

(a) *Sine*   (b) *Iran*   (c) *Himalayas*

(d) *Andes*   (e) *North America*

Fig. 12.9. The data sets in Table 12.14 rendered as gray-scale images. The intensity of each pixel of the image corresponds to the relative height at that location.

Table 12.15. *The number of critical points of the four triangulated spheres.*
The # Mon column gives the number of 2-fold (monkey) saddles. Note that
#Min − #Sad − 2#Mon + #Max = 2 in each case, as it should be.

	# Min	# Sad	# Mon	# Max
Sine	10	24	0	16
Iran	1,302	2,786	27	1,540
Himalayas	2,132	4,452	51	2,424
Andes	20,855	38,326	1,820	21,113
North America	15,032	30,733	464	16,631

points using the procedure described in Section 6.2.3. Table 12.15 lists the number of critical points of each type. As we start with grid data and add diagonals in a consistent manner, each vertex other than the dummy vertex has degree 6. Therefore, monkey saddles are the only multiple saddles that may

Table 12.16. *Running times in seconds.*

	filtration	persistence	QMS
Sine	0.06	0.13	0.03
Iran	0.46	0.90	0.56
Himalayas	0.89	1.74	1.01
Andes	2.62	4.90	2.60
North America	3.28	5.84	5.26

occur in the data. In the current implementation, we use the persistence algorithm, as described in Chapter 7. The data, however, are two-dimensional, and we may alternatively compute persistence using two passes and no cycle search. The second pass would use a union-find data structure and the dual of the triangulation. However, Table 12.16 shows that the slower algorithm used is quite fast, obviating the need for a specialized implementation. All timings were done on a Sun Ultra-10 with a 440 MHz UltraSPARC IIi processor and 256 megabyte RAM, running *Solaris 8.* Therefore, we use the same library to compute the persistence of both α-complex and grid filtration and constructing the QMS complex. Table 12.16 also gives the time for constructing the filtration and the QMS complex.

12.5.3 Discussion

We show the terrain of *Iran* along with its QMS complex in Figure 12.10. We display the QMS complex of this data set only as it is small. Already, there is too much detail that prevents us from seeing the features of the terrain. The multitude of small mountains and lakes clutter the image, partitioning the terrain into small regions. This image serves as a motivation for using persistence and computing hierarchical MS complexes. The situation here is similar to our failure to gain insights into the topology of spaces by simply computing their Betti numbers in Chapter 6. Like homology, Morse theory is powerful enough to capture the complete structure of the data. We need persistence as a mining tool for uncovering nuggets of information in the resulting mountain of data that is provided by the theory.

12.6 The Linking Number Algorithm

In this section, we present some experimental timing results and statistics on the linking number algorithm. We also provide visualizations of basis cycles

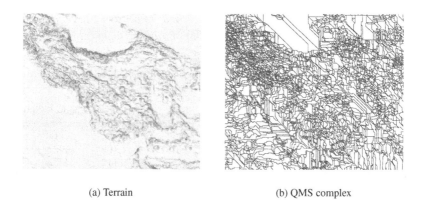

(a) Terrain   (b) QMS complex

Fig. 12.10. Iran's Alburz mountain range borders the Caspian sea (top flat area), and its Zagros mountain range shapes the Persian Gulf (left bottom).

in a filtration. All timings were done on a Sun Ultra-10 with a 440 MHz UltraSPARC IIi processor and 256 megabyte RAM, running the *Solaris 8.*

12.6.1 Implementation

I have implemented all the algorithms in Chapter 10, except for the algorithm for computing $\lambda \bmod 2$. My implementation differs from the exposition in three ways. The implemented component tree is a standard union-find data structure with the union by rank heuristic, but no path compression (Cormen et al., 1994). Edges are tagged with the union time and the least common ancestor is found by two traversals up the tree. Although this structure has an $O(n \log n)$ construction time and an $O(\log n)$ query time, it is very simple to implement and extremely fast in practice. We also use a heuristic to reduce the number of p-linked cycles by storing bounding boxes at the roots of the augmented union-find data structure. Before enumerating p-linked cycles, we check to see if the bounding box of the new cycle intersects with that of the stored cycles. If not, the cycles cannot be linked, so there's no need for enumeration. Finally, we only simulate the barycentric subdivision by storing a direction with each edge.

12.6.2 Timings and Statistics

We use the molecular data from Section 12.1 for experimentation. To compute linking, we first need to compute the canonical basis for each data set. Tables

Table 12.17. *Number of 1-cycles, time in seconds to construct the component tree, and the computation time and number of p-linked pairs (alg), p-linked pairs with intersecting bounding boxes (heur), and links.*

	# cycles	tree	time in seconds alg	heur	links	# pairs alg	heur	links
hopf	1,653	0.00	0.00	0.00	0.00	1	1	1
SOD	1,108	0.00	0.00	0.01	0.04	1,108	692	0
1grm	2,005	0.00	0.01	0.01	0.01	112	0	0
möbius	2,710	0.00	0.01	0.01	0.01	0	0	0
LTA	7,176	0.02	0.06	0.12	1.77	296,998	6,320	0
1mbn	8,036	0.01	0.04	0.04	0.04	522	107	0
FAU	8,293	0.01	0.12	0.07	0.07	1,255,396	34	0
KFI	8,465	0.01	0.05	0.04	0.33	87,956	25,251	0
1qb0	9,327	0.01	0.04	0.05	0.05	765	84	0
BOG	10,106	0.01	0.05	0.04	0.08	170,338	305	0
1hiv	10,032	0.02	0.04	0.05	0.15	8,709	8,426	0
1hck	15,603	0.03	0.08	0.09	0.24	12,338	11,244	0
TAO	52,902	0.12	0.38	0.42	6.83	98,543	4,455	0

12.5 and 12.9 in Section 12.2 give the time to compute and canonize 1-cycles. Table 12.17 gives timings and statistics for the linking algorithm. The table shows that the component tree and augmented trees are very fast in practice. It also shows that the bounding box heuristic for reducing the number of p-linked pairs increases the computation time negligibly, if at all. The heuristic is quite successful, moreover, in reducing the number of pairs we have to check for linkage, eliminating 99.8% of the candidates for data set *BOG*. The differences in total time of computation reflect the basic structure of the data sets, as well as their sizes. *TAO* has a large computation time, for instance, as the average size of the p-linked surfaces is approximately 266.88 triangles, compared to about 1.88 triangles for data set *1hck*.

Discussion. The experiments demonstrate the feasibility of the algorithms for fast computation of linking. The experiments fail to detect any links in the protein data, however. This is to be expected, as a protein consists of a single component, the primary structure of a protein being a single polypeptide chain of amino acids. Links, on the other hand, exist in different components by definition. Proteins may have "links" on their backbone, resulting from disulphide bonds between different residues. We need other techniques to intelligently detect such links.

13

Applications

In this chapter, we sample some of the potential applications of topology to problems in disparate scientific domains. Some of these questions motivated the theoretical concepts in this book to begin with, so it is reasonable to scrutinize the applicability of the work by revisiting the questions. I am not an expert in any of these domains. Rather, my objective is to demonstrate the utility of the theory, algorithms, and software by giving a few illustrative examples. My hope is that researchers in the fields will find these examples instructive and inspiring, and utilize the tools I have developed for scientific inquiry. Applied work is an on-going process by nature, so I present both current and future work in this chapter, including nonapplied future directions.

13.1 Computational Structural Biology

The field of *computational structural biology* explores the structural properties of molecules using combinatorial and numerical algorithms on computers. The initial impetus for the work in this book was understanding the topologies of proteins through homology. In this section, I look at three applications of my work to structural biology: feature detection, knot detection, and structure determination.

13.1.1 Topological Feature Detection

In Chapter 6, the small protein gramicidin A motivated our study of persistence, as we were incapable of differentiating between noise and feature in the data captured by homology. The primary topological structure of this protein is a single tunnel. Figure 13.2 illustrates the speed with which one may identify this tunnel using persistent homology. A glance at the topology map of the data set *1grm* in Figure 13.1 tells the user that there is a single persistent 1-cycle.

Fig. 13.1. Topology map of gramicidin A (*1grm*) with cross-hair at (1016, 4768).

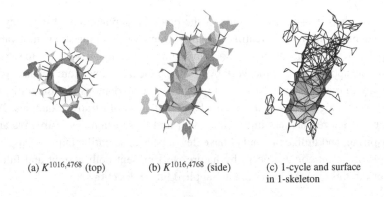

(a) $K^{1016,4768}$ (top)   (b) $K^{1016,4768}$ (side)   (c) 1-cycle and surface
                                                                    in 1-skeleton

Fig. 13.2. Detecting the topological feature of *1grm* using *CView*. The user selects complex (1016, 4768) (a,b) and visualizes the complex's single tunnel (c).

After clicking in the cycle's k-triangle, the user may view the complex from different viewpoints, as shown in Figure 13.2(a,b), and examine the 1-cycle and its spanning surface within the 1-skeleton of the persistent complex (c).

Not all molecular structures are as simple as this protein. The Zeolite *BOG*, for example, has a richer topology map, as shown in Figure 13.3. Observe that the structure features two groups of highly persistent 1-cycles. Again, the user may select to keep both groups of 1-cycles by choosing a point in the appropriate triangular region, as shown in Figure 13.4(a,b). The two sets of tunnels interact to produce a basis of 44 1-cycles. The user may elect to discard the set of 12 1-cycles by increasing persistence, as shown in Figure 13.4(c). The 8 longer-living tunnels (d), however, survive.

Zeolites are crystalline solids with very regular frameworks. This regularity of structure translates to simplicity of topology maps. Proteins, on the other

Fig. 13.3. Topology map of *BOG*

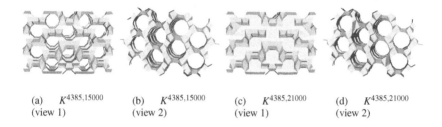

(a) $K^{4385,15000}$ (b) $K^{4385,15000}$ (c) $K^{4385,21000}$ (d) $K^{4385,21000}$
(view 1)   (view 2)   (view 1)   (view 2)

Fig. 13.4. Two views of persistent complexes with index 4385. Increasing persistence from 15,000 to 21,000, we eliminate the first group of tunnels and preserve the second.

hand, do not exhibit regular structure in general. Their topology maps are not simple as a consequence. Figure 13.5 shows the topology map of *1hck*, as well as the graph of its persistent β_1 numbers. We can no longer identify the features immediately, as p-persistent cycles exist for almost every value of p. We were able to distinguish between noise and feature for *BOG* because there were groups of 1-cycles with persistence significantly higher than the other 1-cycles. These groups are easily recognizable in the histogram of the persistence of 1-cycles for *BOG* in Figure 13.6(a). We cannot perceive the same grouping in the histogram for *1hck* (b), however. Persistence, in other words, is not a silver bullet. Rather, it is yet another tool for exploring the complex structure of proteins.

The examples above all use index-based persistence. Alternatively, one may examine structures using time-based persistence (see Section 6.1 for definitions). Currently, I have implemented algorithms for computing time-based persistent Betti numbers.

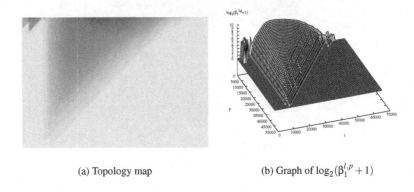

(a) Topology map   (b) Graph of $\log_2(\beta_1^{l,p} + 1)$

Fig. 13.5. The persistent Betti numbers of *1hck*.

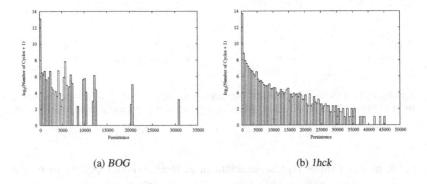

(a) *BOG*   (b) *1hck*

Fig. 13.6. Persistence histograms. *BOG*'s histogram (a) shows some grouping, but *1hck*'s (b) does not.

13.1.2 Knotting

We also wish to detect whether proteins are knotted or have linking in their structures. I have already described algorithms for detecting linking in Chapter 10. The linking number algorithms give us a signature function for a protein. We may also look for alternate signature functions for describing the topology of a protein. The approach here is to exploit the fast combinatorial representation to compute other knot and link invariants. Future directions include computing polynomial invariants, such as the *Alexander polynomial* for detecting knots (Adams, 1994).

13.1.3 Structure Determination

One method used for determining the architecture of a protein is *X-Ray crystallography* (Rhodes, 2000). After forming a high-quality crystal of a protein, we analyze the *diffraction pattern* produced by X-irradiation to generate an *electron density map*. The sequence of amino acids in the protein must be known independently. We then fit the atoms of the residues into the computed electron density map via a series of refinements. The result is a set of Cartesian coordinates for every non-hydrogen atom in the molecule.

Usually, we use these coordinates, augmented with van der Waals radii, to produce filtrations for proteins, the input to the algorithms in this book. We wish to use persistence also as a tool for refining the resolved protein. We guide modifications to the structure of the protein and the radii of the atoms by using persistent complexes. We then produce a synthetic electronic density map for the new coordinates and radii, and compare it to the original density map.

We may also construct three-dimensional MS complexes of the electron-density data for denoising using persistence. I will discuss general denoising of density functions in Section 13.3.

13.2 Hierarchical Clustering

In Chapter 2, we looked at α-shapes as a method for describing the connectivity of a space. As we increase α, the centers of the balls in our data sets are connected via edges and triangles. We may view the connections as a hierarchical clustering mechanism. Persistence adds another dimension to α-shapes, giving us a two-parameter family of shapes for describing the clustering of point sets.

Edelsbrunner and Mücke (1994) first noted the possibility of using α-shapes as a method for studying the distribution of galaxies in our universe. Dyksterhouse (1992) took initial steps in this direction. Persistence gives us additional tools for examining the clustering of galaxies in the universe. Figure 13.7 displays a simulated data set due to Marc Dyksterhouse. Each of the 1,717 vertices represents a galaxy and is a component (0-cycle) of the complex. The figure also displays the manifolds of the 0-cycles: the path through which galaxies will be connected in the future. We may use this information to construct a hierarchical description of the galaxies. In addition, we can examine the persistent topological features of the filtration of the universe. Voids, for example, correspond to empty areas of space.

Another instance of using persistence for hierarchical clustering is to clas-

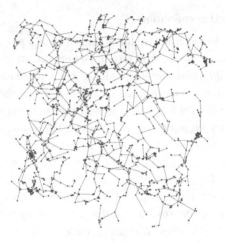

Fig. 13.7. A simulated universe, its 0-cycles, and manifolds.

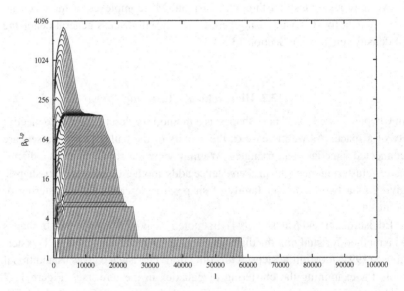

Fig. 13.8. Graph of $\beta_0^{l,p}$ projected on the (l, β_0) plane for new data set *1mct*: Trypsin complexed with inhibitor from bitter.

sify proteins according to their hydrophobic surfaces. Here, we sample hydrophobic points along the surface of a protein. We then compute an α-complex filtration from these points and examine the persistent components. Figure 13.8 shows the graph of the β_0 for this data set. The graph is projected onto the (l, β_0) plane, with the p axis coming out of the page. There are clear groups of persistent components, indicated by the horizontal lines across the graph. We hope to compare and contrast proteins using the graphs generated by this procedure. This idea is due to Thomas LaBean, from the Department of Computer Science at Duke University.

13.3 Denoising Density Functions

The second large class of applications of this work is denoising density functions. We use hierarchical MS complexes to eliminate noise in sampled data intelligently, changing the topology of the level-sets of the space by smoothing the geometry. In this section, I briefly describe future directions for such applications.

13.3.1 Terrain Simplification

In Chapter 9, I described algorithms for constructing the MS complex in two dimensions. I also provided evidence of the feasibility of this approach by implementing the algorithm for computing QMS complexes. My immediate plans are to complete this implementation. A hierarchy of two-dimensional MS complexes of a terrain gives us control over the level of detail in the representation. We may partition an increasingly smoother terrain into increasingly larger regions of uniform flow using the arcs of the MS complexes. Researchers may use this hierarchy to model natural phenomenon using multilevel adaptive refinement algorithms (O'Callaghan and Mark, 1984). Interestingly, eliminating minima using persistent MS complexes corresponds to filling *watersheds* (lakes) incrementally (Jenson and Domingue, 1988). Watersheds need to be filled for computing water flow on terrains.

13.3.2 Iso-Surface Denoising

In three dimensions, volume data give rise to two-dimensional level sets or *iso-surfaces*. As before, inherent limitations of the data acquisition devices add noise to the data. The noise is often manifested as tiny bubbles near the main component of the iso-surface, as shown in Figure 13.9. It is trivial to compute a filtration of a volume grid by tetrahedralizing the volume and using a three-dimensional manifold sweep. We need a three-dimensional MS complex, however, to modify the density values in a sensible fashion. A three-dimensional MS complex is more complicated than its two-dimensional counterpart, however, and is much harder to compute. Furthermore, it is not clear

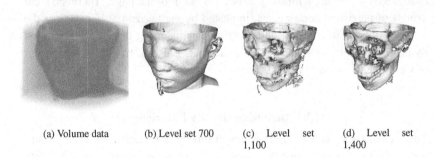

(a) Volume data   (b) Level set 700   (c) Level set   (d) Level set
                                                1,100   1,400

Fig. 13.9. A 63 by 63 by 92 density volume and three level sets. The data are from
the Visible Human Project (National Library of Medicine, 2003) and are rendered with
Kitware's VolView.

that a simplification algorithm, such as the one presented in Section 6.2.4, will
be always successful. There are, therefore, many interesting challenges in this
area for future research.

13.3.3 Time-Varying Data

Often, we are interested in data varying with time. For example, the wind
velocity on Earth, measured through time, describes a time-varying function
on a two-manifold, the sphere. We may view time as another dimension
of space, converting d-dimensional time-varying data to $(d+1)$-dimensional
data. We then denoise the data through time by constructing a hierarchy of
$(d+1)$-dimensional MS complexes. For the example above, we will need
three-dimensional MS complexes. Four-dimensional data also arise in practice. For instance, researchers are currently simulating solid propellant rockets
(Heath and Dick, 2000). The temperature, pressure, and velocity are computed
for a time-interval at every point inside the rocket. Viewing time as space,
we obtain a four-dimensional data set for which we need a four-dimensional
MS complex. Once again, generalizing the MS complex to higher dimensions
seems to be a rich avenue for future research.

13.3.4 Medial Axis Simplification

In two dimensions, the *medial axis* is the locus of all centers of circles inside
a closed planar 1-manifold that touch the boundary of the manifold in two or
more points (Blum, 1967). The medial axis has been used heavily as a de-

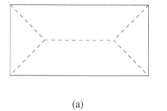 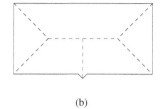

(a)   (b)

Fig. 13.10. The dashed medial axis of the solid polygon (a) is ill-conditioned as a small perturbation changes the resulting axis dramatically (b).

scriptor of shapes for pattern recognition, solid modeling, mesh generation, and pocket machining. This descriptor, however, is *ill-conditioned*, as a small perturbation in the data changes the description radically. I illustrate the sensitivity of the medial axis with an example in Figure 13.10. By restating the problem in terms of persistence, we may be able to denoise the data and, in turn, simplify the medial axis, obtaining a robust description of the data.

We can extend the definition of the medial axis to *n*-dimensional manifolds by using *n*-dimensional spheres, instead of circles. The definition remains sensitive to noise in all dimensions and therefore still requires a method for simplification.

13.4 Surface Reconstruction

Another direction for future work is using persistence for surface reconstruction. I introduced this problem as an example of a topological question in Chapter 1. We may employ the control persistence gives us over the topology of a space to reconstruct surfaces from sampled points.

Figure 13.11 shows a single-click reconstruction of the *bunny* surface. Note that I selected a complex with a tunnel. The bunny was not sampled on its base across the two black felts it rests on, as a laser range-finder scanner was used for acquiring the samples. A good reconstruction, therefore, has two holes or a single tunnel. Such knowledge, however, is not always available.

I believe that a successful reconstruction algorithm must be interactive, iterative, and adaptive. Abstractly, we wish to identify a coordinate (l, p) such that the complex $K^{l,p}$ contains a reconstruction of the point set. We may enrich the solution space by computing radii for the points. For example, we can estimate the local curvature at each point, assigning the inverse curvature as the radius of the point. We then recompute the filtration with the new radii. Sta-

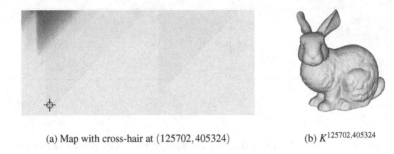

(a) Map with cross-hair at $(125702, 405324)$ (b) $K^{125702,405324}$

Fig. 13.11. Surface reconstruction with *CView*. The selected coordinates on the topology map (a) give a good approximation (b).

tistical analysis of persistence values can give us candidate persistence cutoffs. We use these values to simplify the complex in each dimension independently. Persistence may also guide modifications to the computed radii, giving us a multi-stage refinement algorithm.

13.5 Shape Description

In Section 12.3, we saw that persistence intervals could be used as a compact and general shape descriptor for a space. We are motivated, therefore, to explore shape classification with persistent homology. Homology used in this manner, however, is a crude invariant. It cannot distinguish between circles and ovals, between circles and rectangles, or even between Euclidean spaces of different dimensions. Further, it cannot identify singular points, such as corners, edges, or cone points, as their neighborhoods are homeomorphic to each other. A solution to this apparent weakness of homology is to apply it not to a space $\mathbb{X}$ itself, but rather to spaces constructed out of $\mathbb{X}$ using tangential information about $\mathbb{X}$ as a subset of $\mathbb{R}^n$ (Carlsson et al., 2004). For example, the line in Figure 13.12 has a tangent complex with two components. The "V" shape, on the other hand, has a singular point, resulting in a tangent complex with four components. In practice, we wish to obtain information about a shape when we only have a finite set of samples from that shape. We are faced, therefore, with the additional difficulty of recovering the underlying shape topology, as well as approximating the tangential spaces that we define (Colllins et al., 2004).

(a) Line   (b) V

Fig. 13.12. The line (a) has a tangent complex with two components. The "V" space (b) has a tangent complex with four components.

13.6 I/O Efficient Algorithms

Most of the applications I have described so far in this chapter are only practical if the algorithms can process massive amounts of data. In recent years, advances in computer technology and acquisition devices have made high-resolution data available to the scientific community. For instance, the *Digital Michelangelo Project* at Stanford University sampled the statue *David* using a 0.25-millimeter laser scanner. The reconstructed surface consists of more than two billion triangles (Levoy et al., 2000). Similarly, detailed terrain data for much of the earth's surface is publicly available at a 10-meter resolution from the U.S. Geological Survey. At this scale, data sets for even small portions of the planet will be at least hundreds of megabytes in size. Internal memory algorithms are often unable to handle such massive data, even when executing on fast machines with large memories. It becomes critical, therefore, to design I/O efficient external memory algorithms to analyze massive data (Arge et al., 2000).

Bibliography

C. C. Adams. *The Knot Book: An Elementary Introduction to the Mathematical Theory of Knots.* W. H. Freeman and Company, New York, 1994.

S. I. Adyan. The algorithmic unsolvability of problems concerning recognition of certain properties of groups. In *Doklady Academy Nauk SSSR*, volume 103, pages 533–535. Soviet Academy of Sciences, 1955.

S. I. Adyan and G. S. Makanin. Investigations on algorithmic questions of algebra. In *Proceedings of the Steklov Institute of Mathematics*, volume 3, pages 209–219, 1986.

N. Amenta and M. Bern. Surface reconstruction by Voronoi filtering. *Discrete Comput. Geom.*, 22:481–504, 1999.

L. Arge, L. Toma, and J. S. Vitter. I/O-efficient algorithms for problems on grid-based terrains. In *Proc. Workshop Algor. Engin. Exper.*, 2000.

C. L. Bajaj, V. Pascucci, and D. R. Schikore. Visualization of scalar topology for structural enhancement. In *Proc. 9th Ann. IEEE Conf. Visualization*, pages 18–23, 1998.

T. F. Banchoff. Critical points and curvature for embedded polyhedral surfaces. *Am. Math. Monthly*, 77:475–485, 1970.

H. M. Berman, J. Westbrook, Z. Feng, G. Gilliland, T. N. Bhat, H. Weissig, I. N. Shindyalov, and P. E. Bourne. The protein data bank. *Nucleic Acids Research*, 28: 235–242, 2000.

R. L. Bishop and S. I. Goldberg. *Tensor Analysis on Manifolds.* Dover Publications, Inc., New York, 1980.

R. A. Bissell, E. Córdova, A. E. Kaifer, and J. F. Stoddart. A checmically and electrochemically switchable molecular shuttle. *Nature*, 369:133–137, 1994.

A. Blum. A transformation for extracting new descriptors of shape. In *Proc. Symp. Models for Perception of Speech and Visual Form*, pages 362–380, 1967.

W. M. Boothby. *An Introduction to Differentiable Manifolds and Riemannian Geometry.* Academic Press, San Diego, CA, second edition, 1986.

J. W. Bruce and P. J. Giblin. *Curves and Singularities.* Cambridge University Press, New York, second edition, 1992.

G. Carlsson, A. Zomorodian, A. Collins, and L. Guibas. Persistence barcodes for shapes, 2004. To be published in Proc. Symp. Geom. Process.

H. Carr, J. Snoeyink, and U. Axen. Computing contour trees in all dimensions. In *Proc. 11th Ann. Sympos. Discrete Alg.*, pages 918–926, 2000.

CATH. Protein structure classification, 2003. http://www.biochem.ucl.ac.uk/bsm/cath/.

C. P. Collier, E. W. Wong, Belohradský, F. M. Raymo, J. F. Stoddart, P. J. Kuekes, R. S.

Williams, and J. R. Heath. Electronically configurable moleculear-based logic gates. *Science*, 285:391–394, 1999.

A. Colllins, A. Zomorodian, G. Carlsson, and L. Guibas. A barcode shape descriptor for curve point cloud data, 2004. To be published in Proc. Symp. Point-Based Graph.

T. H. Cormen, C. E. Leiserson, and R. L. Rivest. *Introduction to Algorithms*. The MIT Press, Cambridge, MA, 1994.

T. E. Creighton. *Proteins. Structures and Molecular Principles*. Freeman, New York, 1984.

B. Curless and M. Levoy. A volumetric method for building complex models from range images. In *SIGGRAPH 96 Conference Proceedings*, pages 303–312, 1996.

M. Davis. *The Undecidable*. Raven Press Books, LTD., Hewlett, NY, 1965.

M. de Berg and M. van Kreveld. Trekking in the alps without freezing and getting tired. In *Proc. 1st Europ. Sympos. Alg*, pages 121–132, 1993.

M. de Berg, M. van Kreveld, M. Overmars, and O. Schwarzkopf. *Computational Geometry: Algorithms and Applications*. Springer-Verlag, New York, 1997.

W. de Leeuw and R. van Liere. Collapsing flow topology using area metrics. In *Proc. 10th Ann. IEEE Conf. Visualization*, pages 349–354, 1999.

B. Delaunay. Sur la sphère vide. *Izv. Akad. Nauk SSSR, Otdelenie Matematicheskii i Estestvennyka Nauk*, 7:793–800, 1934.

C. J. A. Delfinado and H. Edelsbrunner. An incremental algorithm for Betti numbers of simplicial complexes on the 3-sphere. *Comput. Aided Geom. Design*, 12:771–784, 1995.

T. K. Dey, H. Edelsbrunner, G. Guha, and D. V. Nekhayev. Topology preserving edge contraction. *Publ. Inst. Math. (Beograd) (N.S.)*, 66:23–45, 1999.

D. Dummit and R. Foote. *Abstract Algebra*. John Wiley & Sons, Inc., New York, 1999.

M. D. Dyksterhouse. An alpha-shape view of our universe. Master's thesis, University of Illinois at Urbana-Champaign, Urbana, IL, 1992.

H. Edelsbrunner. The union of balls and its dual shape. *Discrete Comput. Geom.*, 13: 415–440, 1995.

H. Edelsbrunner and E. P. Mücke. Simulation of simplicity: A technique to cope with degenerate cases in geometric algorithms. *ACM Trans. Graphics*, 9:66–104, 1990.

H. Edelsbrunner and E. P. Mücke. Three-dimensional alpha shapes. *ACM Trans. Graphics*, 13:43–72, 1994.

H. Edelsbrunner and A. Zomorodian. Computing linking numbers in a filtration. *Homology, Homotopy and Applications*, 5(2):19–37, 2003.

H. Edelsbrunner, D. G. Kirkpatrick, and R. Seidel. On the shape of a set of points in the plane. *IEEE Trans. Inform. Theory*, IT-29:551–559, 1983.

H. Edelsbrunner, D. Letscher, and A. Zomorodian. Topological persistence and simplification. *Discrete Comput. Geom.*, 28:511–533, 2002.

H. Edelsbrunner, J. Harer, and A. Zomorodian. Hierarchical Morse-Smale complexes for piecewise linear 2-manifolds. *Discrete Comput. Geom.*, 30:87–107, 2003.

D. Eisenbud. *Commutative Algebra with a View Toward Algebraic Theory*. Springer, New York, 1995.

J. El-Sana and A. Varshney. Topology simplification for polygonal virtual environments. *IEEE Trans. Visualization Comput. Graphics*, 4:133–144, 1998.

E. Flapan. *When Topology Meets Chemistry : A Topological Look at Molecular Chirality*. Cambridge University Press, New York, 2000.

J. D. Foley, A. van Dam, S. K. Feiner, J. F. Hughes, and R. L. Phillips. *Computer Graphics: Principles and Practice*. Addison Wesley, Reading, MA, second edition, 1996.

A. T. Fomenko and S. V. Matveev. *Algorithmic and Computer Methods for*

Three-Manifolds. Kluwer Academic Publishers, New York, 1997.

J. B. Fraleigh. *A First Course in Abstract Algebra.* Addison-Wesley, Reading, MA, fourth edition, 1989.

FSSP. Fold classification based on structure-structure alignment of proteins, 2003. http://www2.ebi.ac.uk/dali/fssp/.

M. Garland and P. S. Heckbert. Surface simplification using quadric error metrics. In *SIGGRAPH 97 Conference Proceedings*, pages 209–216, 1997.

P. J. Giblin. *Graphs, Surfaces, and Homology.* Chapman and Hall, New York, second edition, 1981.

T. Granlund. The GNU multiple precision arithmetic library, 2003. http://www.swox.com/gmp.

L. Guibas and J. Stolfi. Primitives for the manipulation of general subdivisions and the computation of Voronoi diagrams. *ACM Trans. Graph.*, 4:74–123, 1985.

W. Haken. Theorie der Normalflächen. *Acta Math.*, 105:245–375, 1961.

D. Harel and R. E. Tarjan. Fast algorithms for finding nearest common ancestors. *SIAM J. Comput.*, 13:338–355, 1984.

J. Hass, J. C. Lagarias, and N. Pippenger. The computational complexity of knot and link problems. *J. ACM*, 46:185–211, 1999.

A. Hatcher. *Algebraic Topology.* Cambridge University Press, Cambridge, UK, 2001.

T. He, L. Hong, A. Varshney, and S. Wang. Controlled topology simplification. *IEEE Trans. Vis. Comput. Graph.*, 2(2):171–184, June 1996.

M. T. Heath and W. A. Dick. Virtual prototyping of solid propellant rockets. *Comput. Sci. Engr.*, 2:21–32, March–April 2000.

M. Henle. *A Combinatorial Introduction to Topology.* Dover Publications, Inc., New York, 1997.

J. L. Hennessy and D. A. Patterson. *Computer Architecture: A Quantitative Approach.* Morgan Kaufmann Publishers, Inc., San Francisco, CA, second edition, 1989.

L. Holm and C. Sander. Mapping the protein universe. *Science*, 273:595–602, 1995.

H. Hoppe, T. DeRose, T. Duchamp, J. McDonald, and W. Stuetzle. Mesh optimization. In *SIGGRAPH 93 Conference Proceedings*, pages 19–26, 1993.

IZA Structure Comission. Database of zeolite structures, 2003. http://www.iza-structure.org.

W. Jaco and J. L. Tollefson. Algorithms for the complete decomposition of a closed 3-manifold. *Illinois J. Math.*, 39:358–406, 1995.

S. Jenson and J. Domingue. Extracting topographic structure from digital elevation data for geographic information system analysis. *Photogrammetric Engineering and Remote Sensing*, 54(11):1593–1600, 1988.

R. Kirby and L. Siebenmann. On the triangulation of manifolds and the Hauptvermutung. *Bull. Amer. Math. Soc.*, 75:742–749, 1969.

D. E. Knuth. Theory and practice, IV. In *Selected Papers on Computer Science*. CSLI Publications, Stanford, CA, 1996.

T. H. LaBean, H. Yan, J. Kopatsch, F. Liu, E. Winfree, J. H. Reif, and N. C. Seeman. Construction, analysis, ligation, and self-assembly of DNA triple crossover complexes. *J. Am. Chem. Soc.*, 122:1848–1860, 2000.

M. Levoy, K. Pulli, B. Curless, S. Rusinkiewicz, D. Koller, L. Pereira, M. Ginzton, S. Anderson, J. Davis, J. Ginsberg, J. Shade, and D. Fulk. The digital Michelangelo project: 3D scanning of large statues. In *SIGGRAPH 00 Conference Proceedings*, pages 131–144, 2000.

D. Lischinski. Incremental Delaunay triangulation. In P. Heckbert, editor, *Graphics Gems IV*, pages 47–59. Academic Press, Boston, MA, 1994.

A. A. Markov. Insolubility of the problem of homeomorphy. In *Proc. Int. Congress of*

Math., pages 14–21. Cambridge University Press, 1958.

E. Martz. Protein Explorer 1.80b, 2001. http://www.proteinexplorer.org.

W. S. Massey. *A Basic Course in Algebraic Topology*. Springer-Verlag, New York, 1991.

Y. V. Matiyasevich. Investigations on some algorithmic problems in algebra and number theory. In *Proceedings of the Steklov Institute of Mathematics*, pages 227–253, 1986.

G. McCarthy. *Topology: An Introduction with Application to Topological Groups*. Dover Publications, Inc., New York, 1988.

J. McCleary. *User's Guide to Spectral Sequences*. Cambridge University Press, Cambridge, UK, second edition, 2000.

B. Meyer. *Object-Oriented Software Construction*. Prentice Hall, Upper Saddle River, NJ, second edition, 2000.

J. Milnor. Two complexes which are homeomorphic but combinatorially distinct. *Ann. of Maths.*, 74:575–590, 1961.

J. Milnor. *Morse Theory*. Princeton University Press, New Jersey, 1963.

E. Moïse. Affine structures in 3-manifolds. *Ann. of Maths.*, 58:458–480, 1953.

F. Morgan. *Riemannian Geometry: A Beginner's Guide*. A K Peters, Ltd., Wellesley, MA, 1998.

J. R. Munkres. *Elements of Algebraic Topology*. Addison-Wesley, Reading, MA, 1984.

A. G. Murzin, S. E. Brenner, and C. Hubbard, T. Chothia. SCOP: A structural classification of proteins database for the investigation of sequences and structures. *J. Mol. Biol.*, pages 536–540, 1995.

National Geophysical Data Center. Ngdc 5-minute gridded elevation data selection, 1988. http://www.ngdc.noaa.gov/mgg/global/seltopo.html.

National Library of Medicine. The visible human project, 2003. http://www.nlm.nih.gov/research/visible/.

S. Negami. Diagonal flips of triangulations on surfaces, a survey. *Yokohama Math. J.*, 47:1–40, 1999.

J. F. O'Callaghan and D. M. Mark. The extraction of drainage networks from digital elevation data. *Computer Vision, Graphics and Image Processing*, 28, 1984.

B. O'Neill. *Elementary Differential Geometry*. Academic Press, San Diego, CA, second edition, 1997.

C. Orengo, A. Michie, S. Jones, D. T. Jones, M. B. Swindells, and J. M. Thornton. CATH—a hierarchic classification of protein domain structures. *Structure*, 5(8): 1093–1108, 1997.

C. Papakyriakopoulos. A new proof of the invariance of the homology group of a complex. *Bull. Soc. Math. Grèce*, 22:1–154, 1943.

B. Paul and B. Bederson. Togl: a Tk OpenGL widget, 2003. http://togl.sourceforge.net/.

J. Popović and H. Hoppe. Progressive simplicial complexes. In *SIGGRAPH 97 Conference Proceedings*, pages 217–224, 1997.

V. V. Prasolov. *Intuitive Topology*. American Mathematical Society, Providence, RI, 1995.

M. O. Rabin. Recursive unsolvability of group theoretic problems. In *Annals of Mathematics*, volume 67, pages 172–194. American Mathematical Society, 1958.

A. A. Ranicki, editor. *The Hauptvermutung Book*. Kluwer Academic Publishers, New York, 1997.

RCSB. Protein data bank, 2003. http://www.rcsb.org/pdb/.

G. Rhodes. *Crystallography Made Crystal Clear*. Academic Press, New York, 2000.

E. S. Roberts. *Programming Abstractions in C*. Addison-Wesley, Reading, MA, 1997.

D. Rolfsen. *Knots and Links*. Publish or Perish, Inc., Houston, TX, 1990.

J. Rossignac and P. Borrel. Multi-resolution 3D approximations for rendering. *Modeling in Computer Graphics*, pages 455–465, June–July 1993.

W. J. Schroeder, J. A. Zarge, and W. E. Lorensen. Decimation of triangle meshes. In *SIGGRAPH 92 Conference Proceedings*, pages 65–70, 1992.

SCOP. Structural classification of proteins, 2003. http://scop.berkeley.edu/.

H. Seifert. Über das Geschlecht von Knoten. *Math. Annalen*, 110:571–592, 1935.

Stanford Graphics Laboratory. The Stanford 3D Scanning Repository, 2003. http://www-graphics.stanford.edu/data/3Dscanrep/.

W. R. Taylor. A deeply knotted protein structure and how it might fold. *Nature*, 406: 916–919, 2000.

W. P. Thurston. *Three-Dimensional Geometry and Topology, Volume 1*. Princeton University Press, New Jersey, 1997.

X. Tricoche, G. Scheuermann, and H. Hagen. A topology simplification method for 2D vector fields. In *Proc. 11th Ann. IEEE Conf. Visualization*, pages 359–366, 2000.

G. Turk and M. Levoy. Zippered polygon meshes from range images. In *SIGGRAPH 94 Conference Proceedings*, pages 311–318, 1994.

F. Uhlig. *Transform Linear Algebra*. Prentice Hall, Upper Saddle River, NJ, 2002.

M. van Kreveld, R. van Oostrum, C. Bajaj, V. Pascucci, and D. Schikore. Contour trees and small seed sets for iso-surface traversal. In *Proc. 13th Ann. Sympos. Comput. Geom.*, pages 212–220, 1997.

J. van Leeuwen. Finding lowest common ancestors in less than logarithmic time. Unpublished report, 1976.

G. Voronoï. Nouvelle applications des paramètres continues à la théorie des formes quadratique. *J. Reine Angew. Math.*, 133 and 134:97–178 and 198–287, 1908.

S. Wasserman, J. Dungan, and N. Cozzarelli. Discovery of a predicted DNA knot substantiates a model for site-specific recombination. *Science*, 229:171–174, 1985.

J. R. Weeks. *The Shape of Space*. Marcel Dekker, Inc., New York, 1985.

M. Woo, J. Neider, and T. Davis. *OpenGL programming guide*. Addison-Wesley Developers Press, Reading, MA, 1997.

Z. Wood and I. Guskov. Topological noise removal. In *Proceedings of Graphics Interface*, pages 19–26, 2001.

Zeolyst International. Zeolite FAQ, 2003. http://www.zeolyst.com/html/faq.html.

A. Zomorodian and G. Carlsson. Computing topological persistence, 2004. To be published in Proc. 20th Ann. ACM Sympos. Comput. Geom.

Index

Printed in the United States
By Bookmasters